Mastering UI Development with Unity

An in-depth guide to developing engaging user interfaces with Unity 5, Unity 2017, and Unity 2018

Ashley Godbold

BIRMINGHAM - MUMBAI

Mastering UI Development with Unity

Acquisition Editor: Noyonika Das
Content Development Editor: Roshan Kumar
Technical Editor: Sachin Sunilkumar
Copy Editor: Shaila Kusanale
Project Coordinator: Devanshi Doshi
Proofreader: Safis Editing
Indexer: Pratik Shirodkar
Graphics: Jason Monteiro
Production Coordinator: Shraddha Falebhai

First published: April 2018

Production reference: 1250418

Published by Packt Publishing Ltd.
Livery Place
35 Livery Street
Birmingham
B3 2PB, UK.

ISBN 978-1-78712-552-0

www.packtpub.com

`mapt.io`

Mapt is an online digital library that gives you full access to over 5,000 books and videos, as well as industry leading tools to help you plan your personal development and advance your career. For more information, please visit our website.

Why subscribe?

- Spend less time learning and more time coding with practical eBooks and Videos from over 4,000 industry professionals

- Improve your learning with Skill Plans built especially for you

- Get a free eBook or video every month

- Mapt is fully searchable

- Copy and paste, print, and bookmark content

PacktPub.com

Did you know that Packt offers eBook versions of every book published, with PDF and ePub files available? You can upgrade to the eBook version at `www.PacktPub.com` and as a print book customer, you are entitled to a discount on the eBook copy. Get in touch with us at `service@packtpub.com` for more details.

At `www.PacktPub.com`, you can also read a collection of free technical articles, sign up for a range of free newsletters, and receive exclusive discounts and offers on Packt books and eBooks.

About the author

Dr. Ashley Godbold is a programmer, game designer, artist, mathematician, and teacher. She holds a Bachelor of Science in Mathematics, a Master of Science in Mathematics, a Bachelor of Science in Game Art and Design, and a Doctor of Computer Science in Emerging Media where her dissertation research focused on educational video game design. She also authored *Mastering Unity 2D Game Development: Second Edition* (Packt Publishing). She enjoys playing video games and watching anime with her husband, daughter, and two cats.

About the reviewer

Adam Larson started programming professionally in 2005. He has shipped 14 console games, 2 PC titles, and 8 mobile games. In 2012, he founded a company that focused on using Unity for business applications. He spent the following 5 years building a million-dollar agency that built high-end software. Recently, he moved to another start-up, which is focusing on revolutionizing the banking industry. When he isn't doing something with technology, you will find him spending time with his wife and 3 kids.

Packt is searching for authors like you

If you're interested in becoming an author for Packt, please visit `authors.packtpub.com` and apply today. We have worked with thousands of developers and tech professionals, just like you, to help them share their insight with the global tech community. You can make a general application, apply for a specific hot topic that we are recruiting an author for, or submit your own idea.

Table of Contents

Preface

There are a multitude of built-in UI elements that can be incorporated into a game built in Unity. This book will help you master Unity's UI system by describing indepth the various UI objects, functionalities, and properties, and providing step-by-step examples of their implementation.

Who this book is for

This book is intended for game developers who have worked with Unity and are looking to improve their knowledge of the UI system introduced in Unity 4.6. Individuals looking for in-depth explanations of specific UI elements and individuals looking for step-by-step directions explaining how to implement UI items that appear in multiple game genres will also find this book helpful.

What this book covers

Chapter 1, *Designing User Interfaces*, covers basic information related to designing user interfaces. Additionally, a detailed explanation of setting the aspect ratio and resolution of a Unity project is discussed.

Chapter 2, *Canvases, Panels, and Basic Layouts*, begins exploring the development of a user interface by appropriately laying out UI elements within a Canvas. Panels will be used and an introduction to Text and Images will be provided. The examples included in this chapter show how to lay out a basic HUD, create a permanent background image, and develop a basic pop-up menu.

Chapter 3, *Automatic Layouts*, discusses how to implement the various automatic layout components to streamline the UI building process. The examples included within this chapter utilize the automatic layout functionality to create a selection menu in the HUD and a gridded inventory.

Chapter 4, *The Event System and Programming for UI*, explains how to program interactions for graphical and hardware user interfaces. The examples covered in this chapter explain how to use the keyboard to make menus appear and disappear, how to pause the game, and how to create a drag and drop inventory system.

Chapter 5, *Buttons*, explores the various properties of buttons. The examples in this chapter walk through how to set up keyboard and controller navigation of buttons, how to load scenes when buttons are pressed, how to create animated button transitions, and how to make buttons swap their images.

Chapter 6, *Text, Images, and TextMesh Pro-Text*, discusses the properties of images and text more thoroughly and demonstrates how to affect their properties via code. The examples at the end of the chapter show how to create a dialog box with text that animates as if it was being typed in, how to create a custom font, how to make horizontal and circular progress meters/health bars, and how to create text that wraps with a gradient.

Chapter 7, *Masks and Other Inputs*, covers a myriad of UI inputs, as well as masks. Examples showing how to make a scrolling menu and a drop-down menu with images are covered at the end of the chapter.

Chapter 8, *Animations and Particles in the UI*, is all about animating the UI. The examples in this chapter show how to animate menus to fade in and out, and how to make a complex loot box animation with particles that appear in front of the UI elements.

Chapter 9, *World Space UI*, showcases how to create UI elements that exist within the game scene as opposed to on the "screen" in front of all in-game items. The examples cover how to create an interactive UI for a 2D scene and interactive, hover health bars for a 3D scene.

Chapter 10, *Mobile-Specific UI*, showcases interactions that are specific to mobile and touchscreen devices. The examples in this chapter show how to recognize when a portion of the screen is tapped on, how to zoom when the pinch action is performed, how to create press-and-hold or long-press interactions, and how to create static and floating on-screen control pads.

To get the most out of this book

To complete the examples discussed in this text, you will need the following:

- Unity version 5.6 or higher
- A PC with Windows 7, 8, or 10 (64-bit) or a Mac with OS X 10.9 or higher
- An internet connection to access the Unity Asset Store
- Basic knowledge of Unity and C# programming is recommended

Download the example code files

You can download the example code files for this book from your account at www.packtpub.com. If you purchased this book elsewhere, you can visit www.packtpub.com/support and register to have the files emailed directly to you.

You can download the code files by following these steps:

1. Log in or register at www.packtpub.com.
2. Select the **SUPPORT** tab.
3. Click on **Code Downloads & Errata**.
4. Enter the name of the book in the **Search** box and follow the onscreen instructions.

Once the file is downloaded, please make sure that you unzip or extract the folder using the latest version of:

- WinRAR/7-Zip for Windows
- Zipeg/iZip/UnRarX for Mac
- 7-Zip/PeaZip for Linux

The code bundle for the book is also hosted on GitHub at https://github.com/PacktPublishing/Mastering-UI-Development-with-Unity. In case there's an update to the code, it will be updated on the existing GitHub repository.

We also have other code bundles from our rich catalog of books and videos available at https://github.com/PacktPublishing/. Check them out!

Download the color images

We also provide a PDF file that has color images of the screenshots/diagrams used in this book. You can download it here: https://www.packtpub.com/sites/default/files/downloads/MasteringUIDevelopmentwithUnity_ColorImages.pdf.

Conventions used

There are a number of text conventions used throughout this book.

CodeInText: Indicates code words in text, database table names, folder names, filenames, file extensions, pathnames, dummy URLs, user input, and Twitter handles. Here is an example: "The following script, AddSprite.cs, is attached to the UI Image."

A block of code is set as follows:

```
using System.Collections;
using System.Collections.Generic;
using UnityEngine;
using UnityEngine.UI;
```

When we wish to draw your attention to a particular part of a code block, the relevant lines or items are set in bold:

```
// Use this for initialization
    void Start () {
        theImage.sprite=theSprite;
        theImage.preserveAspect=true;
    }
```

Bold: Indicates a new term, an important word, or words that you see onscreen. For example, words in menus or dialog boxes appear in the text like this. Here is an example: "You can add an **Event System** manager to a **GameObject** by selecting **Add Component** | **Event** | **Event System** on the object's **Inspector**."

Warnings or important notes appear like this.

Tips and tricks appear like this.

Get in touch

Feedback from our readers is always welcome.

General feedback: Email `feedback@packtpub.com` and mention the book title in the subject of your message. If you have questions about any aspect of this book, please email us at `questions@packtpub.com`.

Errata: Although we have taken every care to ensure the accuracy of our content, mistakes do happen. If you have found a mistake in this book, we would be grateful if you would report this to us. Please visit `www.packtpub.com/submit-errata`, selecting your book, clicking on the Errata Submission Form link, and entering the details.

Piracy: If you come across any illegal copies of our works in any form on the Internet, we would be grateful if you would provide us with the location address or website name. Please contact us at `copyright@packtpub.com` with a link to the material.

If you are interested in becoming an author: If there is a topic that you have expertise in and you are interested in either writing or contributing to a book, please visit `authors.packtpub.com`.

Reviews

Please leave a review. Once you have read and used this book, why not leave a review on the site that you purchased it from? Potential readers can then see and use your unbiased opinion to make purchase decisions, we at Packt can understand what you think about our products, and our authors can see your feedback on their book. Thank you!

For more information about Packt, please visit `packtpub.com`.

Designing User Interfaces

When working with UI, it is important to understand a few design basics. This chapter will cover the foundation of designing UI as well as a few key concepts to start you off in the right direction.

In this chapter, we will discuss the following topics:

- Defining UI and GUI
- Describing the four types of interfaces
- Choosing a UI layout and color scheme
- Defining interface metaphors
- Discerning and setting resolution and aspect ratio

This book is not about the art of designing UI. It is a technical text that discusses implementation of UI functionality. However, I do want to discuss some basic design principles of UI design. I don't expect you to be an amazing UI artist after reading this chapter. I do hope that you get some basic understanding of layout and design principles from this chapter, though, so that maybe your artist friends won't make too much fun of you.

UI and GUI

So what exactly do UI and GUI stand for, and what's the difference? UI stands for **user interface**, and GUI (pronounced "gooey") stands for **graphical user interface**. To *interface* means to *interact with*, so the user interface is the set of devices that let the player interact with the game. The mouse, keyboard, game controller, touch screen, and so on are all part of the user interface. Graphical user interface is the subset of the user interface that is represented by graphics. So, onscreen buttons, drop-down menus, and icons are all part of a game's GUI.

This book will focus primarily on GUI design, but it will discuss some non-graphical aspects of user interface controls, like accessing data from the mouse, screen tap, keyboard, or controller.

As GUI is a subset of UI, many people (myself included) tend to just refer to the GUI as UI. In fact, Unity also refers to all the GUI items they provide templates for as UI. "Back in the day", the days before Unity 4.6, to implement visual UI in Unity, you had to use the "legacy GUI controls". These controls used the OnGUI() method. I believe one of the reasons that Unity refers to their new graphical user interface controls as UI rather than GUI is to make a distinction between the old GUI and the new UI. This, and the fact that I feel silly saying "gooey", is also why I refer to the graphical user interface we can implement in Unity as "UI".

 Anything Unity replaces with new functionality gets marked as "legacy". Legacy items are only left available within Unity for backward compatibility.

As a general rule, if you are trying to find any information about working in Unity's UI and find reference to OnGUI(), move along! This code has been deprecated for a reason, and Unity no longer supports it. In fact, Unity explicitly states that you should not use it for a new project. There are a few diehard OnGUI() fans out there who want to hold on to the past, but I couldn't tell you why. In my experience, I have not found anything to be "undoable" in the "new" (it's not that new anymore) UI. While some things you may want to do will not be explicitly provided by the "new" UI system, a little bit of your own code can go a long way.

Four game interface types

When you say "game UI", most people think of the HUD (heads-up display) that appears in front of all the in-game items. However, there are actually four different types of game interfaces: non-diegetic, diegetic, meta, and spatial.

Fagerholt and Lorentzon first described these four different interface types in the 2009 *Beyond the HUD: User Interfaces for Increased Player Immersion in FPS Games: Master of Science Thesis*. Since then, the terminology has been widely used throughout the field of UI game design. You can find the original publication at `http://publications.lib.chalmers.se/records/fulltext/111921.pdf`.

The distinction between the four is determined by a cross of the following two dimensions:

- Diegesis: Is part of the story?
- Spatiality: Is in the game's environment?

The following diagram demonstrates the cross relationship between the two questions and how they define the four types of interfaces:

Diagesis: Is it part of the story?

	Yes	No
Yes	Diegetic	Spatial
No	Meta	Non-Diegetic

Spatiality: Is it in the space of the scene?

Non-diegetic is the category that a game's HUD will fall in. This information exists purely for the player to view, and the characters within the game are not aware of its presence. It exists on the *fourth* wall of the game view and appears to be on the screen in front of everything. The examples of this type of UI are endless, as nearly every game has some non-diegetic UI elements.

Alternatively, a **diegetic** interface is one that exists within the game world and the characters within the game are aware of its presence. Common examples of this include characters looking at inventory or maps. The most commonly referred-to example of diegetic UI is the inventory and health display within *Deadspace*. The inventory displays in a holographic display window that pops up in front of the playable character, and they interact with it as you select their weaponry. His health is also indicated by a meter on his back. The inventory of *Alone in the Dark* (2008) is displayed in a diegetic way as well. While there are some UI elements that only the player can see, the main character views inventory within their jacket pockets and interacts with the items. *Uncharted Lost Legacy* and *Far Cry 2* both use maps that the characters physically hold in the scene and interact with. *Fallout 3* and *Fallout 4* use a diegetic interface to display the inventory and map on the character's Pip-boy, which is permanently attached to their arm. Games also use this type of display when characters are in a vehicle or suit, where various displays appear on the shield, window, or cockpit.

Meta interfaces are interfaces that the characters in the game are aware of, but they are not physically displayed within the scene. Common examples of this are speed displays for racing games. *Forza 7* actually uses a combination of meta and diegetic displays for the speedometer. A meta speed indicator is persistently on the lower-right corner of the screen for the player to see. Since the character is constantly aware of how fast they are driving, they would be aware of this speed indicator, therefore making it a meta interface. There is also a diegetic speedometer in the car's dash that is displayed when playing in first-person view. Another common usage of this type of display is a cell phone that appears on the screen but is implied the playable character is interacting with in. *Persona 5*, *Catherine*, and *Grand Theft Auto 5* all use this interface type for cell phone interactions.

The last type of interface, **spatial**, exists in the scene, but the characters within the game are not aware of it. Interfaces that exist in the scene but that the characters are not aware of are incredibly common. This is commonly used to let the player know where in the scene interactable items are, what the in-game character is doing, or information about characters and items in the scene. For example, in *Legend of Zelda: Breath of the Wild*, arrows appear over the heads of enemies, indicating who Link will attack. Link is not actually aware of these arrows; they are there for the player to know who he is focusing on. *Xenoblade Chronicles 2* uses a spatial interface to indicate where the player can dig; a shovel icon appears over the diggable areas.

Layout

When laying out the UI for your game, I strongly recommend checking other games of the same genre and seeing how they implemented their UI. Play the game and see whether it feels good to you.

If you are unsure of how to lay out your game's UI, I recommend dividing the game's screen into a *guttered grid*, like the one shown in the following diagram, and placing items within the non-guttered areas:

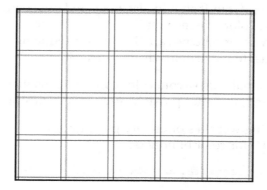

You can use as many grids as you want, but laying out the items with reference to the grid will help ensure that the UI is arranged in a balanced way.

In most cases, the HUD items should remain in the outer edges of the grid. Any UI that displays in the center grids will restrict the player view. So, this area is good for pop-up windows that pause the gameplay.

The device your game will be played on is important when determining layout. If there are a lot of buttons the player will interact with, they are generally best suited for the bottom or side portions of the screen if playing on a mobile device. This is due to the way players hold their phones and top-center part of the screen is the most difficult area to reach with their thumb. Additionally, reaching for this area will cause them to block the majority of the game view with their hand.

You'll note that when you play computer games, they tend to have much smaller and more cluttered UI than mobile and console games. This is due to visibility and interaction. Clicking on small objects with a mouse is significantly easier than tapping them with a finger or selecting them by scrolling through them with the d-pad. Also, the screen resolution is much bigger, allowing for more space to be taken up by the UI as compared to the game.

Fitts' Law is a commonly referenced principle of UI design. The gist of Fitts' law is don't make interactable UI small and far apart to increase user experience. Make the most important interactible items the largest and ensure that they are near each other.

Color schemes

The color you choose for your UI will play an important role in not just its visual appeal, but in the player's interpretation of what the UI does. The colors of the UI should stand out compared to the background, but it should also not stand out so much that it causes eye strain. There is no specific color scheme you have to use for your game, but as a general rule, split complementary color schemes are the best for reducing eye strain while also producing enough contrast to make items distinguishable.

Whenever possible, you should also avoid color combinations that will be indistinguishable to those who are color blind; if it's not possible, use other indicators to make items distinct.

The following websites offer very good information on designing accessible UI for color blindness:

http://blog.usabilla.com/how-to-design-for-color-blindness/

https://www.smashingmagazine.com/2016/06/improving-color-accessibility-for-color-blind-users/

Interface metaphors

When you design your UI, you should use metaphors when possible rather than words. **Metaphors** are symbols whose meanings are universally recognized. For example, most people will recognize the meaning of these buttons to be play, pause, menu, settings, close/cancel, confirm, mute, and save:

There are three main reasons for using these metaphors:

- They are quicker to recognize than text
- They don't clutter the UI as much as their words counter parts
- You don't have to translate them!

The third reason is the reason I use them the most. All the games I produce for the company I work for need to be translated into six different languages, so I avoid using words whenever possible.

Resolution and aspect ratio

The **resolution** of a game is the pixel dimension of the screen. For example, a game could run at 1024x768. This means that the game is 1024 pixels wide and 768 pixels tall. The aspect ratio of a game is the ratio between the width and height (expressed width:height). This **aspect ratio** of a game is determined by dividing the resolution width by resolution height and then simplifying the fraction. So, for example, if your game has a resolution of 1024x768, the aspect ratio would be as follows:

$$\frac{1024px}{768px} = \frac{4}{3}$$

Here, the fraction 4/3 is the aspect ratio 4:3.

The following diagram provides a list of common aspect ratios and related resolutions:

Aspect Ratio	Resolution			
3:2	720x480	1280x854	1440x960	2880x1920
	1152x768			
4:3	640x480	1024x768	1440x1080	1920x1440
	800x600	1280x960	1600x1200	2048x1536
	960x720	1400x1050	1856x1392	
5:3	1280x768	3000x1800		
5:4	1280x1024	2560x2048	5120x4096	
16:9	1024x576	1280x720	1600x900	2560x1440
	1152x648	1366x768	1920x1080	3840x2160
16:10	640x400	1440x900	1920x1200	3840x2400
	1280x800	1680x1050	2560x1600	

The following website provides a list of common resolutions specific to iOS devices: http://iosres.com/. Note that not all the aspect ratios are simplified fractions. For example, 16:10 is not simplified, as the simplified fraction would be 8:5.

When it comes to UI, the resolution of your game will be incredibly important. If you'll build to a single resolution/aspect ratio, the UI will be much easier to deal with. However, if you'll build a game that you want to run on multiple resolutions/aspect ratios (for example, a mobile project), you want your UI to scale appropriately, and you want to be able to easily change the resolution of your game so that you can test that it is scaling properly.

 You can check out https://developer.android.com/guide/practices/screens_support.html#testing for a list of common resolutions specific to Android devices.

Even if you will allow your resolution and aspect ratio to vary, you should still decide on a default resolution. This default resolution represents the resolution of your ideal design. This will be the resolution that your initial design and UI layout is based on, so if the resolution or aspect ratio varies, the UI will try to maintain the same design best as it can.

Changing the aspect ratio and resolution of the game view

You can easily switch between different resolutions and aspect ratios in the **Game** tab. This will allow you to see how your UI scales at the different resolutions and aspect ratios:

1. If you navigate to your **Game** tab, you will see the words **Free Aspect**. Clicking on **Free Aspect** will reveal a menu that shows various aspect ratios and a single **1024x768** resolution that is labeled **Standalone:**

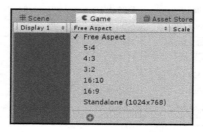

Free Aspect means that the window will scale to whatever resolution you set by changing the size of the game window. So by moving the frame around on the game window, you will change the aspect ratio. You can see this in effect easily by setting your **Editor** layout to one that shows both the **Screen** and **Game** tabs open simultaneously. For example, setting the Layout to 2 by 3 will do this.

2. You can change the layout by selecting the word **Default** that appears in the upper-right hand corner of the Unity Editor.
3. Now the **Game** and **Scene** tabs will both be visible on the left-hand side of your screen. Zoom out of your scene tab very far so that the square representing the camera looks small, as shown:

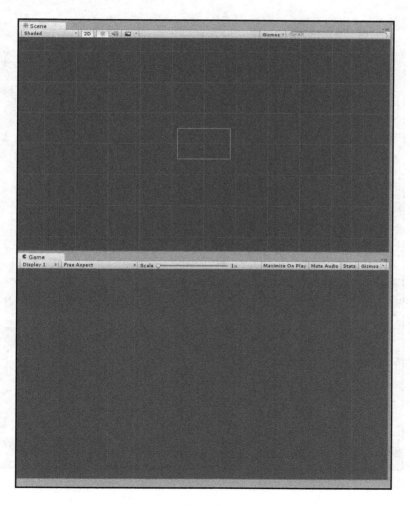

4. Now, reduce the size of the game tab so that it is a very small thin rectangle. You will see that the main camera is now also displaying as a very small thin rectangle, because we are in **Free Aspect** ratio mode:

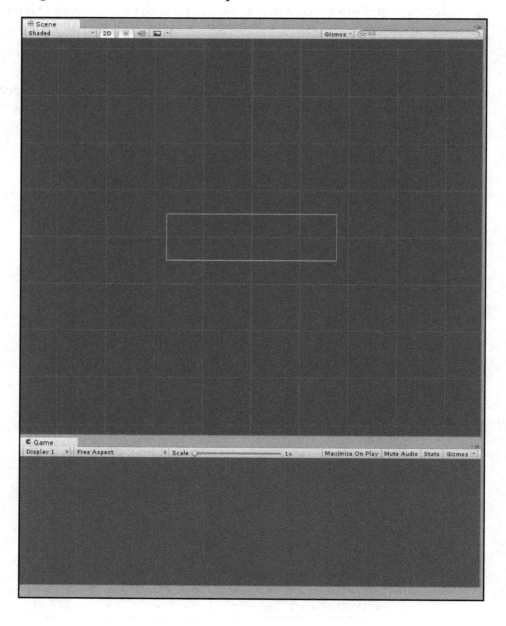

5. You can select another aspect ratio, like **5:4**, and you will see that as you rescale the game window, the blue area representing the actual game will maintain a **5:4** ratio and black bars to fill in any extra spacing. The camera will also maintain that ratio:

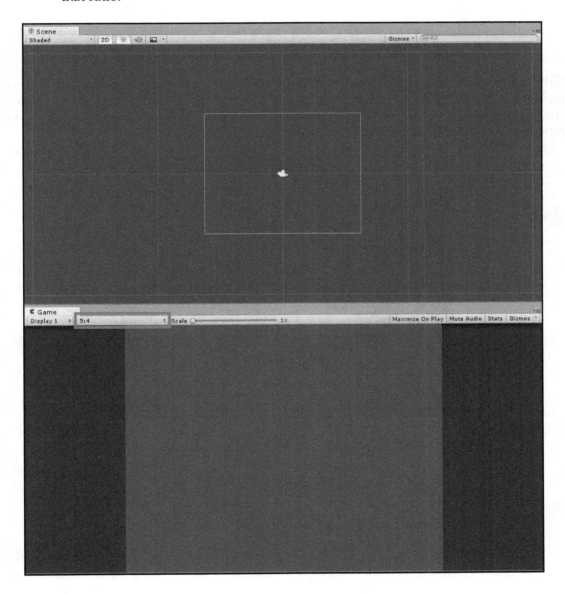

6. **Standalone (1024x768)** will attempt to emulate the 1024x768 resolution. It's pretty likely that the window you have set for the **Game** tab is not big enough to support 1024x768 pixels; if so, it will be scaled as indicated in the following screenshot:

If the resolution or aspect ratio you want to use is not available in the resolution drop-down menu, you can add your own item to this menu by selecting the plus sign. If you want to create a set resolution item, set **Type** to **Fixed Resolution**. If you want to create a set aspect ratio item, set **Type** to **Aspect Ratio**:

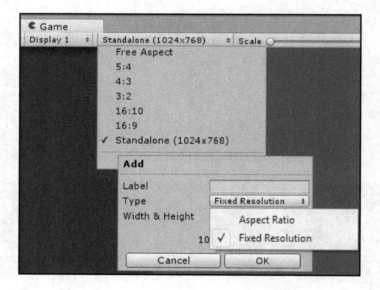

For example, if I wanted to have a resolution item that represented the iPhone 6, add an item with the settings displayed in the following screenshot:

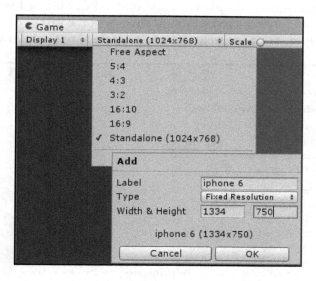

Once you hit **OK**, the **iphone 6** item will be displayed at the bottom of the list. When you select it, the camera and visible area of the **Game** tab will maintain the aspect ratio created by a **1334x750** resolution:

Building for a single resolution

If you are creating a game that you plan to build on the **PC, Mac, & Linux Standalone** target platform, you can force the resolution to always be the same. To do so, go to **Edit | Project Settings | Player**. Your Inspector should now display the following:

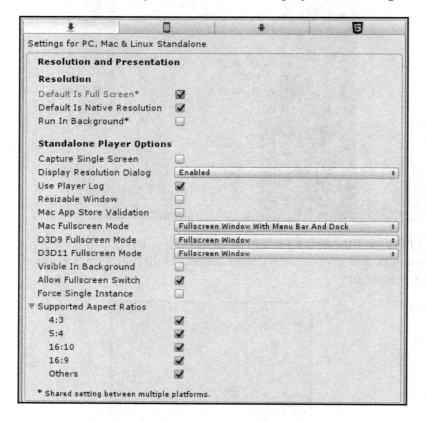

 You may have more or fewer platforms displayed here; it depends on the modules you have installed with Unity.

To force a specific resolution on a PC, Mac, & Linux Standalone game, deselect **Default is Native Resolution**. Then, the options for inputting **Default Screen Width** and **Default Screen Height** will be made available to you, and you can enter the desired resolution values. You must also set **Display Resolution Dialog** to **Disabled**. Then, when you build your game, it will build play in a window of the size you specified.

The following screenshot shows the settings for forcing your game to display at 1024x768 in the **Player** Settings for **PC, Mac, & Linux Standalone**:

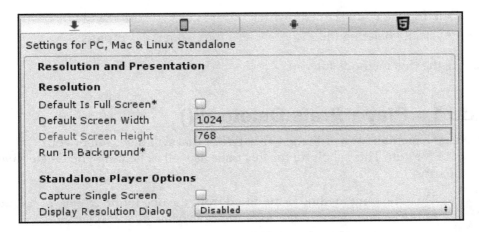

You can also force a specific resolution with a **WebGL** build. There are a few less options to worry about, but the general concept is the same. The following screenshot shows the settings for forcing your game to display at **1024x768** in the Player Settings for **WebGL**:

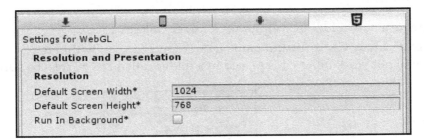

Resetting the resolution

Annoyingly, if you build and run a **PC, Mac, & Linux Standalone** game with one set of resolution settings, and then try to rebuild with a different set of resolution settings, your new settings will not update and the game will still build with the previous resolution. This may seem like a bug, but it is not. The Unity application is saving the screen settings under the `PlayerPref` save data.

If you find that you are unable to manually set your resolution settings, there are two methods you can attempt:

- Deleting the `PlayerPrefs` with `PlayerPrefs.DeleteAll();`
- Physically deleting the `PlayerPrefs` files from the computer

I will outline the two methods for you.

Method 1 – PlayerPrefs.DeleteAll()

You can create a menu item within the Unity Editor that will delete all of your `PlayerPrefs` for you. This is helpful for this issue as well as helping you delete saved data in other scenarios.

 The following method is modified from the one found at `http://answers.unity3d.com/questions/516517/why-doesnt-standalone-build-resolution-settings-af.html`.

To create a menu item within the Unity Editor that will delete all of your `PlayerPrefs`, complete the following steps:

1. Create a new folder in your `Assets` folder called `Editor`.
2. Create a new C# Script and name it `DeletePrefs.cs` within the `Editor` folder. It will not work unless it is placed in a folder called `Editor`, so be sure to do that:

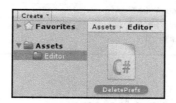

3. Open the `DeletePrefs.cs` script and give it the following code:

```
using UnityEditor;
using UnityEngine;

public class DeletePrefs : EditorWindow {

    [MenuItem("Edit/Delete All PlayerPrefs")]
```

```
public static void DeletePlayerPrefs(){
        PlayerPrefs.DeleteAll();
        Debug.Log("delete prefs");
    }
}
```

4. Save the script.

5. A new option, `Delete All PlayerPrefs`, will now be at the very bottom of the **Edit** menu. Select **Delete All PlayerPrefs**. If performed correctly, you should see `delete prefs` in the **Console** log.

6. Rebuild the game and see whether the new resolution settings "stick".

Method 2 – Deleting PlayerPref files

I have found that Method 1 doesn't always work for me and sometimes my resolution settings are not reset. If you are unable to get Method 1 to work for you (or you just feel like doing it another way), you can find the `PlayerPref` files on your computer and delete them manually. To delete the files manually, complete the following steps:

1. Determine **Company Name** and **Product Name** from **PlayerSettings** by navigating to **Edit | Preferences | Player Settings**:

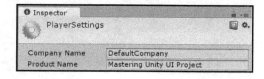

2. Now, select (Windows) **Start** and type `regedit`. Select the `regedit` program when it becomes available to you:

3. The Registry Editor should now be open. Navigate to the folders that represent the **Company Name** and **Product Name** you found in step 1, by the following path:

- **Computer**
- **HKEY_CURRENT_USER**
- **Software**
- The Company Name Found In Step 1 (**DefaultCompany**)
- The Project Name Found In Step 1 (**Mastering Unity UI Project**):

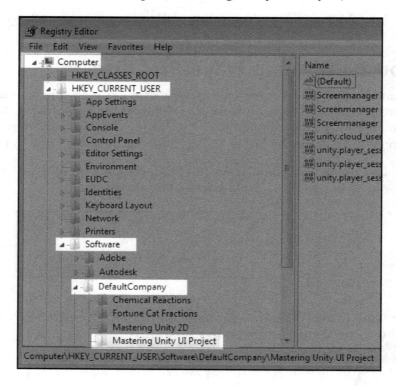

4. Once you select the appropriate folder, you should see the following items on the right-hand side of the Registry Editor:

- **Screenmanager Is Fullscreen**
- **Screenmanager Resolution Height**
- **Screenmanager Resolution Width**

5. Select all three of the listed items and delete them:

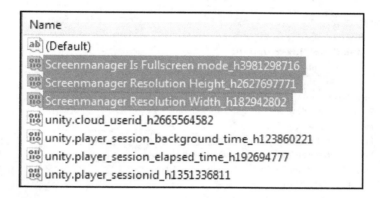

6. Rebuild the game, and the new resolution settings should now be displaying.

 The steps outlined in the previous text demonstrate how to delete the files from a Windows machine. If you have a different operating system, consult the following website for the location of the PlayerPref files: https://docs.unity3d.com/ScriptReference/PlayerPrefs.html.

Building for a single aspect ratio

Forcing a specific aspect ratio is possible in **PC, Mac, & Linux Standalone** builds. To do so, enable **Display Resolution Dialog** and check the aspect ratio you wish to use in the **Supported Aspect Ratios** setting.

The following screenshot shows a game being built with a **4:3** aspect ratio:

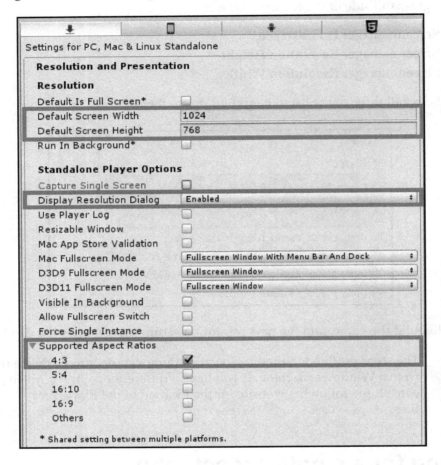

When you build and run your game with the preceding settings, a dialog option will open and the player will be allowed to choose from multiple resolutions that fit that setting. The following screenshot shows the resolution dialog window with multiple **4:3** resolutions available:

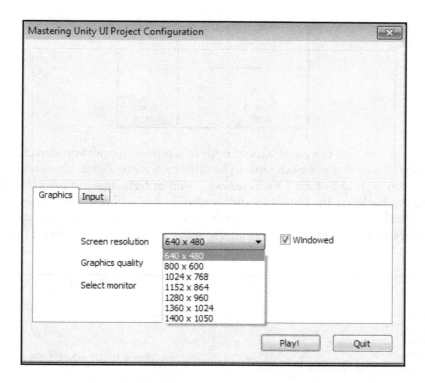

Setting the orientation

When building for mobile devices, you can't specify resolution and aspect ratio. However, you can choose between screen orientations in mobile devices. There are two different orientations: **Landscape** and **Portrait**.

Games built so that they are wider than they are tall are said to have landscape resolution. Games build that are taller than they are wide are said to have portrait resolution. For example, a **16:9** aspect ratio would be a landscape resolution, and a **9:16** aspect ratio would be a portrait resolution, as illustrated:

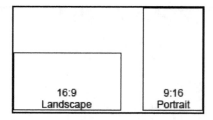

So, while you can't choose the exact aspect ratio of a mobile game, you can choose the orientation, which forces the aspect ratio to be either wider or taller. You can set the orientation by navigating to **Edit | Preferences | Player Settings** and selecting the mobile device. If you are building for both iOS and Android, you will not have to set these properties for both. As you can see from the following screenshot, the asterisk next to the property of **Default Orientation** states that the settings are shared between multiple platforms:

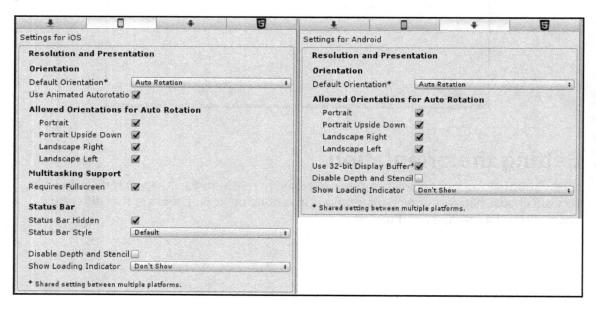

You can set the **Default Orientation** to either **Auto Rotation**, or one of the other rotations, as shown:

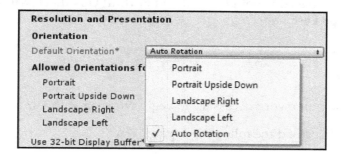

Unity defines the following orientations as the following rotations:

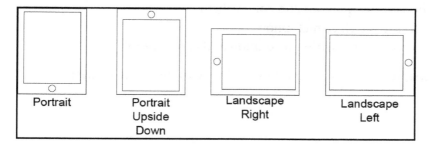

When you select a rotation other than **Auto Rotation** as the **Default Orientation**, the game will only play at that orientation on the device. If you select **Auto Rotation**, you will have the option to select between multiple orientations:

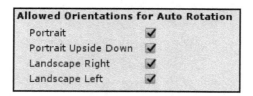

In most cases, it is best to choose only the **Landscape** orientations or only the **Portrait** orientations, but not all four. Generally, allowing all four orientations will cause issues with the game's UI.

Players tend to prefer to be able to rotate their games (especially if they're like me and like to play games in bed while their phone is charging), so unless you have a good reason to stop rotation, it's best to enable both **Portrait** and **Portrait Upside Down** or **Landscape Right** and **Landscape Left**.

Summary

This chapter laid the framework necessary to begin working with UI.

In this chapter, we discussed the following topics:

- Defining UI and GUI
- Describing the four types of interfaces
- Choosing a UI layout and color scheme
- Defining interface metaphors
- Discerning and setting resolution and aspect ratio

In the next chapter, we will jump into working with the Unity UI system.

2
Canvases, Panels, and Basic Layouts

Canvases are the core of all Unity UIs. Every single UI element must be included within a Canvas for it to be able to render within a scene. This chapter covers all that you need to create basic UI in Unity.

It's important to start focusing on setting up a UI that will scale at multiple resolutions and aspect ratios early on, as trying to do so later will cause a lot of headache and extra work. This chapter focuses on creating a UI that scales appropriately.

In this chapter, we will discuss the following topics:

- Creating UI Canvases and setting their properties
- Creating UI Panels and setting their properties
- Using the Rect Tool and Rect Transform component
- Properly setting anchor and pivot points
- How to create and lay out a basic HUD
- How to create a background image
- How to set up a basic pop-up menu

UI Canvas

Every UI element you create must be a child of a **UI Canvas**. To see a list of all UI elements you can create within Unity, select **Create | UI** from the **Hierarchy** window, as shown in the following screenshot:

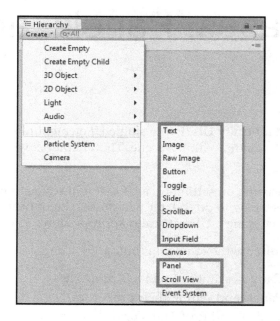

Every one of the UI items highlighted in the preceding screenshot are renderable UI items and must be contained within a Canvas to render. If you try to add any of those UI elements to a scene that does not contain a Canvas, a canvas will automatically be added to the scene, and the item you attempted to create will be made a child of the newly added Canvas. To demonstrate this, try adding a new **UI Text** element to an empty scene. You can do so by selecting **Create | UI | Text**.

This will cause three new items to appear in the Hierarchy list: **Canvas**, **Text**, and **Event System**, where the Text is a child of the Canvas.

Now that you have a Canvas in your scene, any new UI elements you add to the scene will automatically be added to this Canvas.

If you try to take a renderable UI element out of a Canvas, it will not be drawn to the scene.

You can also create an empty Canvas by selecting **Create** | **UI** | **Canvas**. When you create a new Canvas in a scene, if an **Event System** GameObject does not already exist within the scene, one will automatically be created for you (as you saw in the preceding screenshot). We'll discuss the Event System further in Chapter 4, *The Event System and Programming for UI*, but, for now, all you really need to know is the **Event System** allows you to interact with the UI items.

 You can have more than one canvas in your scene, each with their own children.

When you create a Canvas, it will appear as a large rectangle within your scene. It will be significantly larger than that rectangle representing the camera's view:

The Canvas is larger than the Camera, because the Canvas Component has a scaling mode on it. The scaling mode by default equates one pixel within the UI to one Unity unit, so it's a lot bigger. A nice consequence of this large size is that the large size makes it really easy to see your UI items as a somewhat separate entity and keeps it from cluttering up your camera view.

Every newly created Canvas automatically comes with four components: **Rect Transform**, **Canvas, Canvas Scaler, and Graphic Raycaster**, as shown in the following screenshot:

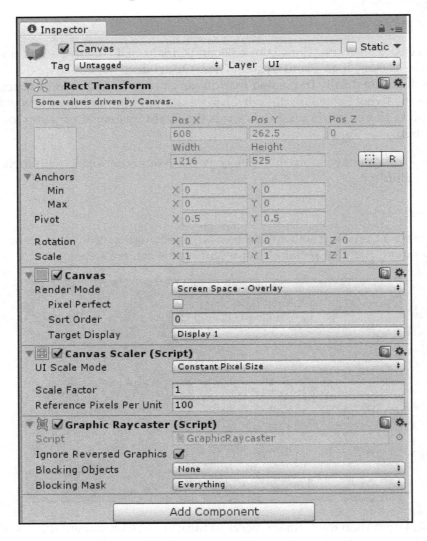

Let's explore each of these components.

Rect Transform component

Every UI GameObject has a **Rect Transform** component as its first component. This component is very similar to the **Transform** component on non-UI GameObject, in that it allows you to place the object within the scene.

You'll note that when you first place a Canvas in the scene, you can't adjust the values within the **Rect Transform**, and there is a message stating **Some values driven by Canvas**, as shown in the preceding screenshot.

This message means you cannot control the position of the Canvas, because of the properties selected in the **Canvas** component. Adjustment of **Rect Transform** is disabled for Canvases that are in **Screen Space-Overlay Render Mode** and **Screen Space-Camera Render Mode** (determined by the **Canvas** component). In these two modes, the values shown are determined by the resolution of the game display and automatically takes up the full screen. When the Canvas is in **World Space Render Mode**, you can adjust the values as you see fit.

We will look at the **Rect Transform** and the various render modes more thoroughly momentarily.

Canvas component

The Canvas component allows you to select the **Canvas Render Mode**. There are three render modes: **Screen Space-Overlay**, **Screen Space-Camera**, and **World Space**. The different render modes determine where in the scene the UI elements will be drawn.

 One reason for creating multiple canvases is to create canvases with different render modes.

Screen Space-Overlay

Screen Space-Overlay is the default rendering mode. When you think of UI, usually the first picture of UI that pops in your head is the type that would be rendered in **Screen Space-Overlay**. This rendering mode overlays all the UI elements within the Canvas in front of everything in the scene. So, UI items like **heads-up-displays** (**HUDs**) and pop-up windows that appear on the same plane and the screen, will be contained within a **Screen Space-Overlay Canvas**.

Remember that when a Canvas is using the **Screen Space-Overlay** render mode, you cannot adjust the **Rect Transform** component of the Canvas. This is because the canvas will automatically resize based on the size of the screen (not the camera):

When you have **Screen Space-Overlay** selected, the following properties become available:

- **Pixel Perfect**: This option can make the UI elements appear sharper and less blurry. This can cause performance issues, so only use it if absolutely necessary.
- **Sort Order**: This option applies only when you have multiple canvases with **Screen Space-Overlay** render modes. The higher the number, the *closer* to the items within the canvas will appear to the person viewing the scene. In other words, higher-numbered canvases will appear *on top* of lower-numbered canvases.
- **Target Display:** If you are creating a PC, Mac, Linux Standalone game, you can have different cameras display on up to eight different monitors. You can also have different UI for each monitor and also where you will tell the Canvas which of the displays it will render on.

Screen Space-Camera

Screen Space-Camera performs similar to **Screen Space-Overlay**, but it renders all UI elements as if they are a specific distance away from the camera. As you can see from the following screenshot, if there is no renderer camera selected, this rendering mode works exactly the same as the **Screen Space-Overlay** mode (as indicated by the warning message):

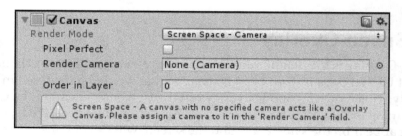

You can add either the **Main Camera** or a second camera as the **Render Camera** in the **Screen Space-Camera** render mode. This is the camera to which the canvas will draw. Once you add a camera to the **Render Camera** slot, the warning message will disappear and new options will be made available to you, as shown in the following screenshot:

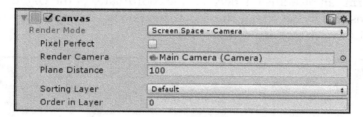

When you have **Screen Space-Camera** selected, the following properties become available:

- **Pixel Perfect**: This is the same option as with **Screen Space-Overlay**.
- **Render Camera**: As stated earlier, this is the camera to which the canvas will draw.
- **Plane Distance**: This property tells the canvas how far away from the camera it should display.
- **Sorting Layer**: This property allows you to choose which **Sprite Sorting Layer** to display the Canvas.
- **Order in Layer**: This property determines the order in the **Sprite Sorting Layer** (chosen earlier) the Canvas will display. This order works similar to the way **Sort Order** works, with higher numbers appearing on top of lower numbers.

This rendering mode is helpful if you want a Canvas to render at a different perspective than your main camera. It is also helpful for creating a static background that will consistently scale with the camera in a 2D game. Since you can use **Sprite Sorting Layer** with this rendering mode, you can make sure the Canvas containing the background always renders behind all other objects in the scene.

Remember, when a Canvas is using the **Screen Space-Camera** render mode, you cannot adjust the **Rect Transform** component of the Canvas. This is because the canvas will automatically resize based on the size of the camera (not the screen).

World Space

The last rendering mode is **World Space**. This mode allows you to render UI elements as if they are physically positioned within the world.

In **Screen Space-Overlay** and **Screen Space-Camera**, you cannot adjust the properties of the **Rect Transform** component. The positions of UI elements within Canvases with those two rendering modes do not translate to world space coordinates and are instead relative to the screen and camera. However, when a Canvas is in **World Space** render mode, the values of the **Rect Transform** can be adjusted, because the coordinates of the UI elements are based on actual positions within the scene. These Canvases do not have to face a specified camera as the other two Canvas types do.

This mode requests an **Event Camera**, rather than a Rendering Camera as **Screen Space-Camera** mode requested. An **Event Camera** is different than a Rendering Camera. Since this Canvas is in the **World Space**, it will be rendered with the Main Camera, just as all the other objects that exist within the scene. The **Event Camera** is the camera that will receive events from the EventSystem. So, if items on this Canvas require interactions, you have to include an **Event Camera**. If the player won't be interacting with the items on the Canvas, you can leave this blank.

The reason you need to specify an **Event Camera** is ray casting. When the user clicks on or touches the screen, a ray (one-directional line) is cast infinitely forward from the point of click (or touch) into the scene. The direction it points in is determined based on the direction the camera is facing. Most of the time, you will set this as your Main Camera, because that is the direction in which the player will expect the events to occur.

When you have **World Space** selected, the following properties become available:

- **Event Camera**: As stated earlier, the camera assigned to this slot determines which camera will receive the events of the Canvas
- **Sorting Layer**: This property is the same as in **Screen Space-Camera**
- **Order in Layer**: This property is the same as in **Screen Space-Camera**

Canvas Scalar component

The **Canvas Scalar** component determines how the items within the canvas will scale. It also determines the pixel density of the items within the UI canvas.

In the Resolution and Aspect Ratio section, we discussed how to build your game at a single resolution or the single aspect ratio. However, most of the time, you will not have the luxury of choosing the resolution or aspect ratio your game will play at. You'll note that I only mentioned specifying the aspect ratio and resolution for the PC, Mac, and Linux Standalone builds, and the WebGL builds. When you build to something that will play on a handheld screen or a TV screen, you cannot guarantee how big that screen will be.

Due to the fact that you cannot guarantee the resolution or aspect ratio of your game, the need for your UI to adjust to various resolutions and scaling is very important; that's why this **Canvas Scalar** component exists.

The Canvas Scalar component has four **UI Scale Modes**:

- **Constant Pixel Size**
- **Scale With Screen Size**
- **Constant Physical Size**
- **World**

The first three UI Scale Modes are available when the **Canvas Render Mode** is set to **Screen Space-Overlay** or **Screen Space-Camera**. The fourth **UI Scale Mode** is automatically assigned when the **Canvas Render Mode** is set to **World Space** (it cannot be changed when set).

Constant Pixel Size

When a Canvas has the **UI Scale Mode** set to **Constant Pixel Size**, every item in the UI will maintain its original pixel size regardless of the size of the screen. You'll note that this is the default setting, so by default UI does not scale; you must turn the setting on for it to scale with altering screen resolutions.

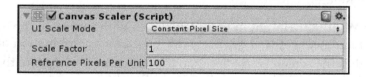

When you change the **UI Scale Mode** to **Constant Pixel Size**, you will see the following properties appear within the inspector:

- **Scale Factor**: This setting creates a scale multiple for all objects within the UI. For example, if you set this number to 2, everything within the UI will then double in size. If you set this number to 0.5, all items will have their size halved.

- **Reference Pixels Per Unit**: This setting determines how many pixels take up a single in-game unit. When this number is set to 100, that means two objects one game unit apart from each other will be 100 pixels apart. Put another way, if two objects are at the same y-coordinate, but one object has an x-coordinate of 1 and the other has an x-coordinate of 2, they are exactly 100 pixels apart. (This property works the same way in all other modes).

Scale with Screen Size

When you have the Canvas Scalar component set to **Scale with Screen Size**, UI elements on the Canvas will scale based on a **Reference Resolution**. If the screen is larger or smaller than this **Reference Resolution**, the items on the Canvas will then scale up or down accordingly. In the Resolution and Aspect Ratio section, I have told you that you should decide on a default resolution that represents the ideal resolution of your UI design. This default resolution will be the **Reference Resolution**.

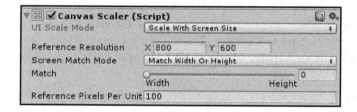

If the aspect ratio of the game does not match with that of the **Reference Resolution**, then things will scale up and down without any problems. If it does not match, then you need to use the **Canvas Scalar** on how to scale items if the aspect ratio changes. This can be done by using the **Screen Match Mode** settings. Below are the three different **Screen Match Modes** that determine how the Canvas will scale if the game's aspect ratio does not match the aspect ratio of the Reference Resolution:

- **Match Width Or Height**: It will scale the UI with respect to the reference height or the reference width. It can also scale based on a combination of both.
- **Expand:** If the screen is smaller than the Reference Resolution, the canvas will be expanded to match that of the Reference Resolution.
- **Shrink:** If the screen gets larger than the Reference Resolution, the canvas will be reduced to match that of the Reference Resolution.

The **Expand** and **Shrink** Screen Match Modes do not have any further properties to edit; they just "do their own thing". However, the **Match Width Or Height** Screen Match Mode does have a **Match** property. This property is a sliding scale that can be adjusted between 0 (**Width**) and 1 (**Height**).

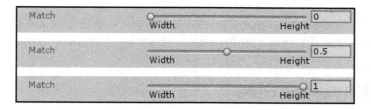

When the value of **Match** is set to 0, the **Canvas Scaler** will force the Canvas to always have the same width specified by the **Reference Resolution**. This will maintain the relative scales and positions of objects along the width of the Canvas. So, objects will not get further away from or closer to each other in the horizontal direction. However, it will completely ignore the height. So, objects can get further from or closer to each other in the vertical direction.

Setting the **Match** value to 1 will accomplish the same thing, but will maintain the positions and scales of the objects along the height, not the width.

Setting the **Match** value to 0.5, will compare the game's width and height to that of **Reference Resolution**, and it will try to maintain the distances between objects in both the horizontal and vertical directions.

The Match value can be any number between 0 and 1. If the number is closer to 1, scaling will favor the height and if it is closer to 0, it will favor the width.

None of these Match settings will be perfect for all games at all aspect ratios and resolutions. The settings you choose will depend on how you want the UI to scale. If you want the relative vertical positions to be maintained, use Height (1). If you want the relative horizontal positions to be maintained, use Width (0). It really just depends on which spacing you care the most about.

I recommend using the following settings based on the orientation of your game:

Orientation	Match Value
Portrait	0 (Width)
Landscape	1 (Height)
Varies	0.5 (Width and Height)

I chose these settings based on whichever of the two numbers on the **Reference Resolution** is the smallest. In **Portrait** mode, the width will be the smallest, so I find it important to maintain the relative position of the items in the width. This is a personal preference and just a recommendation, and it will not necessarily make sense for all games. However, I have found it to be a good rule of thumb for most games.

It is best to avoid making games that will vary between portrait and landscape mode unless you have minimal UI or are very comfortable with creating scalable UI.

Constant Physical Size

When a Canvas has the **UI Scale Mode** set to **Constant Physical Size**, every item in the UI will maintain its original physical size, regardless of the size of the screen. Physical size is referencing the size it would appear to the user if they were to take out a ruler and measure it on their screen. Much like **Constant Pixel Size**, items on Canvases with this **UI Scale Mode** will not scale. If you had a UI item that you wanted to always be a specific width and height, you'd put it on a Canvas that has this **UI Scale Mode**. For example, if you wanted a button to always be 2 inches wide and 1 inch tall, you'd use this mode.

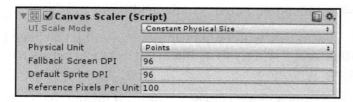

When you change the **UI Scale Mode** to **Constant Physical Size**, you will see the following properties appear within the inspector:

- **Physical Unit**: The unit of measure. You can select from **Centimeters**, **Millimeters**, **Inches**, **Points**, and **Picas**
- **Fallback Screen DPI**: If the DPI is unknown, this is the assumed DPI
- **Default Sprite DPI**: The DPI of all sprites with Pixels Per Unit that are equal to the **Reference Pixels Per Unit**

World

World is the only **UI Scale Mode** available for Canvases set to **World Space**. You'll see from the following screenshot that the mode cannot be changed:

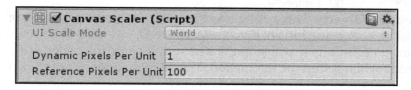

When you change the **UI Scale Mode** to **World**, you will see the following property appear within the inspector:

- **Dynamic Pixels Per Unit**: This is the Pixels Per Unit setting for all dynamic UI items (like text)

Graphic Raycaster component

The Graphic Raycaster allows you to check to see whether objects on the Canvas have been hit by a user input using the EventSystem. As discussed when looking at the **World Space** Canvas Render Mode, when a user touches the screen, a ray is cast forward from the point on the screen at which the player touches. The **Graphic Raycaster** checks these rays and sees if they hit something on the Canvas.

You can adjust the following properties on the **Graphic Raycaster** component:

- **Ignore Reversed Graphics**: If a UI element is facing away from the player, having this selected will stop the hit from registering. If it is not selected, hits will register on back-facing UI objects.
- **Blocking Objects**: This setting specifies which types of items in front of it will block it from being hit. So, if you select **Two D**, any **Two D** object in front of the items on this Canvas will stop the items from being interacted with. However, 3D objects will not stop the interaction. The possible options are shown here:

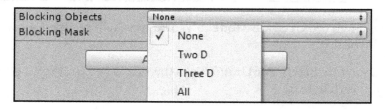

- **Blocking Mask**: Selecting items on this property works similar to the **Blocking Objects** property. This allows you to select items based on their Rendering Layer, so you can get a little more specific. The possible options are shown as follows:

We will discuss Raycasting and the EventSystem more thoroughly in Chapter 4, *The Event System and Programming for UI*.

Canvas Renderer component

The **Canvas Renderer** component is not on a Canvas object but on all other renderable UI objects.

For a UI element to render, it must have a **Canvas Renderer** component on it. All of renderable UI elements that you create via the **Create** menu will automatically have this component attached to them. If you try to remove this component, you will see a warning similar to the following:

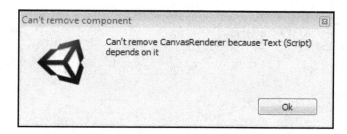

In the preceding screenshot, I tried to remove the Canvas Render a component from a Text UI object. As you can see, it will not let me remove the **Canvas Renderer** component, because the **Text** component relies on it. If I return and remove the text component, I would then be able to remove the Canvas Render a component.

You will note that there are no properties in the **Canvas Renderer** component that can be edited from within the inspector; however, you can access various properties of it from within scripts.

 For further details about properties of the **Canvas Renderer** that can be accessed through script, refer to https://docs.unity3d.com/ScriptReference/CanvasRenderer.html.

UI Panel

The main function of UI Panels is to hold other UI elements. You can create a `Panel` by selecting **Create | UI | Panel**. Its important to note that there is no Panel component. Panels are really just GameObjects that have **Rect Transform**, **Canvas Renderer**, and **Image** components. So, really, a UI Panel is just a UI Image with a few properties predefined for it.

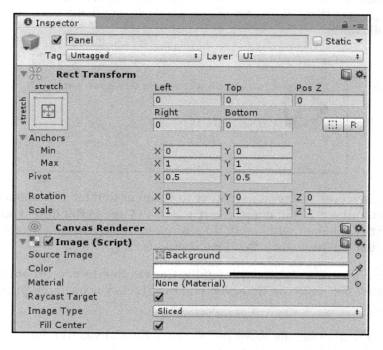

By default, **Panels** start with the **Background** image (which is just a grey rounded rectangle) as the **Source Image** with medium opacity. You can replace the **Source Image** with another image or remove the image entirely.

Panels are very useful when you are trying to ensure that items scale and are appropriately relative to each other. Items that are contained within the same Panel will scale relative to the Panel and maintain their relative position to each other in the process.

We will look at the **Image** component more thoroughly soon, but, now that we are looking at an object that will allow us to edit its **Rect Transform** component, let's explore that component.

Rect Transform

Each UI element has a Rect Transform component. The Rect Transform component works very similarly to the Transform component and is used to determine the position of the object on which it is attached.

Rect Tool

Any of the Transform tools can be used to manipulate UI objects. However, the Rect Tool allows you to scale, move, and rotate any object by manipulating the rectangle that encompasses it. While this tool can be used with 3D objects, it is most useful for 2D and UI objects.

- To move an object with the Rect Tool, select the object and then click and drag inside the rectangle.
- To resize an object, hover over the edge or corner of an object. When the curse changes to arrows, click and drag to resize the object. You can scale uniformly by holding down shift while dragging.
- To rotate, hover at the corner of the objects, slightly outside of the rectangle until the cursor displays a rotating circle at its corner. You can then rotate by clicking and dragging.

Positioning modes

When using the Rect Tool, it is important that you have the correct positioning modes selected. You can select **Center** or **Pivot** and **Global** or **Local**. The modes will toggle by clicking on the buttons:

- When in the **Center** mode, the object will move based on its center point and rotate around its center point.
- When in **Pivot** mode, the object will rotate around its pivot point rather than its center point. You can also alter the position of the pivot point in this mode by hovering over the pivot point, and clicking and dragging to move.

- When in the **Global** mode, the Rect Transform's bounding box will be an non-rotated box that encompasses the entire object.
- When in **Local** mode, the Rect Transform's bounding box will be rotated box that snuggly fits the object.

The following illustration shows the bounding boxes of the Rect Transform for a Panel in **Global Mode** and **Local Mode**. The empty blue circle represents the object's pivot point:

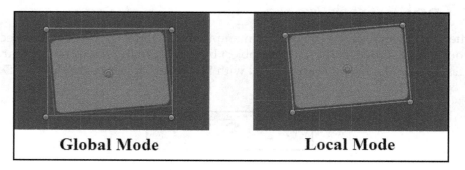

Rect Transform component

As stated earlier, UI elements do not have the standard **Transform** component, they have the **Rect Transform** component. If you compare it to a standard **Transform** component, you will see that it has quite a few more properties.

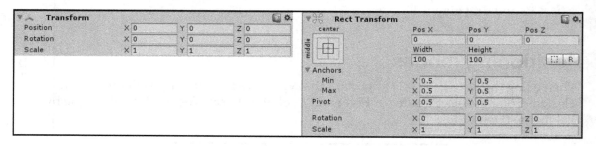

You can use it to change the position, the rotation, and the scale, just as you can with the **Transform**, but there are the added properties of Anchor Presets (represented by the square image in the top left corner), two values for determining dimension: **Anchor Min** and **Max** points, and **Pivot** point.

It's important to note that the **Scale** value is considered the Local Scale. If you rescale the object with the Rect Tool, even with the Local positioning mode, the values within **Scale** will remain at 1.

You may have noted that the labels for the position and dimensional values are different on the preceding illustration than they were on the one provided in the UI Panel Properties section. This is because the labels that represent the position and dimension change depending on the Anchor Preset chosen. We'll discuss how to use these Anchor Preset momentarily, but let's look at some different examples of labels the position and dimensional values can hold.

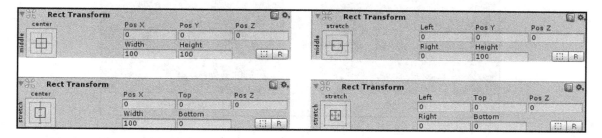

If the **Rect Transform** has its Anchor Preset set to not include stretch, as with the top-left example in the preceding screenshot, the values for position are determined by **Pos X**, **Pox Y**, **Pos Z**, and the dimensions are determined by **Width** and **Height**.

If the **Rect Transform** has its Anchor Preset set to include stretch, as with the other three examples, the positions perpendicular to the stretch and the dimensions parallel to the stretch are labeled with **Left**, **Right**, **Top**, and **Bottom**. These values represent the offset from the border of the parent's **Rect Transform**.

The Anchor Point of an object determines the point from which all the relative positions are measured from. The Pivot Point determines the point from which the scaling and rotating modifiers happen. It will rotate around this point and scale toward this point. We will look at Anchors and Pivots more thoroughly in the Anchors and Pivot section.

Rect Transform edit modes

There are two different edit modes available to you within the **Rect Transform—Blueprint Mode** and **Raw Edit Mode**—as represented by the following icons, respectively:

Blueprint mode will ignore any local rotation or scaling applied to it and will display the Rect Transform bounding box as a non-rotated, non-scaled box. The following screenshot shows the bounding box of a Panel that has been rotated and scaled with Blueprint Mode turned off and turned on:

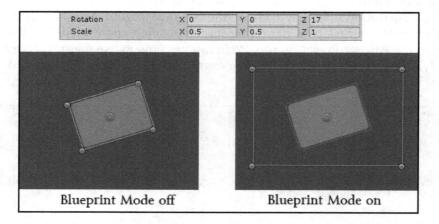

Rotation	X	0	Y	0	Z	17
Scale	X	0.5	Y	0.5	Z	1

Blueprint Mode off   Blueprint Mode on

Raw Edit Mode will allow you to change the anchor and pivot points of a UI object without the object moving or scaling based on the changes you have made.

Anchor and Pivot Point

Every UI object has a set of Anchor Handles and a Pivot Point. These objects used together will help ensure that your UI is positioned appropriately and scales appropriately if the resolution or aspect ratio of your game changes.

The **Anchor Handles** are represented by four triangles in the form of an X, as shown in the following diagram:

The Anchors can be in a group together forming a single Anchor, as shown in the preceding diagram, or they can be split in to multiple Anchors, as follows:

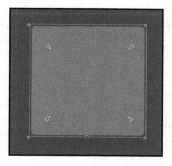

The Anchors will always form a rectangle. So, the sides will always line up.

The **Rect Transform** has properties for Anchor **Min** and Anchor **Max** points. These represent the position of the Anchor Handles relative to the parent's Rect Transform, as percentages. So, for example, a 0 in an x value represents all the way to the left, and a 1 represents all the way to the right. You can see from the following screenshot how adjusting the x value will move it left and right, relative to the parent:

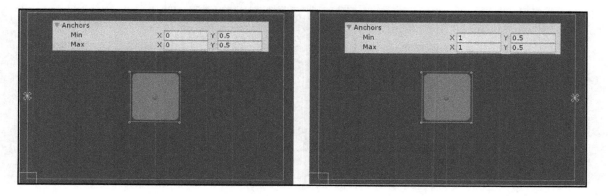

The **Rect Transform** has a Property for **Anchor Presets** and **Anchors Min** and **Max** Points. The Anchor represents the point at which the UI element is connected to its parent's Rect Transform:

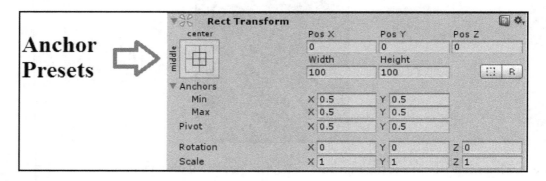

As a Canvas has no parent, you'll see that the Anchor Preset is empty. This is true, regardless of the Canvas Render Mode chosen:

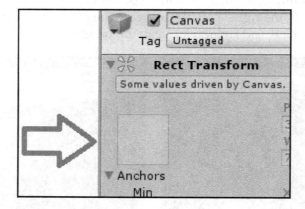

Click on the box holding representing the Anchor Presets icon will display a list of all the possible **Anchor Presets**.

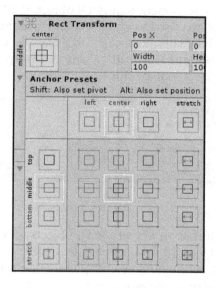

If you click on one of the presets, it will move the anchors to the position displayed in the screenshot. You can also adjust the position and pivot point using the anchor preset. The images will change if you hold down *Shift* and/or *Alt*. Holding *Shift* will show positions for the pivot point represented by blue dots, holding *Alt* will show how the position will change, and holding both will show the pivot point and the position change.

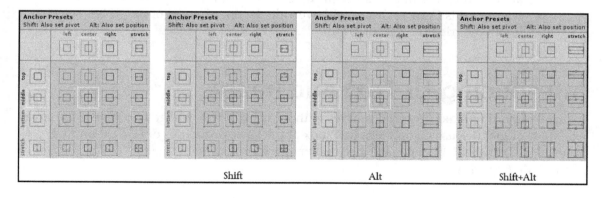

Canvas Group component

You can add a Canvas Group component to any UI object. It allows you to adjust specific properties of the UI object it is attached to and all of its children at once, rather than having to adjust these properties individually. You can add a Canvas Group component to any UI object by selecting **Add Component** | **Layout** | **Canvas Group** (you can also just search for Canvas Group) from the UI object's **Inspector**.

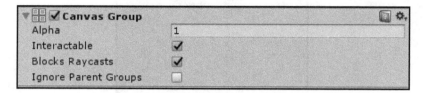

You can adjust the following properties using a **Canvas Group** component:

- **Alpha**: This is the transparency of the UI objects within the Canvas Group. The number is between 0 and 1 and represents a percentage of opaqueness; 0 is completely transparent, while 1 is completely opaque.
- **Interactable**: This setting states whether or not the objects within the group can accept input.
- **Blocks Raycast**: This setting determines if the objects within the group will block the raycast from hitting things behind it.
- **Ignore Parent Groups**: If this Canvas Group is on an object that is a child of another object with a **Canvas Group** component, this property determines whether this Canvas Group will override the one above it or not. If it is selected, it will override the parent group.

Introducing UI Text and Image

It's kind of hard to make any UI examples without using text or images. So, before we cover examples of that discuss layout, let's first look at the basic properties of UI Text and UI Images. UI Text and UI Images are discussed more thoroughly in Chapter 6, *Text, Images, and TextMesh Pro-Text*.

When you create a new Text object using **Create** | **UI** | **Text**, you will see that it has a **Text** Component.

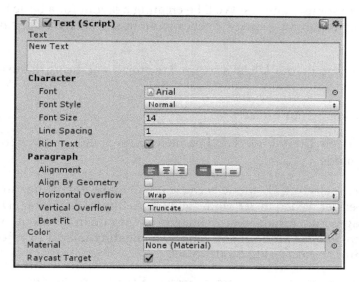

You can change the displayed text by changing the words in the New **Text** box. In Chapter 6, *Text, Images, and TextMesh Pro-Text*, we'll take a closer look at the individual properties of the **Text** component, but, for now, it should be fairly obvious what most of the properties do.

When you create a new Image object using **Create** | **UI** | **Image**, you will see that it has an **Image** component.

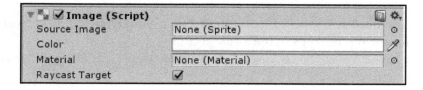

Remember that a Panel is essentially an **Image**, but with a few properties prefilled. When you create an **Image**, however, there are no pre-filled properties.

We'll work with the Source Image property in this chapter, which allows you to change the displayed image. We'll look at the other properties in Chapter 6, *Text, Images, and TextMesh Pro-Text*.

Examples

Now let's jump into some examples! We'll be creating a layout for a basic **heads-up-display (HUD)** and a background image that stretches with the screen and scales at multiple resolutions.

Before we begin setting up our UI, let's set up our project and bring in the art assets we will need.

We'll begin by setting up our project:

1. Create a new Unity Project and name it `Master Unity UI Project`. Create it in the 2D mode.

> We're selecting 2D Mode because it will make importing our UI sprites a lot easier. When in 2D Mode, all images import as Sprite (2D and UI) images rather than Texture images, as they do in 3D Mode. You can change to 3D Mode at any time by navigating to **Edit** | **Project Settings** | **Editor** and changing Mode to 3D.

2. Create three new folders named **Scenes**, **Scripts**, and **Sprites**:

> You don't need the `Editor` folder, but, if you'd like it, it was created following the steps in the `Method 1:` `PlayerPrefs.DeleteAll()` section of `Chapter 1`, *Designing User Interfaces*.

3. Create a new scene and name it `Chapter2.unity`; ensure that you save it in the `Scenes` folder.

4. We'll be using art assets that I've modified from free art assets found at the following:

   `https://opengameart.org/content/free-game-gui`
   `https://opengameart.org/content/cat-dog-free-sprites`

   Let's bring the sprites in to our project and prepare them to be used within our UI. You can get the original source files from the links provided so that you can follow along with the book; I recommend using the edited images provided in the source files of the text. In the `Chapter2/Sprites` folder, you'll find the `catSprites.png`, `pinkBackground.png`, and `uiElements.png` images.

5. We'll be importing the sprites to the project and slicing the sprite sheets into their separate image regions. If you already know how to slice sprite sheets, do so now for the `catSprites` image and the `uiElements` image and proceed to the *Laying out the Basic HUD* section. If you are not familiar with the process, follow these steps:

6. Drag the three sprites into the **Sprites** folder.

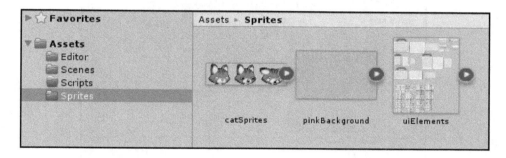

7. Select the `catSprites` image, hold *Ctrl*, and click on the `uiElements` image so that both are selected.

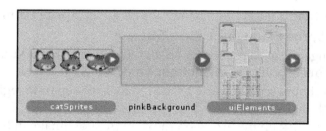

8. Now, in the **Inspector**, select **Multiple** for **Sprite Mode**. Then hit **Apply**. This will cause both the `catSprites` and the `uiElements` images to be considered a sprite sheet.

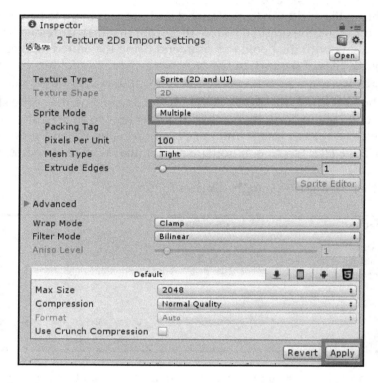

9. Note that the **Inspector** says that **2 Texture 2Ds** are selected, because we have selected two images.
10. Now select the `catSprites` image and open the **Sprite Editor**.
11. With the **Sprite Editor** open, select **Slice**.
12. Now change the slice properties so that the **Slice Type** is **Automatic** and the sprite **Pivot** is applied to the **Bottom**. Once done, hit **Slice**.
13. You should now see the sprite broken in to three separate regions. Hit **Apply** to save the changes.
14. Now if you click on the arrow on the `catSprites` image in the project folder view, you should see the individual images.

15. Complete steps 10–14 for the `uiElements` image, but make the pivot point in the **Center**.

Now that we have our project and sprites set up, we can begin with the UI examples.

Laying out a basic HUD

We will make a HUD that will look like the following:

It will be expanded upon in the upcoming chapters, but, for now, it'll have a pretty simple layout that will focus on parent–child relationships and anchor/pivot point placement.

To create the HUD shown in the preceding image, complete the following steps:

1. Create a new Canvas using **Create** | **UI** | **Canvas**.
2. In the Canvas **Inspector**, change the name to `HUD Canvas`.

I like to break my Canvases up into the following categories: HUD, Background, and Popups. I find that this keeps my various UI elements well organized.

3. It is best to set up all of your **Canvas Scaler** component information before you even begin adding elements to the UI. If you try to do it afterward, you may find that your UI elements will start rescaling. We'll work with an ideal resolution of `1024x768`. If you look at the **pinkBackground** image (that we'll apply in the next example), it has a resolution of `2048x1536`; `1024x768` has the same aspect ratio as the background image. So, set your **Canvas Scaler** component to the following settings:

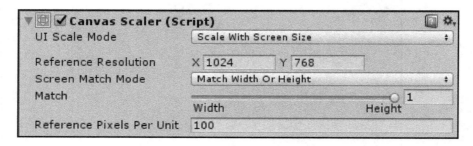

We have set the **Screen Match Mode** to **Match Width Or Height** with the **Match** settings set to `1` so that it maintains the ratios in the vertical direction. If you remember from the *Scale with Screen Size* section, I find that this works best for most games made with a landscape resolution.

4. Set your game view Aspect to Standalone `1024x768` so that you will see everything scaled appropriately. (Refer to the *Changing the Aspect Ratio and Resolution of the Game View* section for directions.)
5. Since we only have one Canvas, when we add any new UI elements to our scene, they will automatically be made children of our HUD Canvas. Create a new Panel using **Create | UI | Panel**, and rename it **HUD Panel**. You will see that it is a child of the HUD Canvas. This Panel will represent the rectangle that holds all the HUD elements.

6. Click on the **Anchor Presets** icon and select the top-left Anchor Preset while holding down *Shift + Alt*.

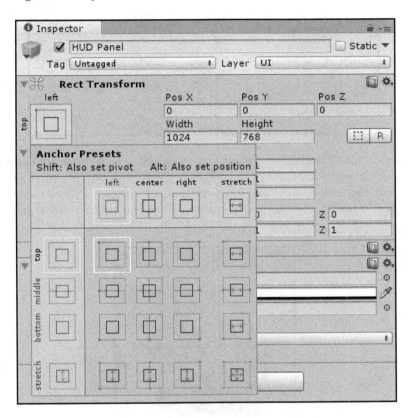

7. Expand the `uiElements` image by selecting the arrow on its right. Locate the `uiElements_1` subimage:

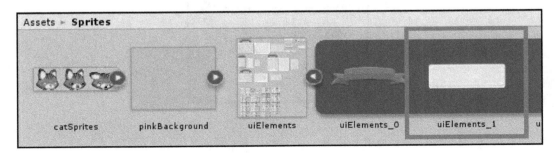

8. Drag `uiElements_1` to the **Source Image** slot of the **Image** component on the **HUD Panel**:

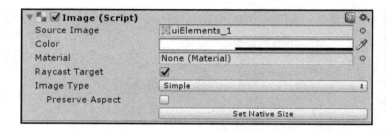

9. Currently, the Panel is very faint and stretches across the whole scene. Let's make it easier to see by increasing the opacity. Click on the white rectangle in the **Color** slot of the **Image** component to open up a color picker. Move the Alpha slider all the way to the right or input the value 255 in the alpha value slot:

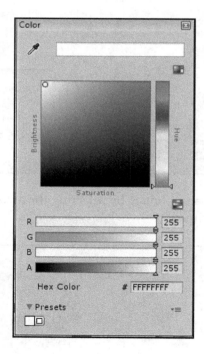

As shown in the preceding screenshot, it should be a lot easier to see the Panel now:

10. Click on the checkbox next to the **Preserve Aspect** setting in the **Image** component:

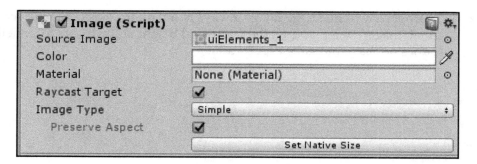

11. The Panel will now take up only the top portion of the scene:

12. This property will make the image always maintain the aspect ratio of the original image, even if you set the width and height of the Image to something that does not have the same aspect ratio.

13. You'll note, from the **Rect Transform** component, that the **Width** and **Height** are still set to 1024 and 768, respectively. You can also see more easily from the **Scene** view that the Rect Transform expands past the viewable region of the image. So, the object is much larger than it appears to be.

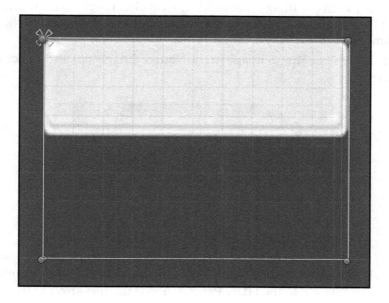

14. Let's rescale the **Rect Transform** of the Panel so that it matches the size we are looking for and hugs the viewable image better. Change the **Width** to 300 and the **Height** to 102. The Rect Transform won't be a perfectly snug fit in the vertical direction, but it will be pretty close.

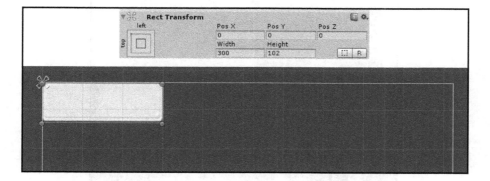

15. We now have the main Panel set up. Since all other images will be contained within the HUD Panel, we want to make them children of the HUD Panel. That way, when the screen rescales, the other images will remain "inside" the HUD Panel and will maintain their size relative to the HUD Panel.

16. Let's start with the Image that holds the cat character's head. Right-click on the HUD Panel and select **UI | Image**. You'll see that it is a child of the HUD Panel. Rename it `Character Holder`.

17. Place the `uiElement_6` image in the **Source Image** slot and select **Preserve Aspect**.

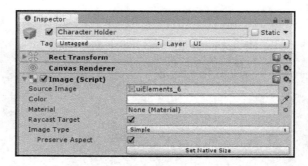

18. Since the **Character Holder** image is a child of the **HUD Panel**, any anchoring we set will be relative to the HUD Panel. Choose the **left-stretch** Anchor Preset while holding *Shift + Alt*. Also, set the position and dimension variables, as shown:

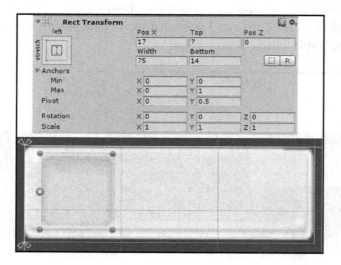

19. Let's add the image for the cat head. We want it to fully fill out the slot represented by the `Character Holder` image. So, we will make it a child of the **Character Holder** image. Right-click on `Character Holder` and select **UI | Image**. Change its name to `Character Image`.

20. Now add the `catSprites_0` subimage to the **Source Image** of the **Image** component and select **Preserve Aspect**.

21. Set the **Anchor Preset** to **stretch-stretch** while holding *Shift + Alt*:

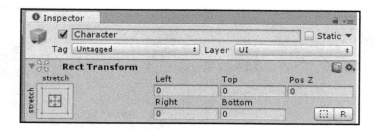

22. Since we ensured that we have the **Rect Transform** of the `Character Holder` fit snuggly around the holder's image, it should make the cat's head fit perfectly within the holder image without having to adjust any settings!:

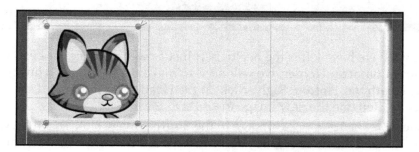

23. Now we are ready to start making the health-bar. We will create it similar to the way we made the `Character Holder` and `Character`. Right-click on the HUD Panel and select **UI** | **Image**. Rename the new image `Health Holder`.

24. Place the `uiElement_20` image in the **Source Image** slot and select **Preserve Aspect**.

25. Set the **Rect Transform** properties as shown in the following image and ensure that you hold *Shift + Alt* when selecting the **Anchor Preset**:

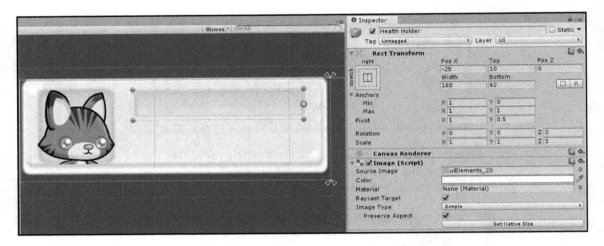

26. Now all we have left is the health bar! Just as we made the cat head image a child of the Character Holder, we will need to make the health bar's image a child of the **Heath Bar Holder**. Right-click on the Heath Bar Holder and select **UI** | **Image**. Rename the new image to `Health Bar`.

27. Place the `uiElement_23` image in the **Source Image** slot. This time we will not be selecting **Preserve Aspect**, because we want the image to scale this image horizontally.

28. Set the **Rect Transform** properties, as shown in the following screenshot, and ensure that you hold *Shift + Alt* when selecting the **Anchor Presets**:

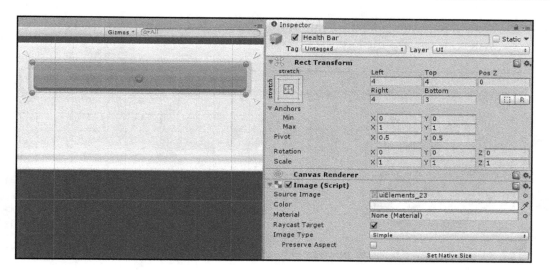

29. Note that a little padding was added so that you can see the edges of the **Health Holder.**

30. We're almost done. Right now, the pivot point of the image is right at the center. This means if we try to scale it, it will scale toward the center. We want it to be able to scale toward the left, however. So, open the **Anchor Presets** and while holding *Shift* only, select middle-left. This will cause only the pivot point to move.

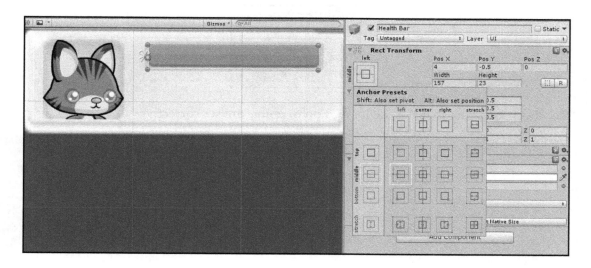

31. Now when we adjust the **Scale X** value on the **Rect Transform**, the health bar will scale toward the left:

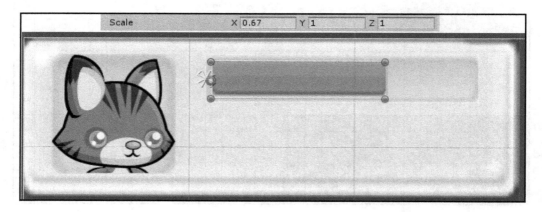

That's it for our HUD example! Try changing your Game view's aspect ratio to different settings so that you can see the Panel scale appropriately and see all the object relative positions maintained.

If your HUD is doing some wonky stuff when you change the Game's aspect ratio, ensure that your objects have the correct parent-child relationship. Your parent–child relationships should be as follows:

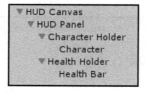

Also, check to ensure that the anchor and pivot points are set correctly.

Placing a background image (2D game)

Placing a background image that scales with the screen is not too difficult as long as you use the appropriate Canvas properties. We will expand upon our HUD example and place a background image in the scene.

We'll need to ensure that this background image doesn't just display behind other UI elements, but also displays behind any game objects we may put in our scene.

To make a background image that displays behind all UI elements as well as all game elements, complete the following steps:

1. Create a new Canvas using **Create | UI | Canvas**. I like to use different Canvases to sort my different UI elements, but the need for a new Canvas stems from more than personal preference, in this case. We need a new Canvas, because we need a Canvas with a different **Render Mode**. This Canvas will use the **Screen Space-Camera** Render Mode.
2. In the Canvas **Inspector**, change the name to `Background Canvas`.

3. Change the **Render Mode** to **Screen Space-Camera** and drag the **Main Camera** into the **Render Camera** slot:

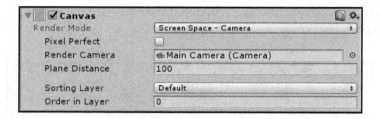

4. To ensure that this Canvas appears behind all other UI elements and all the 2D sprites in the game, we will need to use the **Sorting Layers**. In the top-right corner of the Unity Editor, you will see a drop-down menu labelled **Layers**. Select it and select **Edit Layers**:

5. Expand the **Sorting Layers** by selecting the arrow. Add a new **Sorting Layer** by selecting the plus sign. Name this new layer as **Layer Background**:

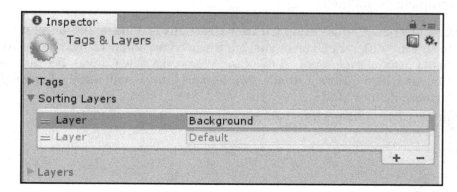

6. Sorting layers work so that whichever is on the top of this list will render the furthest back in the scene. So if you wanted to add a foreground layer, you'd add it below **Default**. Default is the layer that all new sprites will automatically be added to, so unless you create new layers, the **Background** layer will be behind any new sprite you create. If you do create new layers, ensure that the **Background** layers stay on the top of this list.

7. Reselect **Background Canvas** and now change the **Sorting Layer** to **Background**:

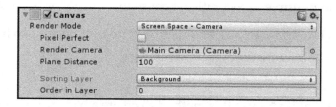

8. Now all we need to do is add the background image. Right-click on the **Background** Canvas and select **UI | Image**. Rename the new image to **Background Image**.

9. Place the **pinkBackground** image in the **Source Image** slot. This time we will not be selecting **Preserve Aspect**, because we want the image to be able to squash and stretch as the game screen resizes and always fill the scene.

10. Set the Rect Transform properties as shown and ensure that you hold *Shift + Alt* when selecting the **Anchor Presets**:

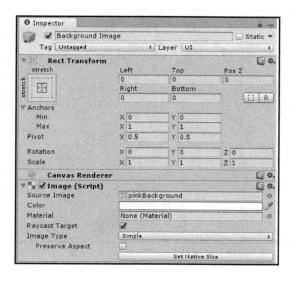

That's it! Try changing the Game view's aspect ratio around and resizing the screen in **Free Aspect** mode so that you can see the background image always filling the screen. Also, try adding some non-UI 2D sprites to the scene and see how they render on top of the background.

One thing that is not ideal about this example is that the background image is being allowed to change its aspect ratio. You'll see that the image looks pretty bad at some aspect ratios because of this. This background image will not be a good choice for a game that would be released on multiple aspect ratios. I chose this image for two reasons:

You can see how it's important to pick an image that doesn't depend so highly on aspect ratio.

It was free!

I highly recommend that if you use this method to create a background image, you use one with a pattern that doesn't so obviously display distortion.

Setting up a basic pop-up menu

The last example we will cover in this chapter will utilize the **Canvas Group** component. We won't be able to really see this component in action until we start programming in Chapter 4, *The Event System and Programming for UI*, but we can lay the groundwork now. We'll also get a bit more practice with laying out UI with this example.

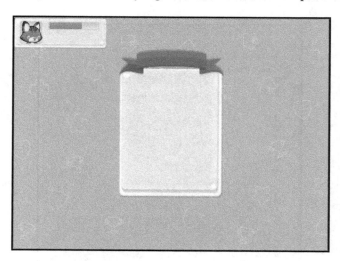

To create the pop-up menu shown in the preceding image, complete the following steps:

1. Create a new Canvas using **Create | UI | Canvas**.
2. In the Canvas Inspector, change the name to `Popup Canvas`.
3. I want to use the same properties for the **Canvas Scaler** on this Canvas that I used for the `HUD Canvas`. Instead of setting up all that again, I'll use a shortcut and copy the **Canvas Scaler** from the `HUD Canvas`. To do so, select the cog in the right-hand corner of the **Canvas Scaler** component on the `HUD Canvas` and select **Copy Component**.
4. Now select the cog in the right-hand corner of the **Canvas Scaler** component on the `Popup Canvas` and select **Paste Component Values**.
5. We will add a panel that will hold all the items, similar to the way we did with the HUD. This will ensure that everything stays together as it should. Right-click on `Popup Canvas` and select **UI | Panel**. Rename the new Panel as **Pause Panel**.
6. Place the `uiElement_32` image in the **Source Image** slot, give it a full alpha value, and select **Preserve Aspect**.
7. Set the **Rect Transform** properties, as shown in the following screenshot, and ensure that you hold *Shift + Alt* when selecting the **Anchor Presets**:

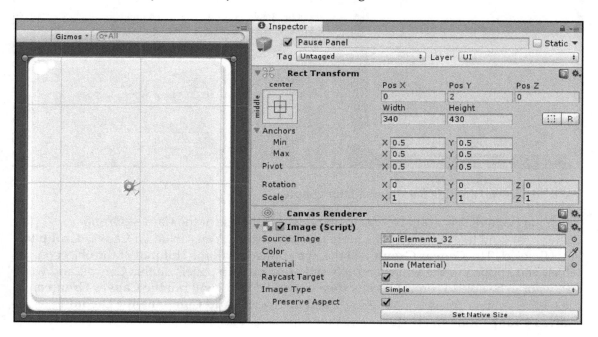

8. Now let's give the Panel a nice banner at the top. Right-click on `Popup Panel` and select **UI | Panel**. Rename the new Panel to `Pause Banner`.

9. Place the `uiElement_27` image in the **Source Image** slot and select **Preserve Aspect**.

10. Set the Rect Transform properties, as shown in the following screenshot, and ensure that you hold *Shift + Alt* when selecting the **Anchor Presets**:

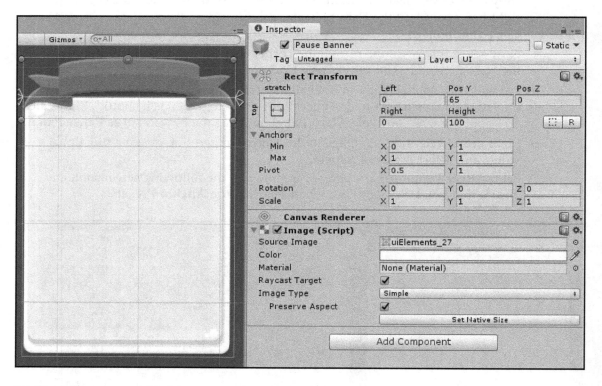

We'll add the text to this banner in a later chapter.

The main point of this example was to demonstrate the use of the **Canvas Group** component (and to give you a little more layout practice). You can add a **Canvas Group** to any UI object. The **Canvas Group** will then be applied to all the children of the object on which you applied it. We will eventually put more pop-up panels on this Canvas, and we will want to be able to control each of them separately, so I will put the **Canvas Group** on the `Pause Panel`. Select `Pause Panel`, and then select **Add Component | Layout | Canvas Group** (you can also just search for Canvas Group).

That's it for now! Change the values of Alpha in the **Inspector** of the **Pause** Panel, and you will see that as you change it, both the **Pause** Panel and the **Pause Banner** alpha values change. This is great for pop-up menus you want to hide a show without having to program each item individually. Once we spend more time with this **Pause** Panel, it will have a lot more items on it, and we will be happy that we don't have to program each piece individually.

Summary

Wow! This chapter was intense! There was a lot to cover, as this chapter set the groundwork that will be used throughout the rest of this book.

In this chapter, we discussed the following topics:

- Creating UI Canvases and setting their properties
- Creating UI Panels and setting their properties
- Using the Rect Tool and Rect Transform component
- Properly setting anchor and pivot points
- Creating and laying out a basic HUD
- Creating a background image
- Setting up a basic pop-up menu

The next chapter will cover how to create different automatic layouts that will let us line up our UI in grids.

Automatic Layouts

3

Now that we have the basics of manually positioning, scaling, and aligning UI elements with the Rect Transform and anchors, we can explore how to use automatic layouts. Automatic layouts allow you to group your UI elements so that they will position automatically in relation to each other.

There are quite a few scenarios in which you will want Unity to automatically control the layout of your UI objects. If you are generating UI items via code and a number of items may change, but you still want them to line up, scale, and position properly, you can use automatic layouts. Also, if you want perfectly spaced UI objects, automatic layouts will help you create this perfect spacing without having to do any position calculating yourself. These automatic layouts work well for things like inventory systems aligned in a grid or list.

In this chapter, we will discuss the following topics:

- Using Layout Group components to automatically space, position, and align a group of UI objects
- Using the Layout Element component, the Content Size Fitter component, and Aspect Ratio Fitter component to resize UI elements
- How to set up a horizontal HUD selection menu
- How to set up a grid inventory

All the examples shown in this section can be found within the Unity project provided in the code bundle. They can be found within the scene labeled Chapter3Text in the Assets/Scene/ExamplesInText/Chapter3Text/ folder.

Each example image has a caption stating the example number within the scene.

In the scene, each example is on its own Canvas and some of the Canvases are deactivated. To view an example on a deactivated Canvas, simply select the checkbox next to the Canvas' name in the **Inspector**:

Types of Automatic Layout Groups

When a UI object has an automatic layout group component attached to it, all of its children will be aligned, resized, and positioned based on the parameters of the layout component. There are three automatic layout group options: **Horizontal Layout Group**, **Vertical Layout Group**, and **Grid Layout Group**.

The following screenshot shows three panels (represented by gray rectangles), each with six UI image children (represented by the black rectangles): the first panel has a Horizontal Layout Group component, the second panel has a Vertical Layout Group component, and the third panel has a Grid Layout Group component:

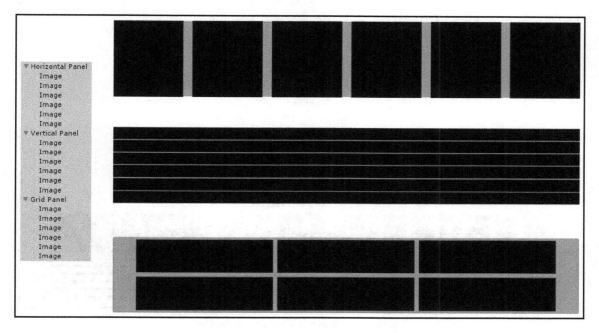

Automatic Layout Groups Example 1 in the Chapter3Text Scene

From the preceding screenshot, you can see clearly what the three types of Automatic Layout Groups accomplish. You can use any combination of the three to create nested, perfectly spaced layouts, as follows:

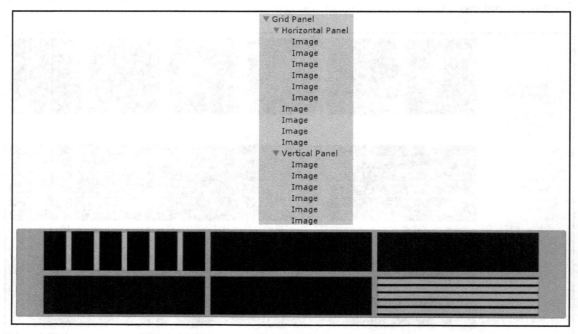

Automatic Layout Groups Example 2 in the Chapter3Text Scene

Let's look at each of these layout groups individually and explore their various properties.

Horizontal Layout Group

All the children of a UI object with a **Horizontal Layout Group** component will be automatically placed side by side. If you allow the Horizontal Layout Group to resize the children, the children will be positioned and scaled so that they are fully within the bounds of the parent object's Rect Transform. Padding properties can be adjusted, however, if you'd like them to go outside the bounds of the parent's Rect Transform.

The order in which the children appear in the Hierarchy determines the order in which they will be laid out by the Horizontal Layout Group. The children will be laid out from left to right. The topmost child in the hierarchy will be placed in the leftmost position and the bottommost child in the hierarchy will be placed in the rightmost position:

Horizontal Layout Groups Example 1 in the Chapter3Text Scene

To add a Horizontal Layout Group component to a UI object, select **Add Component | Layout | Horizontal Layout Group (Script)** from within the object's **Inspector**. If you click on the arrow next to the **Padding** property, you should see the following:

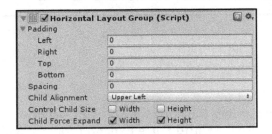

Let's explore each of the properties further.

Padding

The **Padding** property represents the padding around the edges of the parent object's Rect Transform. Positive numbers will move the child objects inward and negative numbers will move the child objects outward.

As an example, the following screenshot shows three panels with various padding values applied. The first Panel has no padding, the second panel has a positive padding on all four sides, and the third Panel has positive padding on the left, right, and bottom but a negative padding on the top:

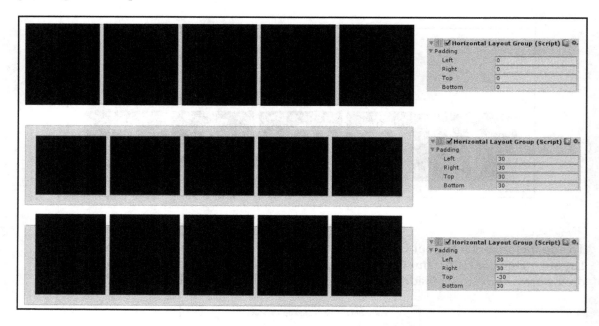

Horizontal Layout Groups Example 2 in the Chapter3Text Scene

Spacing

The **Spacing** property determines the horizontal spacing between the child objects. This may be overridden if you use the **Child Force Expand** property without the **Control Child Size Property**, and the children may have larger spacing.

Child Alignment

The **Child Alignment** property determines where the group of children will be aligned. There are nine options for this property, as shown:

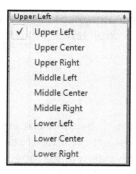

As an example, the following diagram shows three overlapping panels that fill the screen. The Rect Transform area for these parent Panels is represented by the selected Rect Transform. The first panel has an **Upper Left** Child Alignment. Its children are represented by the white squares. The second panel has a **Middle Center** Child Alignment, and its children are represented by gray squares. The third panel has a **Lower Right** Child Alignment, and its children are represented by black squares:

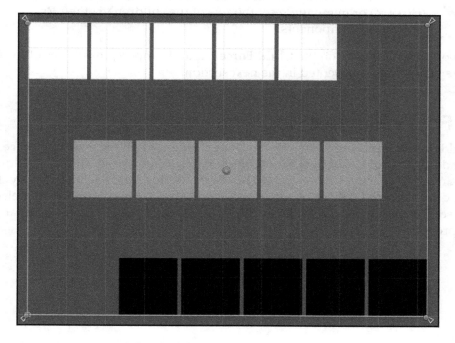

Horizontal Layout Groups Example 3 in the Chapter3Text Scene

It is important to note that the **Child Alignment** property only shows an effect if the children (along with spacing) don't completely fill in the Rect Transform, as with the preceding diagram.

Control Child Size

These Control Child Size options allow the automatic layout to override the current Width or Height of the child objects. If you select it without selecting the corresponding **Child Force Expand** property, your child objects will no longer be visible (unless it has a Layout Element component with **Preferred Width** specified).

If you do not set this property, it is possible that the children will draw outside of the parent's Rect Transform, that is, if too many children exist.

 This property changes the width and height property of the child objects' Rect Transforms. So, if you select and then deselect it, the children will not go back to their original sizes. You will have to either use **Edit | Undo** (*Ctrl + Z*) or manually reset the size of the children via their Rect Transform components.

Since this property depends on the **Child Force Expand** property, examples of the **Control Child Size** property are presented in the next section.

Child Force Expand

The **Child Force Expand** property will cause the children to fill the available space. If the corresponding **Control Child Size** is not selected, this property will shift the children so that they and their spacing fill the space. This may override the **Spacing** property. If the corresponding **Control Child Size** is selected, it will stretch the children in the selected direction so that they and their spacing completely fill the space. This will maintain the **Spacing** property.

In the following screenshot, all three panels have a Horizontal Layout Group component with a **Middle Left Child Alignment** and different combinations of **Child Control Size** and **Child Force Expand** selected. The top Panel has only **Child Force Expand Width** selected, the middle Panel has **Control Child Size Width** and **Child Force Expand Width** selected, and the last panel has both **Control Child Size** properties selected and both **Child Force Expand** properties selected:

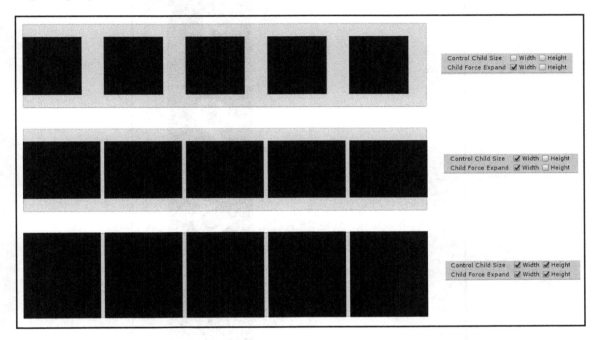

Horizontal Layout Groups Example 4 in the Chapter3Text Scene

Vertical Layout Group

The Vertical Layout Group component works very similarly to the Horizontal Layout Group and has all the same properties, except that children of a UI object with a **Vertical Layout Group** component will be automatically placed on top of each, rather than side by side.

As with the Horizontal Layout Group, the order in which the children appear in the Hierarchy determines the order in which they will be laid out by the Vertical Layout Group. The children will be laid out from top to bottom in the same order in which they appear in the Hierarchy:

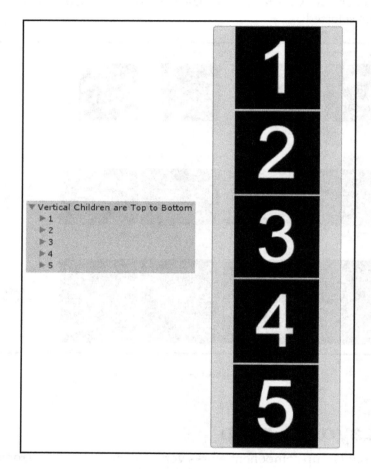

Vertical Layout Groups Example in the Chapter3Text Scene

To add a Vertical Layout Group component to a UI object, select **Add Component** | **Layout** | **Vertical Layout Group** from within the object's Inspector. If you click on the arrow next to the **Padding** property, you should see the following:

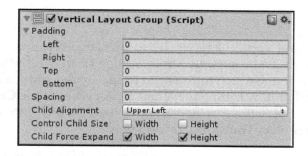

Since the properties of the Vertical Layout Group component are identical to those of the Horizontal Layout Group, we won't explore each of the properties further. For an explanation of each of the properties, refer to the Horizontal Layout Group section.

Grid Layout Group

The **Grid Layout Group** component allows you to organize child objects in columns and rows in (you guessed it) a grid layout. It works similarly to Horizontal and Vertical Layout Groups but has a few more properties that can be manipulated.

To add a Grid Layout Group component to a UI object, select **Add Component | Layout | Grid Layout Group** from within the object's Inspector. If you click on the arrow next to the **Padding** property, you should see the following:

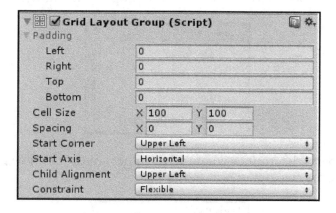

A few of the properties of the Grid Layout Group are the same as the other two Layout Groups, but let's look more closely at the properties unique to the Grid Layout Group component.

Cell Size

Unlike the Horizontal and Vertical Layout Groups, which determine the size of the children either by their Rect Transform component or by scaling them to fit inside the parent's Rect Transform, the Grid Layout Group requires you to specify the width and height of the child objects. You accomplish this by setting the **X** and **Y** properties of the **Cell Size** property. This will automatically apply the specified **X** and **Y** sizes to each of the children's **Width** and **Height** property of their Rect Transform, respectively.

Due to the **Cell Size** property and the lack of a **Control Child** size property, the children are not guaranteed to fit within the parent's Rect Transform. If too many children exist, it is possible they will be drawn outside the parent's Rect Transform. So, if you have a grid filling up dynamically that can change throughout the gameplay and want the grid to always fit within a specific area, you will have to prepare for that scenario of overflow.

The Grid Layout Group allows you to specify both an **X** and **Y** **Spacing**. The **X Spacing** is the horizontal spacing, and the **Y Spacing** is the vertical spacing. These values will not be overridden by further property choices, as they can be with the Horizontal and Vertical Layout Groups.

Start Corner and Start Axis

The **Start Corner** property determines where the very first child in the Hierarchy will be placed. There are four choices for the Start Corner property, as shown:

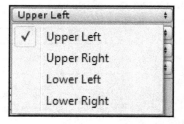

The **Start Axis** property determines where all the other children will be placed relative to the first child. There are two options, as follows:

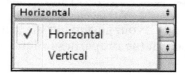

A **Start Axis** property set to **Horizontal** means that the children will be laid out, starting with the first child, in a horizontal fashion. If the **Start Corner** is one of the Left options, the children will be placed from left to right. If the **Start Corner** is one of the Right options, the children will be placed from right to left. Once the new row is filled, it will continue to the next row and will restart on the same side as the **Start Corner**. If the **Start Corner** is one of the Upper options, the rows will continue downward. If the **Start Corner** is one of the Lower options, the rows will continue upward.

The following screenshot demonstrates the flow of the children, with a **Horizontal Start Axis** based on the different **Start Corner** options:

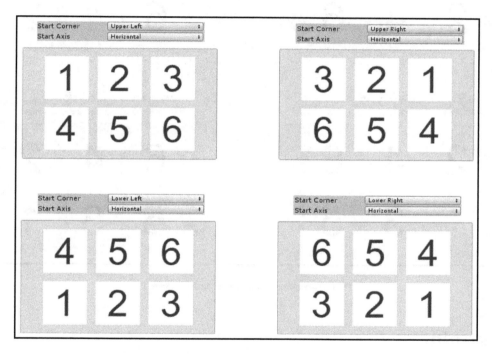

Grid Layout Groups Example 1 in the Chapter3Text Scene

A **Start Axis** property set to **Vertical** means that the children will be laid out starting with the first child and then in a vertical fashion. Whether the children will be placed from top to bottom or from bottom to top is determined in the same way as it is when this property is set to Horizontal, based on the position of the **Start Corner**. Then, when a column is filled, the children will be placed from left to right or from right to left based on the position of the Start Corner.

The following screenshot demonstrates the flow of the children, with a **Vertical Start Axis** based on the different **Start Corner** options:

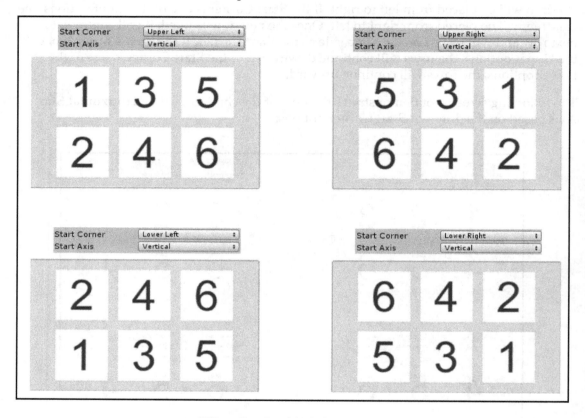

Grid Layout Groups Example 2 in the Chapter3Text Scene

Constraint

The **Constraint** property allows you to specify the number of rows or columns the grid will have. There are three options, as shown:

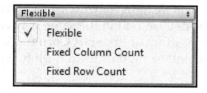

The **Fixed Column Count** and **Fixed Row Count** allow you to specify an amount of columns or rows, respectively. If you select either of these options, a new property, **Constraint Count**, will become available. You then specify how may columns or rows you want. When you select **Fixed Column Count**, the number of rows will be variable. When you select **Fixed Row Count**, the number of columns will be variable.

The **Flexible** option automatically calculates the amount of rows and columns for you based on the **Cell Size** and the **Start Axis** chosen. It will begin laying out the children in the defined pattern until there is no space left on the chosen axis. It will then continue on. Whichever axis is specified in the **Start Axis** will have a fixed amount of children, and the other axis will be variable. So, for example, if the **Start Axis** is set to **Horizontal** and three children can fit horizontally within the defined space, there will be three columns and the amount of rows will be determined by how many total children there are.

Layout Element

The **Layout Element** component allows us to specify a range of size values of an object if it is being sized with an automatic layout. If the parent object tries to size it outside of these preferences, the Layout Element will override any sizing information being sent from the parent object.

To add a **Layout Element** component to a UI object, select **Add Component | Layout | Layout Element** from within the object's **Inspector**. The **Layout Element** has the following properties:

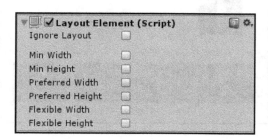

To use these properties, you first select their checkboxes to enable them; boxes will become available so that you can enter your desired values:

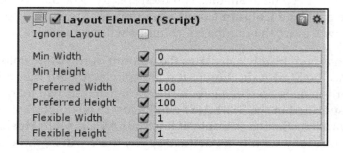

Ignore Layout

The **Ignore Layout** property can be used to have the object ignored by any automatic layout components of the parent object. A child with this property selected can be moved and resized freely, and all other children will be laid out without regard for the ignored child.

In the following example, the panel has a **Horizontal Layout Group** component and five child objects. The first child, labeled with a 1, has a **Layout Element** component with the **Ignore Layout** property selected:

Layout Element Example 1 in the Chapter3Text Scene

You can see, since the **Ignore Layout** property is selected for the first child, that it can be moved around outside of the parent Panel and it was ignored when the position and scale of the other children were determined. It also maintained its original Rect Transform scale.

If the **Ignore Layout** property is deselected, the first child will be added to the Horizontal Layout Group with the other children.

The Width and Height properties

The **Layout Element** component has three sets of properties that can be used to specify the way you want the object to resize. These properties will override the size being assigned to the child by the parent object if the assigned size is outside of the provided values.

 It is important to note that these properties will not override the **Cell Size** settings of the Grid Layout Group component. *They will have no effect on a child within a Grid Layout Group.*

Min Width and Height

The **Min Width** and **Min Height** properties are the minimum width and height a child object can achieve. If the parent object is scaled down, the child will scale down until it meets its **Min Width** or **Min Height**. Once it meets its **Min Width** or **Min Height** property, it will no longer scale in that direction.

In the following diagram, the panel has a **Horizontal Layout Group** component and five child objects. The first child, labeled with a 1, has a **Layout Element** component with **Min Width** and **Min Height** properties set:

Layout Element Example 2 in the Chapter3Text Scene

You can see that the parent object's **Horizontal Layout Group** tried to scale all the children down with it as it scaled down itself. The other four children scaled, but since the first child had a **Min Width** and **Min Height** property set, it refused to scale down any further.

Preferred Width and Height

The **Preferred Width** and **Preferred Height** properties are a little confusing, because they perform differently depending on the settings you have for the parent's layout group. There is no official **Max Width** and **Max Height** setting, despite there being a **Min Width** and **Min Height** setting. The **Preferred Width** and **Preferred Height** properties, however, can be used to specify the maximum size the child object will achieve, but only if the correct settings on the parent's layout group are selected.

The following diagram contains three Panels with **Vertical Layout Group** components and various settings. Their children also have various settings for **Preferred Height** within a **Layout Element** component:

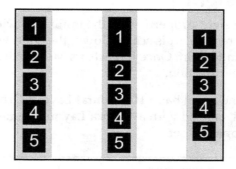

Layout Element Example 3 in the Chapter3Text Scene

The first parent Panel has a **Vertical Layout Group** component with **Control Child Size Width** and **Height** selected as well as **Child Force Expand Width** and **Height**. None of its children have a **Preferred Width** or **Preferred Height** setting within a **Layout Element** component. The first panel will act as the default for reference when comparing the others.

The second parent Panel has the same properties as the first—a **Vertical Layout Group** component with **Control Child Size Width** and **Height** selected as well as **Child Force Expand Width** and **Height**. However, its first child has a **Preferred Height** setting of 100 within a **Layout Element** component.

You can see that because the second parent Panel has **Child Force Expand Height** selected, the **Preferred Height** of 100 in the **Layout Element** component of the first child is causing the first child to be exactly 100 units taller than the other four children. So, when the **Child Force Expand** property is selected on the parent, the child with the **Preferred Height** will not use **Preferred Height** as its maximum possible height; it will add that value to the height assigned by the parent's layout group component.

The third Panel has a **Vertical Layout Group** component with **Control Child Size Width** and **Height** selected as well as **Child Force Expand Width**. It does not have **Child Force Expand Height** selected as the other two do. All of its children have a **Preferred Height** setting of 100 within a **Layout Element** component.

If you compare the children in the third Panel to the children in the first Panel (the default), you can see that the children are shorter. This is because their **Preferred Height** is set to a smaller number than the height that the Vertical Layout Group component attempts to assign to them. So, when the **Child Force Expand Height** property is deselected, the children will use their **Preferred Height** setting in the expected way—making it the maximum size the children should attain.

Therefore, if you want the **Preferred Width** or **Preferred Height** settings to work as a maximum attainable width or height, you will need to deselect the corresponding **Child Force Expand** property on the parent object.

Flexible Width and Height

The **Flexible Width** and **Flexible Height** properties represent a percentage, where the percentage is the size of the child relative to the other children. Since these values are percentages, a value of 0 would represent 0% and a value of 1 would represent 100%.

As with the **Preferred Width** and **Height**, this setting doesn't work as expected unless the **Child Force Expand** property is deselected. In the following example, the two Panels and children have nearly identical settings. The only difference between the two is that the top parent Panel has the **Child Force Expand Width** property selected and the bottom parent Panel does not. So, you can see that the values set for **Flexible Width** of the children are ignored if **Child Force Expand Width** is selected on the parent:

Layout Element Example 4 in the Chapter3Text Scene

The children in the preceding diagram have the following **Flexible Width** settings, from left to right: 0, 0.5, 0.75, 1, and 1.5. You can see that the children have scaled relative to each other based on the percentages. The first child is not visible because it has a **Flexible Width** of 0.

Fitters

There are two fitter layout components. These components make the Rect Transform of the object on which they are attached fit within a specified area.

Content Size Fitter

The **Content Size Fitter** component allows you to force the size of the parent to fit around the size of its children. This fitting can be based on the minimum or preferred size of the children.

To add a **Content Size Fitter** component to a UI object, select **Add Component** | **Layout** | **Content Size Fitter** from within the object's **Inspector**. The **Content Size Fitter** component has the following properties:

You can choose the following properties for the **Horizontal Fit** and the **Vertical Fit**:

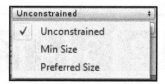

If the **Unconstrained** property is selected, **Content Size Fitter** will not adjust the size of the object along that axis.

If the **Min Size** property is selected, the **Content Size Fitter** will adjust the size of the object based on the minimum size of the children. This minimum size is determined by the **Min Width** and **Min Height** properties of the **Layout Element** component of the children.

The children do not have to have a **Layout Element** component if the parent has a **Grid Layout Group** component for this property to work. If this property is selected for an object with a **Grid Layout Group** component, the Rect Transform of the parent will hug the children based on the **Cell Size** and **Padding** properties, as in the following diagram:

Content Size Fitter Example in the Chapter3Text Scene

If the **Preferred Size** property is selected, the **Content Size Fitter** will adjust the size of the object based on the preferred size of the children. This preferred size is determined by the **Preferred Width** and **Preferred Height** properties of the **Layout Element** component of the children. If the object has a **Grid Layout Group** component, this setting will perform in the exact same way as **Min Size**.

Aspect Ratio Fitter

The **Aspect Ratio Fitter** component works similarly to the **Layout Element** component, as it allows overriding the size constraints being sent to it. It will force the UI object on which it is attached to resize based on an aspect ratio.

To add an Aspect Ratio Fitter component to a UI object, select **Add Component** | **Layout** | **Aspect Ratio Fitter (Script)** from within the object's **Inspector**. The Aspect Ratio Fitter component has the following properties:

The **Aspect Ratio** property is the aspect ratio that the Rect Transform will maintain. If you want to do an aspect ratio like 4:3, you can simply enter $4/3$ in the box, and it will convert it to the decimal value:

You can choose the following properties for the **Aspect Mode** property:

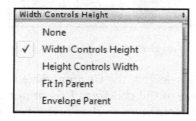

If the **None** property is selected, the Aspect Ratio Fitter will not adjust the size to fit within the **Aspect Ratio**.

If the **Width Controls Height** property is selected, the Aspect Ratio Fitter will adjust the size of the height based on the width of the object.

If the **Height Controls Width** property is selected, the Aspect Ratio Fitter will adjust the size of the width based on the height of the object.

If the **Fit In Parent** property is selected, the Aspect Ratio Fitter will adjust the size of the object to fit within its parent object but will maintain the **Aspect Ratio**. This will make the child object stay within the bounds of the parent.

If the **Envelope Parent** property is selected, the Aspect Ratio Fitter will adjust the size of the object to cover its parent object but will maintain the **Aspect Ratio**. This is similar to the **Fit In Parent** property, except that instead of staying within the bounds of the parent, it can go outside the bounds.

If you try to add an **Aspect Ratio Fitter** component to a child of a parent with a layout group, you'll see the following message:

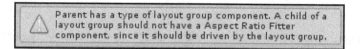

While you can ignore it and do it anyway, it doesn't work entirely as expected. The recommended workaround is to add the **Aspect Ratio Fitter** component to a child of the child within the group. For example, in the following diagram, a panel was added as a child of the **Horizontal Layout Group**. Then, a child with an **Aspect Ratio Fitter** component was added to the panel so that the child could have the 4:3 **Aspect Ratio**:

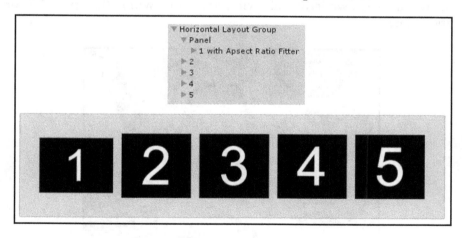

Aspect Ratio Fitter Example in the Chapter3Text Scene

Examples

We'll continue working in the scene created in the Chapter 2, *Canvases, Panels, and Basic Layouts*, examples and will use the art assets imported for them. In addition to the art already added to our project, we'll be using art assets that I've modified from free art assets found at https://opengameart.org/content/platformer-pickups-pack.

The download from the previous link provides many individual images. I could have used those, but for performance reasons, it is best to use sprite sheets when possible. So you can find the sprite sheet labeled `foodSpriteSheet.png` in the code bundle.

To combine all the images into a sprite sheet, I've used the program Texture Packer, which can be found at `https://www.codeandweb.com/texturepacker`.

Before you begin with the following examples, complete the following steps:

1. Import the `foodSpriteSheet.png` sprite sheet into your project's `Asset/Sprites` folder.
2. Change the **Sprite Mode** of `foodSpriteSheet.png` to **Multiple**. Use the Sprite Editor to automatically slice the sprite sheet.
3. Automatic slicing results in a blank image being created in the sprite sheet. Find the rectangle shown in the following screenshot within the **Sprite Editor**; select and delete it:

4. Once you apply your changes, you should have the following in your `Sprites` folder:

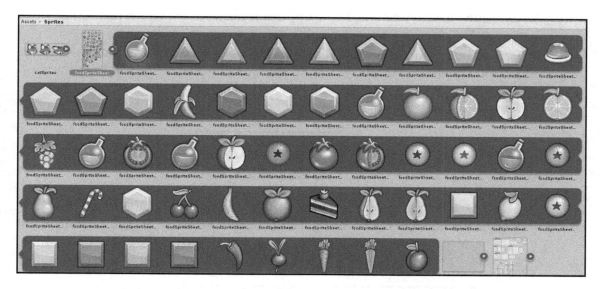

5. Duplicate your Scene named `Chapter2` by pressing *Ctrl + D*. The duplicated scene will automatically be named `Chapter3`. Open the `Chapter3` scene and complete the following examples within that scene.

Laying Out an HUD Selection Menu

The first example we will cover in this chapter is a HUD selection menu in the lower-right corner of the screen that uses the **Horizontal Layout Group** component:

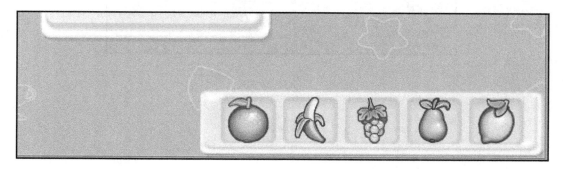

To create the HUD group shown in the preceding screenshot, we have to complete the following steps:

1. Currently, we have a Panel in the upper-left corner of the screen named HUD Panel. For clarity's sake, rename this Panel as Top Left Panel.
2. We will be creating a new HUD Panel to hold our fruity inventory. We want to put our new HUD item in the HUD Canvas. Right-click on the Canvas named HUD Canvas in the Hierarchy and select **UI** | **Panel**.
3. Rename the new Panel as Bottom Right Panel:

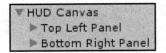

4. Change the Rect Transform properties of the Bottom Right Panel so that the Panel is anchored in the lower-right corner, has a **Width** of 500, and has a **Height** of 100. Remember to hold down *Shift + Alt* when selecting the lower-right anchor preset:

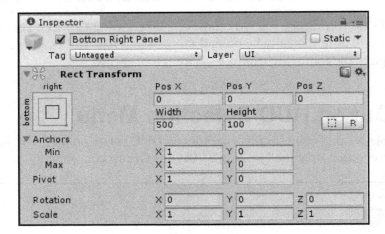

You should see the following in your **Game view**:

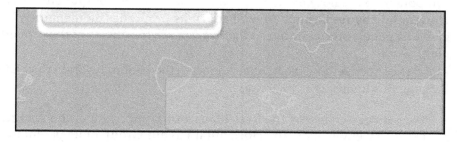

5. Now, we will replace the image with one of the uiElements.png sprites. Drag uiElements_1 into the **Source Image** property of the **Image** component. Change the **Color** property so that it has full opacity:

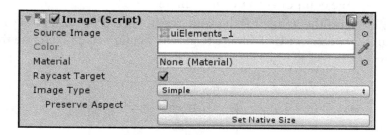

You should now see the following in your **Game view**:

6. To create the layout we want, we need to add a **Horizontal Layout Group** component to the `Bottom Right Panel`. Select **Add Component** | **Layout** | **Horizontal Layout Group**. We will adjust its properties momentarily. First, let's give this panel some children so that we can see the effects of the properties take place.

7. Right-click on the `Bottom Right Panel` in the Hierarchy and select **UI** | **Image**. Rename this image as `ItemHolder`.

We won't be changing the **Rect Transform** component of this **Image**, because we will allow the **Horizontal Layout Group** of its parent to control its size, position, and anchor.

8. This image will be the background holder for the item. So, drag `uiElement_6` into its **Image** component's **Source Image**.

9. Now, let's add the image for the fruit. Right-click on `ItemHolder` in the Hierarchy and select **UI** | **Image** to give it a child image. Rename this Image as `Food`:

10. To ensure that we aren't just looking at a white block, let's replace the **Source Image** with one of the food images from `foodSpriteSheet.png`. I've used `foodSpriteSheet_18`, which is a full orange:

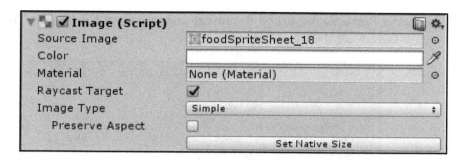

You should see something that looks like this:

If your orange and its holder are in a different place than mine, don't worry. When we start adding more children and adjusting the Horizontal Group Layout, everything should pop into its proper place.

11. We don't want our orange image to have its aspect ratio distorted, and we also want to ensure that it always fills the `ItemHolder` image without expanding past it. So, let's adjust a few properties on the Rect Transform and Image components. First, let's ensure that the orange's image will always fill the slot and not expand past it by changing its Rect Transform anchor preset to stretch-stretch. This won't appear to have changed much, but it will help our orange scale properly if we change the screen size. Also, to ensure that there is a little bit of spacing between the edge of the container and the food, change the **Left, Top, Right**, and **Bottom** properties to 5.

12. Now, select **Preserve Aspect** on the **Image** component of the orange. Your Food image should have the following properties:

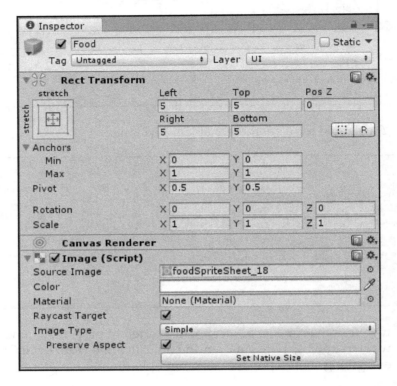

13. Now we're ready to start adding some more children. Select the ItemHolder Image in the Hierarchy and press *Ctrl + D* four times so that there is a total of five ItemHolders:

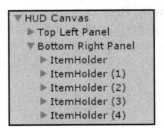

You should see the following in the **Game view**:

14. I, personally, don't like my objects to have names with the numbered parentheses in them, so I'll rename all the duplicated Images to ItemHolder without the number. Select ItemHolder (1), hold *Shift*, and select ItemHolder (4) so that you have all of them selected. Now, in the Inspector, type ItemHolder in the name slot and press *Enter*. They should all be renamed to ItemHolder now:

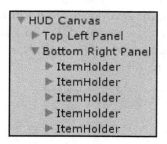

15. Now, let's adjust the properties on the **Horizontal Layout Group** component of the Bottom Right Panel. Select the Bottom Right Panel and in its **Horizontal Layout Group** component, give it the following properties:

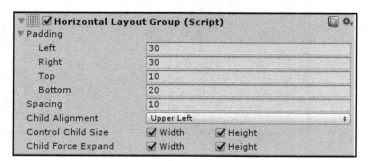

You will now be able to see the following:

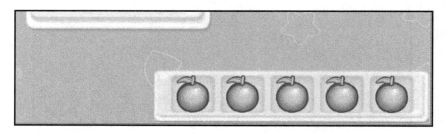

By adjusting the **Padding** properties, we brought the group of objects off the edge of the parent Panel. We spaced them apart by changing the **Spacing** property, and we ensured that the sizes of the `ItemHolder` images were adjusted to fit onto the parent Panel by enabling **Control Child Size Width** and **Height**.

16. Now, all that's left to do is swap out the orange images for four other items. Select the `Food` image of the second through fourth `ItemHolders` and change their **Source Image** to a different food. I used `foodSpriteSheet_13`, `foodSpriteSheet_22`, `foodSpriteSheet_34`, and `foodSpriteSheet_45` to get the following results:

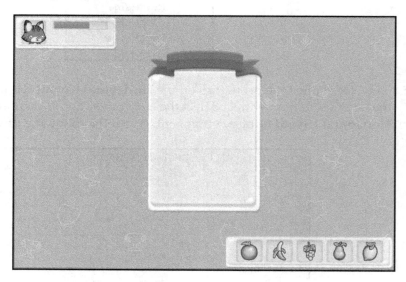

As you can see from this example, **Horizontal Layout Group** components and (similarly) **Vertical Layout Group** components aren't too difficult to set up and are extremely useful for creating well-organized lists.

Laying Out a Grid Inventory

The last example we'll cover in this chapter is the creation of a gridded inventory system using a **Grid Layout Group** component and the **Content Fitter** component. We'll add text to the banner in a later chapter:

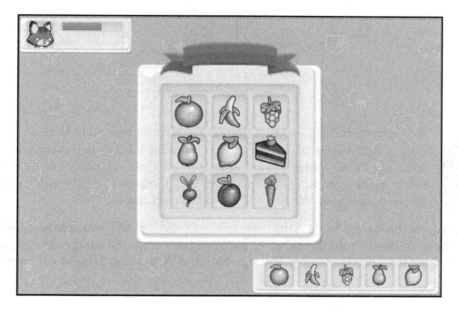

To create the gridded inventory system shown in the preceding screenshot, complete the following steps:

1. The shell that holds this inventory system looks remarkably similar to our `Pause Panel` (refer to the screenshot in step 16 of the previous example). Since they are so similar, and there is no reason to reinvent the wheel, we will just duplicate the `Pause Panel` we created in `Chapter 2`, *Canvases, Panels, and Basic Layouts*, and adjust some of its settings to get the square shape. Select `Pause Panel` in the Hierarchy and press *Ctrl + D* to duplicate it. Now, rename the duplicate as `Inventory Panel`. Rename its child **Image** to `Inventory Banner`:

> ▼ Popup Canvas
>   ▼ Pause Panel
>   Pause Banner
>   ▼ Inventory Panel
>   Inventory Banner

Remember that we added a Canvas Group component to the `Pause Panel` in `Chapter 2`, *Canvases, Panels, and Basic Layouts*. By duplicating it to create the **Inventory Panel**, the `Inventory Panel` has a Canvas Group component as well. This component will allow us to easily hide and show the two panels, which we will do in the next chapter.

2. To get the square look of the `Inventory Panel` in the example screenshot, we need to deselect the **Preserve Aspect** property from the **Image** component and adjust the Rect Transform. Change both the **Width** and **Height** values to `500`:

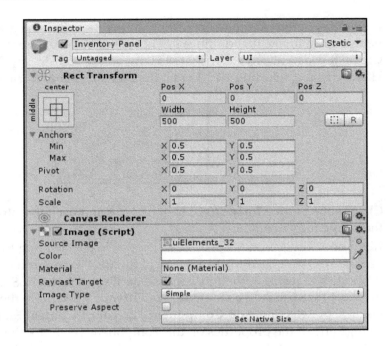

You should now see the following in your **Game view**:

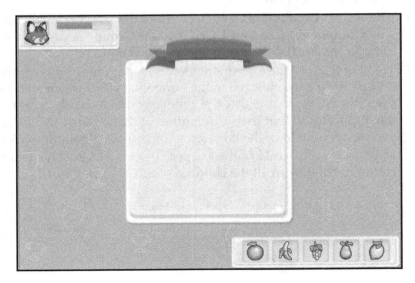

3. If you look at the example screenshot, you will see that the group of inventory items has an image that outlines it. This will act as the parent object of our grid. Create this parent object by right-clicking on the `Inventory Panel` in the Hierarchy and selecting **UI | Panel**. Rename this Panel to `Inventory Holder`:

```
▼ Popup Canvas
  ▶ Pause Panel
  ▼ Inventory Panel
      Inventory Banner
      Inventory Holder
```

4. Change the **Source Image** to `uiElement_38` and use the **Color** property to make the image fully opaque.

5. Right now, the `Inventory Holder` is completely covering the `Inventory Panel`. We don't need to change any of the **Rect Transform** component properties to resize it, though, because we'll use a **Content Size Fitter** component to adjust the size. Add a **Content Size Fitter** component to the `Inventory Holder` by selecting **Add Component | Layout | Content Size Fitter**. Don't change any of the properties on this component yet. Since the `Inventory Holder` has no children, adjusting the **Horizontal Fit** and **Vertical Fit** now will cause it to "disappear".

6. Add a **Grid Layout Group** component to the `Inventory Holder` by selecting **Add Component | Layout | Grid Layout Group**. Once again, don't adjust the settings yet. We'll do this once we add the children.

7. You'll note, from the example screenshot, that the children of the inventory are set up just like the children in the horizontal HUD we created in the previous example. So, we'll duplicate the children of the `Bottom Right Panel` and move the duplicates so that they are children of the `Inventory Holder`. Select the first `ItemHolder` child of the `Bottom Right Panel`, hold down Shift, and select the last `ItemHolder` child of the `Bottom Right Panel`. This will select all the children. Now, with all the children selected, press *Ctrl + D* to duplicate them.

8. Click on and drag the duplicated `ItemHolders` in the Hierarchy from the `Bottom Right Panel` to the `Inventory Holder`, making them children of `Inventory Holder`:

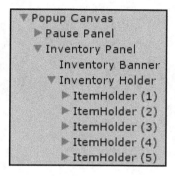

9. Select `ItemHolder (5)` and duplicate it four times so that there is a total of nine `ItemHolder` children. Select all the `ItemHolder` children and rename them to `ItemHolder` so that they no longer have the number in the name:

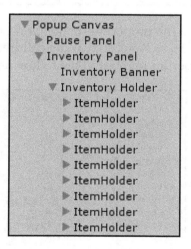

You should now see something like this in your **Game view**:

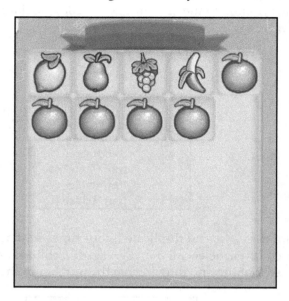

10. Now, let's adjust the properties on the Grid Layout Group component on the `Inventory Holder` Panel so that the children will be laid out in a 3x3 grid. Adjust the properties to those in the following screenshot:

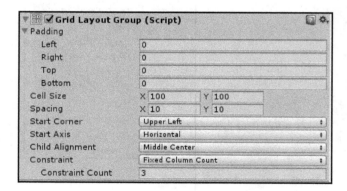

11. You should now see the following in your **Game view**:

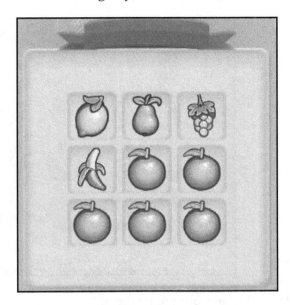

We put spacing between each of the cells using the **Spacing** property, centered the children in the object using the **Child Alignment Middle Center** property, and gave it a 3x3 layout using **Fixed Column Count Constraint** and by setting **Constraint Count** to 3.

12. Now that `Inventory Holder` has children, we can change the settings of its Content Size Fitter. Set **Horizontal Fit** and **Vertical Fit** to **Min Size**:

You should now see the following in your **Game view**:

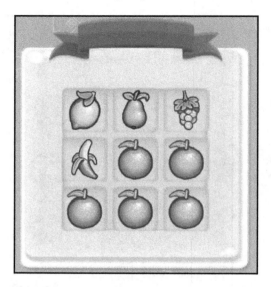

It's a little hard to see, but the image of `Inventory Holder` is now snug with the `ItemHolder` images. We want a bit of padding, though.

13. Add padding to the sides of the `ItemHolder` objects by adjusting the **Padding** properties in the **Grid Layout Group**, as shown:

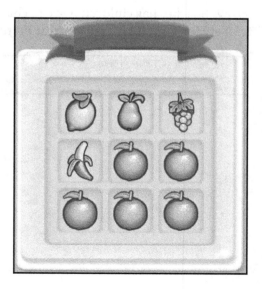

14. Now that everything is lined up and positioned properly, the only thing left to do is change the order of the images and change the images of the last four slots. To change the order of the images, simply change their order in the Hierarchy; the **Grid Layout Group** component will automatically reposition the items within the scene for you. To get the result in the example image, I changed the **Source Image** of the last four `Food` items to `foodSpriteSheet_41`, `foodSpriteSheet_52`, `foodSpriteSheet_55`, and `foodSpriteSheet_53`. These changes result in the following completed `Inventory Panel`:

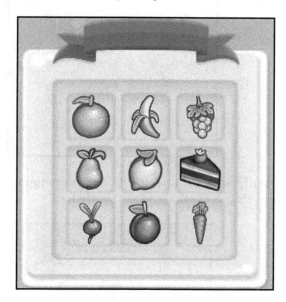

That's it. You should now have a perfectly laid out inventory grid.

With the **Grid Layout Group** component set up along with our **Content Size Fitter**, we can now change a number of items in the Grid, and the `Inventory Holder` will automatically resize to fit a number of items, as you can see here:

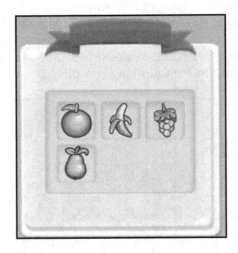

This actually works really well, until we try to add more items to the inventory. You'll see, once we have 10 items, that everything looks pretty bad:

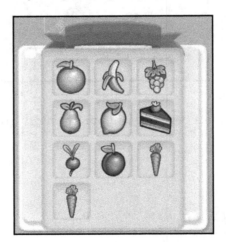

There are a few things we can do to handle this, including changing the cell size and using a mask along with a **Scroll Rect**. We'll discuss how to make those changes in `Chapter 7`, *Masks and Other Inputs*. For now, though, just leave your inventory at nine items so that everything looks nice.

After completing all the examples in the last two chapters, you should have the following:

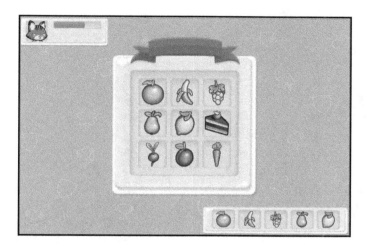

Summary

Now we know all sorts of techniques for laying out our UI elements. The information covered in this chapter, and the last one, has provided enough tools to create almost any UI layout that you can imagine.

In this chapter, we discussed the following topics:

- Using Layout Group components to automatically space, position, and align a group of UI objects
- Using the Layout Element component, the Content Size Fitter component, and Aspect Ratio Fitter component to resize UI elements
- How to set up a horizontal HUD selection menu
- How to set up a grid inventory

In the next chapter, we will learn how to access UI components via code and how to use the Event System to allow the player to interact with the UI objects.

4

The Event System and Programming for UI

One of the key features of the Unity UI system is the ability to easily program how the UI elements receive interactions from the player via events. The Event System is a robust system that allows you to create and manage events.

In this chapter, we will discuss the following topics:

- How to access UI elements and their properties via code
- What the Event System is and how to work with it
- How to customize input axes with the Input Manager
- What an Input Module is and which ones are provided by Unity
- How to use the Event Trigger component to receive events on UI objects
- What Raycasters are and what types of Raycasters are provided by Unity
- How to show and hide pop-up panels using keyboard inputs
- How to pause the game
- How to create a drag and drop inventory system

Accessing UI elements in code

All the UI elements can be accessed and manipulated in code similar to other GameObjects. To access a UI element in code, you must include the `UnityEngine.UI` namespace and the correct variable type.

UnityEngine.UI namespace

A **namespace** is a collection of classes. When you include a namespace in your class, you are stating that you want to access all the variables and methods (functions) in your class. Namespaces are accessed at the top of a script with the `using` keyword.

By default, all new C# scripts include the `System.Collections`, `System.Collections.Generic`, and `UnityEngine` namespaces. To access the properties of UI elements via code, you must first use the `UnityEngine.UI` namespace.

Therefore, at the top of your C# script, you will need to include the following line to signify that you want to use the `UnityEngine.UI` namespace:

```
using UnityEngine.UI;
```

Without using the namespace, any variable type related to UI elements will be colored red in MonoDevelop, and you will be given a compiler error. Once you include the namespace, the variable type will change to blue colored text, signifying that it is an available variable type, and the compiler error will disappear.

UI variable types

Each variable type is a class within the `UnityEngine.UI` namespace. Therefore, each of these variable types, in turn, have their own set of variables and functions that can be accessed. We'll discuss each variable type more thoroughly in the future sections and chapters, but, for now, let's just look at the standard template for accessing a property of a UI element in code.

In the `Chapter4Text` scene available in the provided project, you will see a UI Image named `UI Variables Example`. It does not have a sprite assigned to it and appears as a white square. The following script, `AddSprite.cs`, is attached to the UI Image:

```
using System.Collections;
using System.Collections.Generic;
using UnityEngine;
using  UnityEngine.UI;

public class AddSprite : MonoBehaviour {
    public Image theImage;
    public Sprite theSprite;

    // Use this for initialization
    void Start () {
        theImage.sprite=theSprite;
        theImage.preserveAspect=true;
    }
}
```

The UI-specific pieces of code are highlighted in the preceding code. Note that the `UnityEngine.UI` namespace is included at the top of the class.

There are two public variables defined in the class: `theImage`, which is an `Image` type and `theSprite`, which is a `Sprite` type. The `theImage` variable is referencing the UI Image in the scene and the `theSprite` variable is referencing the sprite that will be become the source image of the UI Image.

The `Image` variable type is within the `UnityEngine.UI` namespace and represents UI Image GameObject.

The `Sprite` variable type is not a UI element and is included in the `UnityEngine` namespace.

Within the `Start()` function, the properties of the Image component on `theImage` are referenced by typing a period and then the property after the variable name. You can access any property that appears in a UI element's corresponding component in this way. You can also access properties that are not listed in the component this way.

The `AddSprite` script attached to the `UI Variables Example (Image)` appears in the inspector, as shown in the following screenshot:

Now when the scene is played, the sprite will change from a blank white square to an image of a banana with its aspect ratio preserved.

The Event System

In `Chapter 2`, *Canvases, Panels, and Basic Layouts*, we learned that when the first Canvas is added to a scene, a GameObject named `EventSystem` is automatically added to the Hierarchy. The Event System allows you to easily receive player interaction and send those interactions to objects in your scene through events. Note that I said "objects in your scene" and not "UI objects". The Event System allows you to send events to non-UI items, too!

 Before we proceed, I'd like to note my use of EventSystem (one word) and Event System (two words), because I will be switching back and forth between the two. I want you to know that I am doing it deliberately and am not just randomly deciding that sometimes I hate the spacebar.

I will use EventSystem (one word) to reference the actual GameObject that appears in the Heirarchy of your scene and Event System (two words) to reference the system that handles events.

The Event System does quite a few things for you other than just sending events to objects. It also keeps track of the currently selected GameObject, the Input Modules, and Raycasting.

The `EventSystem` GameObject initializes, by default, with three components: the **Transform**, **Event System** Manager, and **Standalone Input Module**, as shown in the following screenshot:

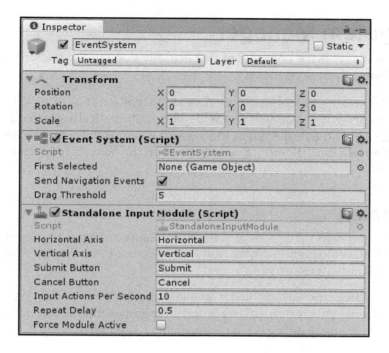

Since EventSystem is a GameObject, it physically exists within the scene (even though it has no renderable component making it visible) and therefore has a **Transform** component like all other GameObjects. You should be familiar with the **Transform** component by now, so we won't discuss it further. However, the other two components do merit further discussion. Let's look at the **Event System** Manager Component more closely now. We'll also discuss the **Standalone Input Module** Component in the *Input Modules* section of this chapter.

You cannot have more than that one EventSystem GameObject in your scene. If you try to add a new one in the scene via **Create | UI | Event System**, a new one will not be added, and the one currently in the scene will be selected for you.

If you manage to add a second EventSystem to your scene (by perhaps using *Ctrl + D* to duplicate the existing one), you will see a warning message on your **Console**.

If you have more than one EventSystem GameObject in your scene, only the first one added will actually do anything. Any additional EventSystems will be non-functional.

Event System Manager

Event System Manager is the component that actually does all the tracking and managing of the various **Event System** elements.

 If you want to work with the **Event System** without using UI, the EventSystem GameObject will not be automatically created for you. You can add an **Event System** Manager to a GameObject by selecting **Add Component** | **Event** | **Event System** on the object's **Inspector**.

First Selected

You know when you start up a game and the **Start Game** button is highlighted for you that hitting *Enter* will start the game without you having to use your mouse? That's what the **First Selected** property does for you.

You can drag and drop any intractable UI element into this slot to make it the first selected UI item in your scene. This is particularly helpful for games that do not use a mouse or touchscreen, but rely solely on a gamepad, joystick, or keyboard.

Send Navigation Events

The **Send Navigation Events** property can be toggled on and off. When this property is enabled, you can navigate between UI elements via a gamepad, joystick, or keyboard. The navigation events that can be used are as listed:

- **Move:** You can select the various UI elements via arrow keys on the keyboard or the control stick on a gamepad (or whichever keys/buttons you have designated as the movement keys). Movement will start at the UI item designated **First Selected**. We will discuss how to specify the order in which UI items are selected using movement in Chapter 5, *Buttons*.
- **Submit:** Commit to the UI item selected.
- **Cancel:** Cancel the selection.

Drag Threshold

The **Drag Threshold** property represents the number of pixels a UI object can be moved before it is considered being "dragged". People don't have perfectly steady hands, so when they are trying to click or tap a UI item their mouse or finger may move slightly. This **Drag Threshold** allows the player to move their input slightly (or a lot if you make this number high) before the item they are selecting is being "dragged" rather than "clicked".

Input Manager

Before we discuss the next component on the **Event System** Manger, I want to discuss the Input Manager. The Input Manager is where you define the axes in your game, by assigning them to the buttons on your mouse, keyboard, or joystick (gamepad). This also allows you to use the axis name when coding to easily reference all inputs that you want to perform in an action.

To open **InputManager**, select **Edit | Project Settings | Input**.

If you select the arrow next to **Axes**, you will see the default list of axes:

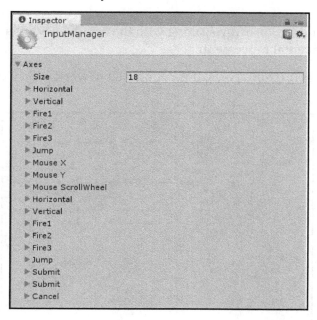

There are 18 total axes by default. Changing the number next to **Size** will give you more or less axes. Expanding axes will reveal the following:

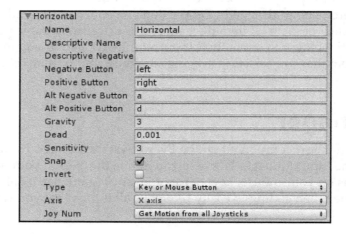

The item entered in the **Name** slot is the one that will appear next to the expandable arrow. In the preceding screenshot, all the keys that allow for horizontal movement have been defined.

Note that the left and right arrows, along with the a and d keys of a keyboard, are defaulted to the **Horizontal** movement.

There is also a second **Horizontal** axis. It is configured to work with a joystick or a gamepad.

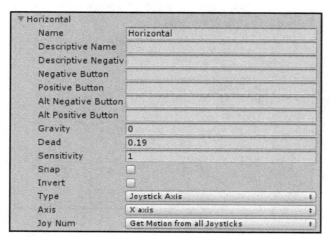

As there are two Axes labeled **Horizontal**, they can both be easily referenced in code with the "Horizontal" label.

 To view a list of the keywords for each keyboard key as well as a description for each of the properties of an axis input, visit https://docs. unity3d.com/Manual/ConventionalGameInput.html.

This will allow you to reference all of these buttons and joysticks together as a group. This is much simpler than having to write code that gets each of the individual keyboard keys along the individual joysticks.

You can delete any of these 18 default axes you want by right-clicking on them and selecting **Delete Array Element**.

 However, be careful when you delete them. You need at least one Submit and one Cancel axis to be able to use the **Standalone Input Manager** (unless you change the **Submit Button** and **Cancel Button** in the **Standalone Input Manager**). For more information, refer to the *Standalone Input Manager* section.

Input functions for buttons and key presses

There are quite a few ways to access key and button presses via code. How you do this depends on whether you have the key specified as an axis in the Input Manager and whether you want the key to register once or continuously. I'll discuss a few in this text, but you can find a full list of the functions at https://docs.unity3d.com/ScriptReference/ Input.html.

A script named KeyPresses is attached to the Main Camera in Text example scene of Chapter4, *The Event System and Programming for UI*, and contains all the code demonstrated in this section if you'd like to play around with key presses.

GetButton

If you have a button defined as an axis in the Input Manager, you can use GetButton(), GetButtonDown(), and GetButtonUp() to determine when a button has been pressed.

`GetButton()` returns true while the button is being held, `GetButtonDown()` returns true only once, on the frame that the button is initially pressed, and `GetButtonUp()` returns true only once, on the frame that the button is released.

Within each of the functions, you place the axis name from the Input Manager within the parentheses within quotes. These functions should be checked in the `Update()` function of a script so that they are continuously being checked for.

So, for example, if you wanted to check whether the *Enter* key is being pressed since it is assigned to a **Positive Button** for the `Submit` axis, you can write the following code to trigger when the *Enter* key is pressed down:

```
void Update () {
    if(Input.GetButtonDown("Submit")){
        Debug.Log("You pressed a submit key/button!");
    }
}
```

Keep in mind that this will not just trigger with the *Enter* key, as the submit axis has a few keys assigned as **Positive Buttons** or **Alt Positive Buttons**.

GetAxis

If you're looking for a function that will trigger continuously without any breaks between firing, you want to use `GetAxis()` rather than `GetButton()`. `GetButton()` is good for buttons you want to hold down but want a slight pause between events firing (think holding down a fire button, and the gun shoots bullets with breaks in between them). `GetAxis()` works better for events involving movement because of this continuous frame-rate independent execution.

`GetAxis()` works a bit differently, as it returns a `float` value rather than a Boolean, such as `GetButton()`. It is also best suited within an `Update()` function. So, for example, you can check whether the horizontal movement is occurring, as follows:

```
void Update () {
    float horizontalValue=Input.GetAxis("Horizontal");
    if(horizontalValue!=0){
        Debug.Log("You're holding down a horizontal button!");
    }
}
```

GetKey

If you want to get a keyboard key press that is not assigned to an axis, you can use
GetKey(), GetKeyDown(), or GetKeyUp() to reference keyboard keys via their KeyCode.

The GetKey() functions work pretty similar to the GetButton() functions. GetKey()
returns true while the key is being held down; GetKeyDown() returns true only once, on
the frame that the key is initially pressed; and GetKeyUp() returns true only once, on the
frame that the key is released.

Each key has its own KeyCode that needs to be referenced in the parentheses of the
GetKey() functions. You can find a list of all the keyboard KeyCodes at https://docs.
unity3d.com/ScriptReference/KeyCode.html.

So, for example, if you wanted to check whether the *8* key from the alphanumeric keyboard
is being pressed, you could write the following code to trigger when the *8* key is pressed
down:

```
void Update () {
    if(Input.GetKeyDown(KeyCode.Alpha8)){
        Debug.Log("You pressed the 8 key for some reason!");
    }
}
```

GetMouseButton()

Just with GetButton() and GetKey(), there are three functions for telling when a mouse
button has been pressed: GetMouseButton(), GetMouseButtonDown(), and
GetMouseButtonUp(). They return true in the same way that the GetButton() and
GetKey() functions do.

You'd place these functions within the Update() function as well. Within the parentheses,
you check to see which button is being pressed; 0 represents a left-click, 1 represents a
right-click, and 2 represents a middle-click.

So, for example, if you wanted to check that the middle mouse button was clicked from the alphanumeric keyboard is being pressed, you could write the following code to trigger when the middle mouse button is pressed down:

```
void Update () {
    if(Input.GetMouseDown(2)){
        Debug.Log("You pressed the middle mouse button!");
    }
}
```

Input Modules

Input Modules describe how the Event System will handle the inputs to the game via the mouse, keyboard, touchscreen, gamepad, and such. You can think of them as the bridge between the hardware and events.

There are four input modules provided by Unity:

- Standalone Input Module
- Hololens Input Module
- Base Input Module
- Pointer Input Module

To utilize these input modules, you attach them to your EventSystem GameObject.

You are not restricted to using these four input modules and can create your own, so if you have an input device that is not covered by one of those four, you'd create your own input module script and then attach it to the Event System.

Until the recent version of Unity, there was another input module called Touch Input Module, which was necessary for touchscreen inputs. However, this module has been depreciated and its functionality is now lumped in the **Standalone Input Module**. If you have an older version of Unity installed, you may see a **Touch Input Module** component attached to your EventSystem GameObject. Since this input module has been depreciated, it will not be discussed in this text.

Let's look at the four input modules provided by Unity in depth.

Standalone Input Module

The **Standalone Input Module** is a pretty robust input module that will work with most of your input devices. It works with a mouse, keyboard, touchscreen, and gamepads.

The Standalone Input Module is automatically added to your `EventSystem GameObject` when it is created. However, you can attach the Standalone Input Module as a component using **Add Component | Event | Standalone Input Module** on the object's **Inspector**. You could do this if you wanted to add a second one, previously deleted it and want to re-attach it, or want to add the **Standalone Input Module** to another `GameObject`.

You'll see that the first four properties of the **Standalone Input Module** are **Horizontal Axis**, **Vertical Axis**, **Submit Button**, and **Cancel Button**. These properties are the reason I wanted to discuss the Input Manager before discussing the Input Modules. The default properties assigned to these slots are **Horizontal**, **Vertical**, **Submit**, and **Cancel**. These assignments are referencing the axes assignments that form the Input Manager.

The **Input Actions Per Second** property defines how many inputs are allowed per second. This is in relation to the keyboard and the gamepad inputs. The default value is `10`. This means that there will be a tenth of a second delay after an input action before the next input action is registered. The **Repeat Delay** property is the amount of time, in seconds, before **Input Actions Per Second** occurs.

Hololens Input Module

The **Hololens Input Module** allows you to receive input from the Microsoft Hololens. It is also a component that can be attached to your `EventSystem`. It can be attached to your `EventSystem` using **Add Component | Event | Hololens Input Module** on the object's **Inspector**. Its properties are very similar to that of the **Standalone Input Module**.

Due to the niche nature of this Input Module, it is outside of the scope of this general UI text, so I will not go into further detail of using the **Hololens Input Module**, but I wanted to make you aware that it is available for you.

There is not a lot of information concerning the **Hololens Input Module** available on Unity's website; however, the following two resources may be helpful to you if you wish to make a game with Microsoft Hololens:

https://forum.unity3d.com/threads/unity-ui-on-the-hololens.394629/

https://docs.unity3d.com/ScriptReference/EventSystems.HoloLensInputModule.html

Base Input Module/Pointer Input Module

The **Base Input Module** and **Pointer Input Module** are modules that are only accessible via code.

If you need to create your own input module, you will create it by extending from the Base Input Module. You can view a full list of the variables, functions, and messages that can be utilized by extending the Base Input Module at https://docs.unity3d.com/ScriptReference/EventSystems.BaseInputModule.html.

The Pointer Input Module is a Base Input Module that is used by the Standalone Input Module described earlier. It can also be used to write custom input modules. You can view a full list of the variables, functions, and messages that can be utilized by extending the Pointer Input Module at https://docs.unity3d.com/ScriptReference/EventSystems.PointerInputModule.html.

Event Trigger

The **Event Trigger** component can be attached to any UI (or non-UI) element to allow the object to receive events. Some of the UI elements are preconfigured to intercept specific events. For example, buttons have the onClick event. However, if you'd like to add an event to an object that either isn't already set up to receive events or you want it to receive different events, you can attach an **Event Trigger** component to the GameObject.

You can attach an Event Trigger component by selecting **Add Component** | **Event** | **Event Trigger**.

One caveat of using the **Event Trigger** component is that the object it is attached to receives all the events, not just the ones you added. So, even if you don't tell the object what to do with the specified event, it will receive that event and acknowledge that the event occurred—it just won't do anything in response. This can have a slow performance in your game. If you are worried about performance, you will want to write your own script that attaches only the events you want to use to your component. The next section, *Event Inputs*, discusses how to achieve this.

If you use an **Event Trigger** component on an object other than a UI element, the object must also have a collider component, and you must include a raycaster on the camera within the scene.

Which collider and raycaster you use depends on whether you are working in 2D or 3D.

If you are working in 2D, you can add a 2D collider to the object with **Add Component | Physics 2D** and then select the appropriate 2D collider from within the object's **Inspector**. You can then add a raycaster to the camera by selecting **Add Component | Event | Physics 2D Raycaster** from within the camera's **Inspector**.

If you are working in 3D, you can add a 3D collider to the object with **Add Component | Physics** and then select the appropriate 3D collider from within the object's **Inspector**. You can then add a raycaster to the camera by selecting **Add Component | Event | Physics Raycaster** from within the camera's **Inspector**.

Let's look at the various event types that the Event Trigger can receive.

Event Types

You can tell the object which type of input event you want to receive by selecting **Add New Event Type**.

Many of these events are tied to the bounding region of the object. The bounding region of a UI object is represented by the area of the Rect Transform. For a non-UI object, the bounding region is represented by a 2D or 3D collider.

Pointer events

Pointer events can be called by the pointer in a **Standalone Input Module**. Remember that a pointer is not exclusively a mouse. The pointer in a **Standalone Input Module** can be a mouse, finger touch, or a reticle tied to gamepad movement.

Two of the event types are related to the position of the pointer in relation to the object's bounding box region. The **PointerEnter** event is called when the pointer enters the bounding box of the object and **PointerExit** is called when the pointer exits the bound box area.

There are three events related to clicking on the object. The **PointerDown** event is called when the pointer is pressed down within the bounding region of the object, and **PointerUp** is called when the pointer is released within the bounding region of the object. It's important to note that with **PointerUp**, the pointer can be pressed outside of the object, held down, and then released inside the object for the **PointerUp** event to trigger. The **PointerClick** event is called when the pointer is pressed and then released within the bounding region of the object.

Drag and Drop events

When working with the various drag and drop events, it's important to differentiate between the object being dragged and the object on which the dragged object is dropped.

The **InitializePotentialDrag** event is called whenever a drag object is found, but before an object is actually being dragged.

The **Drag** event is called on the object being dragged when it is being dragged. A **Drag** event occurs when a pointer is pressed within the bounding box of an object and then moved without releasing. It's ended by releasing the pointer. The **BeginDrag** event is called from the object being dragged when its drag begins and **EndDrag** event is called when its drag ends.

The **Drop** event is different from the **EndDrag** event. The **EndDrag** event is called on the object that was just being dragged. The **Drop** event is called by the object on which the dragged object was dropped. Therefore, the **Drop** event is called by the object touching the dragged when the dragged object stops dragging. So, if you were making a drag and drop menu, you'd add the **Drag** event to the objects you want to drag and the **Drop** event to the slots they will be dragged to.

Selection events

The **Select** event is called when the object is considered the selected object, and **Deselect** is called when the object is no longer considered selected. Each of these events only fire once—the moment the object is considered selected or deselected. If you want an event that will trigger continuously while the object is selected, you can use the **UpdateSelected** event. The **UpdateSelected** event is called every frame.

Other events

The following events are called based on assignments in the Input Manager. Remember that you can assign buttons, keys, and such to axes that define movement, submit, and cancel.

The **Scroll** event is called when the mouse wheel scrolls, and the **Move** event is called when a movement happens. When the button assigned to the `Submit` axis is pressed, the **Submit** event is called, and when the button assigned to the `Cancel` axis is pressed, the **Cancel** event is called.

Adding an action to the event

Once you have actually selected an event type, you must specify what will happen when that event type triggers. The following screenshot shows the results of selecting **Pointer Enter** as an event type:

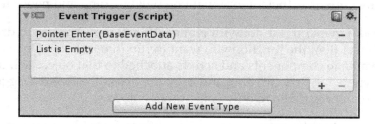

The preceding screenshot shows that an event type of **Pointer Enter** has been selected, but what happens when the pointer enters the object's bounding area yet to be defined. To define what happens when the event triggers, you must select the plus sign (+) at the bottom-right corner of the event's box. You can add multiple things to happen when the event triggers by selecting the plus sign multiple times.

Once an event type has been added to the **Event Trigger**, it cannot be added a second time and will be grayed out in the **Add New Event Type** list.

To remove an event type from the **Event Trigger**, select the minus (-) at the top-right corner of the event type's box.

Once the plus sign is selected, the event type should look as follows:

The first setting on this event is a drop-down menu with the **Runtime Only** (by default), **Editor and Runtime**, and **Off** options. This is where we specify when the event can be triggered. Setting this to **Off** will make the event never trigger. Setting this to **Runtime Only** will have the event trigger when the game is being played. Setting this to **Editor and Runtime** will make events trigger when the game is being played, but it also accepts the triggers in the Editor when the game is not in play mode. I generally just always set this to **Editor and Runtime**, because I usually want my events to always work. However, most of the time, **Runtime Only** is sufficient for what you will be doing and hence it is the default.

Below that drop-down menu is a slot with **None (Object)** in it. You are to drag from the Hierarchy whichever item the function you want to run into this slot. Once that is assigned, a list of all the available components and scripts attached to that object will display in the second drop-down menu. You can drag and drop the object the **Event Trigger** is attached to in this slot and are not restricted to only using other objects.

The following screenshot shows an Image object with an **Event Trigger** added to it and the Pointer Enter event type. The same image is added to the slot, signifying to look at the components available at itself. The image component's sprite property is to change to the image foodSpriteSheet_1 when the pointer enters its **Rect Transform**.

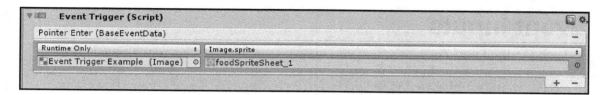

Event Trigger Example in the Chapter4Text Scene

To see this **Event Trigger** in action, view the `Chapter4Text` scene in the provided game project. Hover your mouse over the image; it will look like a potion bottle, and you will see it change to a triangle.

You can also run functions within scripts attached to objects. For example, the next screenshot shows the same image, but now with a `Pointer Click` event as well. `Main Camera` has a script attached to it called **HelloWorld** with a function called `HeyThere()`.

Event Trigger Example in the Chapter4Text Scene

The `HeyThere()` function simply prints `Hello world! This is main camera speaking!` in the **Console**. Each time the potion bottle is clicked on, that function will run, and you'll see the message in the **Console**.

 To run a function from the **Event Trigger**, it must be `public`, have a return type of `void`, and have no more than one parameter.

Event inputs

As stated in the *Event Trigger* section, you may not want to use an **Event Trigger** component, because the **Event Trigger** component causes the object on which it is attached to receive all the events listed in the *Event Trigger* section. So, if you are worried about performance issues, you will want an alternate way to receive events on an object.

All event types that were available to add in the **Event Trigger** can also be added to an object via code without using the **Event Trigger** component. To use an event without the **Event Trigger** component, you must derive your script from the appropriate interface and know the type of event data class that the event uses.

An **interface** is a template that defines all the required functionality that a class can implement. So, by using an interface, you can then use any of the methods or functions that have been defined within that interface. I'll show you some examples of how to do this, but first, let's look at the available events and their required interfaces.

There are three classes that the event data can be derived from: **PointerEventData**, **AxisEventData**, and **BaseEventData**. PointerEventData is the class that contains events associated with the pointer, AxisEventData contains events associated with the keyboard and gamepad, and BaseEventData contains events that are used by all event types.

The list of events available for a **Standalone Input Module** along with their required interfaces and event data class are provided in the following chart. The events are listed in the same order they are listed within the **Event Trigger** component for continuity purposes:

Event	Interface	Event Data Type
OnPointerEnter	IPointerEnterHandler	PointerEventData
OnPointerExit	IPointerExitHandler	PointerEventData
OnPointerDown	IPointerDownHandler	PointerEventData
OnPointerUp	IPointerUpHandler	PointerEventData
OnPointerClick	IPointerClickHandler	PointerEventData
OnDrag	IDragHandler	PointerEventData
OnDrop	IDropHandler	PointerEventData
OnScroll	IScrollHandler	PointerEventData
OnUpdateSelected	IUpdateSelectedHandler	BaseEventData

OnSelect	ISelectHandler	BaseEventData
OnDeselect	IDeselectHandler	BaseEventData
OnMove	IMoveHandler	AxisEventData
OnInitializePotentialDrag	IInitializePotentialDragHandler	PointerEventData
OnBeginDrag	IBeginDragHandler	PointerEventData
OnEndDrag	IEndDragHandler	PointerEventData
OnSubmit	ISubmitHandler	BaseEventData
OnCancel	ICancelHandler	BaseEventData

To write a class with one of these events, you will use the following template:

```
using UnityEngine;
using UnityEngine.UI;
using UnityEngine.EventSystems;
public class ClassName : MonoBehaviour, InterfaceName{
    public void EventName(EventDataTypeName eventData){
        //what happens after event triggers
    }
}
```

The items highlighted in the preceding code will be replaced by the items within the preceding table.

For example, if you wanted to implement a OnPointerEnter event, the code would look as follows after the highlighted code has been replaced with an appropriate event, interface, and event data type:

```
using UnityEngine;
using UnityEngine.UI;
using UnityEngine.EventSystems;
public class ClassName : MonoBehaviour, IPointerEnterHandler{
    public void OnePointerEnter(PointerEventData eventData){
        //what happens after the event triggers
    }
}
```

You *must* include the UnityEngine.EventSystems namespace to write code with event data. The UnityEngine.UI namespace is optional and is only required if you will also be writing your events for UI objects.

Raycasters

Remember that the Event System keeps track of Raycasting along with all the other things we have discussed. Raycasting is used to determine which UI elements are being interacted with by projecting a ray from the user's pointer into the scene. This ray is considered to originate at the camera's plane and then proceed forward through the scene. Whatever this ray hits, receives an interaction. You can have the ray continue on through the first UI element it hits or stop at the first UI element hits. To get a ray to stop at the first UI element it hits, the object must block raycasting. This will stop items behind it from being interacted with.

Graphic Raycaster

When a Canvas is added to the scene, it is automatically given a **Graphic Raycaster** component.

This is the raycasting system that will allow you to interact with all UI objects that are children of that Canvas. It has three properties: **Ignore Reversed Graphics**, **Blocking Objects** and **Blocking Mask**.

The **Reversed Graphics** toggle determines whether or not graphical objects within the Canvas can be interacted with if they are facing backward (in relation to the raycaster). The **Blocking Objects** and **Blocking Mask** allow you to assign the types of objects that are in front of the Canvas (between the camera and the Canvas) that can block raycasting to the Canvas.

Other Raycasters

As stated earlier, if you want to use the **Event System** with a non-UI object, you must attach a Raycaster to a camera within the scene. You can add either a **Physics 2D Raycaster** or a **Physics Raycaster** (or both) to your camera based on whether you are using 2D or 3D.

From within the camera's inspector, you can add the Physics 2D Raycaster by selecting **Add Component | Event | Physics 2D Raycaster** and the Physics Raycaster by selecting **Add Component | Event | Physics Raycaster**.

The two components appear as follows:

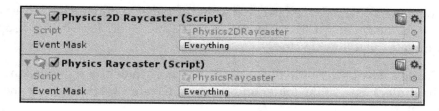

The **Event Mask** property determines which types of objects can receive raycasting.

 If you attempt to add either of these components to a non-camera GameObject, a **Camera** component will automatically be attached to the GameObject as well.

Examples

We will continue to work on the UI we have been building for the last two chapters. To help organize the project, duplicate the Chapter3 scene that you created in the last chapter; it will automatically be named as Chapter4.

Showing and hiding pop-up menus with keypress

So far, we have made two panels that we plan on making pop-ups: Pause Panel from *Chapter 2, Canvases, Panels, and Basic Layout* and Inventory Panel from *Chapter 3, Automatic Layouts*. Right now they are both visible in the scene (even though Pause Panel is hidden behind the Inventory Panel). We want them to pop up when we press specific *p* and *i* on the keyboard. For demonstration purposes, we'll access the keyboard keys differently for each panel.

Remember that both of these panels have Canvas Group components on them. These components will allow us to easily access the panels' alpha, intractable, and blocks raycasts properties.

Using KeyCode with the Inventory Panel

Let's begin with the `Inventory Panel`. We want the panel to pop up and close when the *i* key is pressed on the keyboard. To make the `Inventory Panel` appear and disappear with the *i* key, complete the following steps:

1. Create a new C# script in the `Assets/Scripts` folder by right-clicking within the **Project** view of the folder and selecting **Create | C# Script** from the pop-up panel.
2. Name the script `ShowHidePanels`, and then double-click on it to open.
3. We will now go to the `public CanvasGroup` variable called `inventoryPanel` to represent the panel. We will use a `CanvasGroup` variable type to reference the panel, since we want to access the properties of the **Canvas Group** component. Update your `ShowHidePanels` script to include the following highlighted line of code:

```
using System.Collections;
using System.Collections.Generic;
using UnityEngine;

public class ShowHidePanels : MonoBehaviour {
    public CanvasGroup inventoryPanel;
    // Use this for initialization
    void Start () {

    }

    // Update is called once per frame
    void Update () {

    }
}
```

 The `CanvasGroup` variable type, even though it is used with UI elements, is not in the `UnityEngine.UI` namespace, but the `UnityEngine` namespace, so we do not need to include `UnityEngine.UI` in our namespace script to work with it.

4. Let's create another variable that will keep track of whether or not the Inventory Panel is visible. Add the following code to the next line of the script:

```
public bool inventoryUp=false;
```

5. We want `Inventory Panel` to be hidden when the scene starts playing. When the panel is hidden, it should also not accept interactions or block raycasts. So, update the `Start()` function to include the following code:

```
void Start () {
    inventoryPanel.alpha=0;
    inventoryPanel.interactable=false;
    inventoryPanel.blocksRaycasts=false;
}
```

6. Now, we need to write code that triggers whenever the *i* key on the keyboard is pressed down. We will use the `Input.GetKeyDown()` function so that we get the function called the moment it is pressed down. We will also use `KeyCode.I` to reference the *i* key on the keyboard. Add the following code to your `Update` function to check whether the *i* key is pressed down:

```
void Update () {
    //inventory panel
    if(Input.GetKeyDown(KeyCode.I)){

    }
}
```

7. We want this key to disable and enable the panel, so we will place an `if-else` statement within the code created in the last step that checks whether or not the inventory panel needs to be enabled or disabled. It will accomplish this by checking the current status of the `inventoryUp` variable. Remember that we initialized `inventoryUp` as `false`, so if the inventory is not up, that is, `inventoryUp` is equal to `false`, it will show the Panel and set `inventoryUp` to `true`. If the inventory is up, that is, `inventoryUp` is equal to true, it will hide the Panel and set `inventoryUp` to `false`. Add the following code to your `Update()` function:

```
void Update () {
    //inventory panel
    if(Input.GetKeyDown(KeyCode.I)){
        //not visible
        if(inventoryUp==false){
            inventoryUp=true;
            inventoryPanel.alpha=1;
            inventoryPanel.interactable=true;
            inventoryPanel.blocksRaycasts=true;
        //already visible
        }else{
            inventoryUp=false;
```

```
inventoryPanel.alpha=0;
inventoryPanel.interactable=false;
inventoryPanel.blocksRaycasts=false;
    }
  }
}
```

8. Now, for this code to work, we need to attach it to a `GameObject` within our scene. It really doesn't matter what `GameObject` we attach it to, since we used a public variable to access our `inventoryPanel`. However, since we are planning on using this script to affect both panels, I want to add it to `Main Camera`. Drag and drop the `ShowHidePanels` script into the **Inspector** of `Main Camera`. You should now see the following as a component on your `Main Camera`:

9. Now, we need to assign the `Inventory Panel` GameObject to the slot labelled `Inventory Panel`. Drag and drop the **Inventory Panel** from the Hierarchy into this slot:

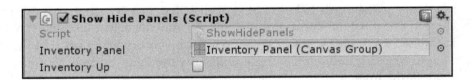

10. Play the game to ensure that the code is working correctly. You should see the inventory panel start out invisible and then turn on and off as you press the *i* key on the keyboard.

Using Input Manager with the pause panel

Now, let's do the same thing for the `Pause Panel`. We'll do this slightly differently than the `Inventory Panel`, using the Input Manager instead of a `KeyCode`. We also need to actually pause the game.

To display the pause panel using the *p* key and pause the game, complete the following steps:

1. First, we need to set up the Input Manager to include a `Pause` axis. Open the Input Manager with **Edit** | **Project Settings** | **Input** and expand the axes by selecting the arrow next to the word **Axes**.

2. By default, your project has `18` axes. You can replace one of these with the new Pause axis if you aren't planning on using them, but we might as well just go ahead and make a new one. Definitely, don't delete the `Submit` and `Cancel` axes, as we have them being referenced in our **Standalone Input Manger**.

   To add a new axis, change the size to `19`. This will duplicate the last axis in the list, `Cancel`, as shown in the following screenshot:

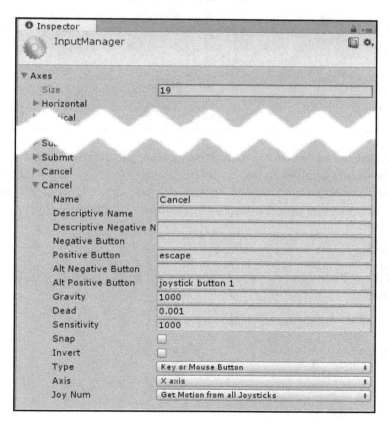

3. Change the second `Cancel` axis to a `Pause` axis by changing the **Name** to `Pause`, the **Positive Button** to `p`, and deleting `joystick button 1` in **Alt Positive Button**, as shown:

4. Now that we have our `Pause` axis set up, we can start writing our code. Let's define some variables to use with the `Pause Panel` similar to the way we defined variables for `Inventory Panel`. Add the following variable definitions at the top of your class under your previous variable definitions:

```
public CanvasGroup pausePanel;
public bool pauseUp=false;
```

5. Add the following to the `Start()` function and make the `Pause Panel` invisible at start:

```
pausePanel.alpha=0;
pausePanel.interactable=false;
pausePanel.blocksRaycasts=false;
```

6. Since we added the `Pause` axis to our Input Manager, we can use `Input.GetButtonDown()` instead of `Input.GetKeyDown()`, like we did with `Inventory Panel`. We want to use `GetButtonDown()` rather than `GetAxis()`, because we want a function that will return true once, not continuously. If it returned continuously (using `GetAxis()`), the panel would flicker in and out while the *p* key was being pressed. Add the following code at the end of your `Update()` function. Note that it's very similar to the code we used for `Inventory Panel`:

```
//pause panel
if(Input.GetButtonDown("Pause")){
    //not visible
    if(pauseUp==false){
        pauseUp=true;
        pausePanel.alpha=1;
        pausePanel.interactable=true;
        pausePanel.blocksRaycasts=true;
    //already visible
    }else{
        pauseUp=false;
        pausePanel.alpha=0;
        pausePanel.interactable=false;
        pausePanel.blocksRaycasts=false;
    }
}
```

7. Now that we've added two new public variables to our script, they should both be showing up in the **Inspector** of our `Main Camera` now. Drag and drop the `Pause Panel` from the Hierarchy to the **Pause Panel** slot.

8. Now, play the game and watch the `Pause Panel` become visible and invisible when you press the *p* key on the keyboard.

Pausing the game

The game doesn't actually pause right now. If we had animations or events running in the scene, they would continue to run even with the pause panel up. There is a really quick way to pause a game and that is by manipulating the time scale of the game. If the time scale is set to 1, time will run as it normally does. If the time scale is set to 0, the time within the game will pause.

Also, our current setup doesn't quite work, as a pause menu would be expected. `Inventory Panel` and `Pause Panel` can be displayed at the same time. If `Inventory Panel` is up, the `Pause Panel` is covered up by it, since it is rendering behind it. Also, the `Inventory Panel` can be activated when the game is "paused".

We'll need to pause the time scale of our game, change the order that our panels render, and disable functionality when the game is paused to have a `Pause Panel` that functions properly. To create a properly functioning `Pause Panel`, complete the following steps:

1. Add the following to the `Update()` function to the `ShowHidePanels` script to pause the time in the game:

```
//not visible
if(pauseUp==false){
    pauseUp=true;
    pausePanel.alpha=1;
    pausePanel.interactable=true;
    pausePanel.blocksRaycasts=true;
    Time.timeScale=0;

//already visible
}else{
    pauseUp=false;
    pausePanel.alpha=0;
    pausePanel.interactable=false;
    pausePanel.blocksRaycasts=false;
    Time.timeScale=1;
}
```

2. Now, let's deal with the fact that `Pause Panel` is behind the `Inventory Panel`. This is an easy fix. Simply change their order in the Hierarchy by dragging `Pause Panel` below the `Inventory Panel`. The items that are listed lower in the Hierarchy appear on top of the ones listed above it within the scene. Now, `Pause Panel` will be above the `Inventory Panel` in the scene:

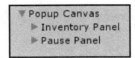

3. The only thing left to do is to disable the ability of `Inventory Panel` to appear and disappear if the `Pause Panel` is up. Adjust the `if` statement that checks for *i* key being pressed to also check whether `pauseUp` is `false`, like so:

```
if(Input.GetKeyDown(KeyCode.I) && pauseUp==false){
```

4. Play the game now and see when if the game is paused, `Inventory Panel` cannot be activated and deactivated. If the `Inventory Panel` is activated when the `Pause Panel` is already up, it cannot be deactivated until after the game is unpaused.

It's important to remember that when you have a `Pause Panel`, other events need to be turned off. Setting the timescale to `0` does not stop the ability for other events to occur; it only really stops animations and any clocks you may have displayed that use the time scale. So, we will need to ensure that any other event we program is turned off when the game is paused.

Dragging and dropping inventory items

We have an `Inventory Panel` that can be displayed and hidden and an HUD inventory. I want to be able to drag objects from my larger `Inventory Panel` to my smaller HUD inventory called `Bottom Right Panel` that we created in the previous chapter.

To make things a little easier for ourselves, let's disable the `ShowHidePanels` script that we added to the `Main Camera` earlier in this chapter. You can do this by deselecting the checkbox next to the script's component on the `Main Camera`:

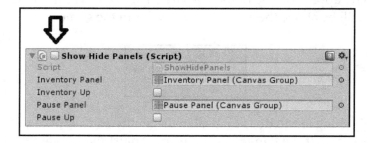

Let's also disable `Pause Panel` so that it will not be in our way. Do this by deselecting the checkbox next to the name of the `Pause Panel` in its Inspector.

Now our panel will stay visible, making it easier for us to debug the code we're about to write.

There are quite a few different ways to make a drag and drop mechanic. To ensure that this chapter provides an example of how to use the **Event Trigger** component, we will write a drag and drop mechanic utilizing it. To create a drag and drop mechanic for the `Inventory Panel` and `Bottom Right Panel`, complete the following steps:

1. Create a new C# script in the `Assets/Scripts` folder called `DragAndDrop` and open it.
2. We will be referencing UI elements in this script, so add the `UnityEngine.UI` namespace to the top of the script with this:

   ```
   using UnityEngine.UI;
   ```

3. We only need to add two variables to this script: one will represent the `GameObject` being dragged, and the other represents the `Canvas` that the items will be dragged on. Add the following public variables to the top of the class:

   ```
   public GameObject dragItem;
   public Canvas dragCanvas;
   ```

4. Before we write any more code, let's go back to the Editor with a bit more prep work. Drag the `DragAndDrop` script to the **Inspector** of the `Main Camera` to attach it as a component:

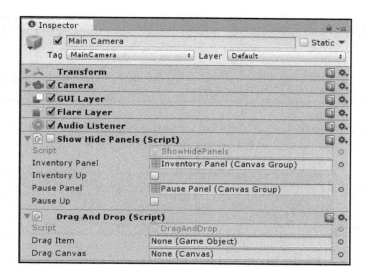

I've chosen to create a script that attaches it to the `Main Camera` rather than the individual inventory items, to reduce the need to duplicate this script.

5. Now, create a new UI Canvas by selecting **Create | UI | Canvas** from the Hierarchy menu. Name the new Canvas `Drag Canvas`.

6. Select `HUD Canvas` and copy its **Canvas Scalar** component by selecting the settings cog in its top-right corner and selecting **Copy Component**.

7. Reselect `Drag Canvas`, and paste the copied **Canvas Scaler** properties to its **Canvas Scalar** component by selecting the settings cog in its top-right corner and selecting **Paste Component Values**.
Once that is done, it should have the following values:

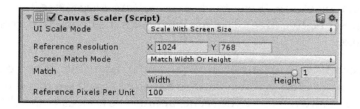

8. Set the **Sort Order** property on the `Drag Canvas` Canvas component to 1. This will cause anything that is on the `Drag Canvas` to render in front of all other Canvases, since the other Canvases have a **Sort Order** of 0:

9. Drag and drop the `Drag Canvas` from the Hierarchy into the **Drag Canvas** slot on the `DragAndDrop` script component on the `Main Camera`:

10. Reopen the `DragAndDrop` script. Create a new function called `StartDrag()`, as follows:

```
public void StartDrag(GameObject selectedObject){
    dragItem=Instantiate(selectedObject, Input.mousePosition,
selectedObject.transform.rotation) as GameObject;
    dragItem.transform.SetParent(dragCanvas.transform);
    dragItem.GetComponent<Image>().SetNativeSize();
dragItem.transform.localScale=1.1f*dragItem.transform.localScale;
}
```

This function will be called when a drag begins. It accepts a `GameObject` as a parameter and then creates a new instance of it at the position of the mouse. It then moves it so that it is a child of `dragCanvas`. Lastly, it sets the size of the Image on the Image component to native size. This resets the scale on the image to its original pixel size. (Refer to `Chapter 6`, *Text, Images, and TextMesh Pro-Text* for more on **Set Native Size**). The last line makes the image 10 percent bigger than its native size.

 After we hook up our `BeginDrag` and `Drag` events, if you comment out the line of code that sets the size to native, you'll see that the Image does not actually render in the scene, because its scale is "wacky" from the original `GameObject` being within a **Layout Group**.

11. Now create a new function called `Drag()`, as follows:

```
public void Drag(){
    dragItem.transform.position=Input.mousePosition;
}
```

This function will be called when an object is being dragged. While the object is dragged, it will keep position with the mouse.

12. Return to the Editor. We will just hook the events to the first object in the `Inventory Panel` for now. Select the first `Food` image in the `Inventory Panel`:

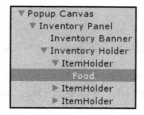

13. Add a new **Event Trigger** component to the `Food` Image by selecting **Add Component | Event | Event Trigger** within its **Inspector**:

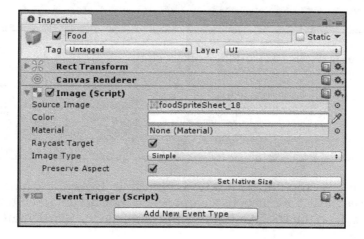

14. Now, add a `BeginDrag` event type and a `Drag` event type to the **Event Trigger** list by selecting **Add New Event Type** | **BeginDrag** and **Add New Event Type** | **Drag**:

15. Now we will hook add an action to the `BeginDrag` list by selecting the plus sign at the bottom-right corner of the **Begin Drag** area:

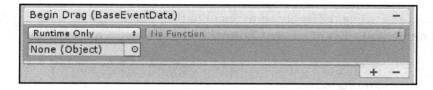

16. Drag the `Main Camera` into the object slot:

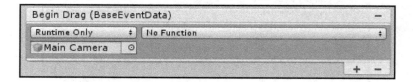

17. The function drop-down list is now intractable. Expand the function drop-down list to see the list of functions, components, and such attached to the **Main Camera**. Find the **DragAndDrop** script and then the **StartDrag(GameObject)** function:

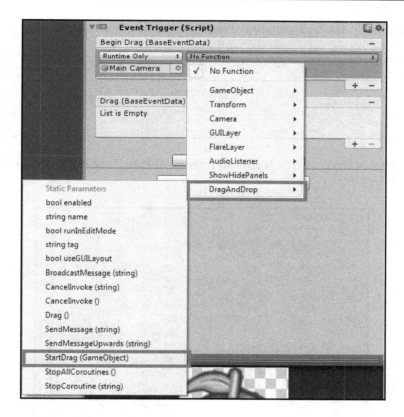

Once you have done so, you should see the following:

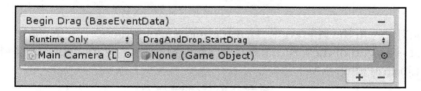

18. Now, we need to assign the `GameObject` parameter. Drag and drop the `Food` Image that this **Event Trigger** component is attached to into the parameter slot:

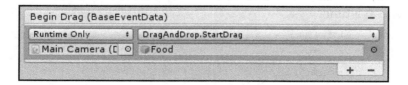

19. Now, set up the `Drag` event list similarly so that it looks like this:

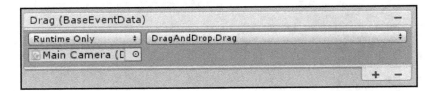

20. If you play the game, you should now be able to drag the orange in the first slot out of its slot:

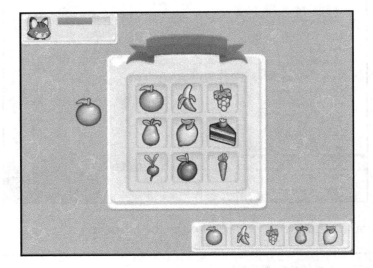

You'll see, in the Hierarchy, that there is a new `GameObject` called `Food(Clone)` that is a child of the `Drag Canvas`. This is the orange that gets created when you begin dragging:

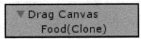

At this point, you can actually make as many of these clones as you want. In a moment, however, we will make it so that there is only one clone in the `Drag Canvas` at a time.

21. Go back to the `DragAndDrop` script and create a new function called `StopDrag()`, as follows:

```
public void StopDrag(){
    Destroy(dragItem);
}
```

This code will destroy the `Food(Clone)` `GameObject` once it is no longer being dragged.

22. Go back to the Editor and reselect the `Food` Image in `Inventory Panel`. Give its **Event Trigger** component an `EndDrag` event type by selecting **Add New Event Type | EndDrag**. It will automatically assign the `Drag()` function from the `DragAndDrop` script to this event, since that was the last selected function:

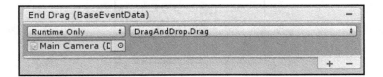

23. Replace the `Drag()` function in the function dropdown with the `StopDrag()` function:

24. Play the game, and you will see that the orange can now be dragged out of its slot and when you release the mouse, it is destroyed.

25. Go back to the `DragAndDrop` script and create a new function called `Drop()`, as shown:

```
public void Drop(Image dropSlot){
    GameObject
droppedItem=dragCanvas.transform.GetChild(0).gameObject;
    dropSlot.sprite=droppedItem.GetComponent<Image>().sprite;
}
```

This function accepts an `Image` as a parameter. This `Image` will be the Image component of the slot that will receive a drop. The first line of the function finds the first child of the `dragCanvas` (at position 0) and then assigns its image to the sprite of the `dropSlot`. Since we have set up the `StopDrag()` functions to destroy the objects being dragged once they stop dragging, we don't have to worry about there being more than one child of the `Drag Canvas`, making this the easiest way to find the object being dragged.

26. Go back to the Editor and select the second `Food` Image in the `Bottom Right Panel`:

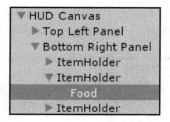

We're using the second `Food` Image, rather than the first, because the first already has an image of an orange in it, and it will be hard to tell that our script worked in that slot.

27. Add a new **Event Trigger** component to the `Food` Image by selecting **Add Component** | **Event** | **Event Trigger** within its Inspector.

28. Add a `Drop` event type to the **Event Trigger** component by selecting **Add New Event Type** | **Drop**:

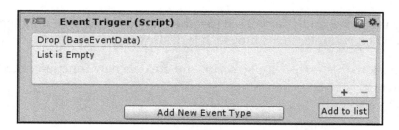

29. Add a new action to the list with the plus sign:

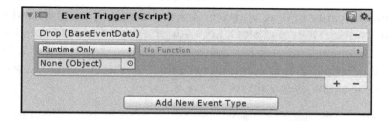

30. Drag `Main Camera` to the object slot and select the `Drop()` function from the `DragAndDrop` script:

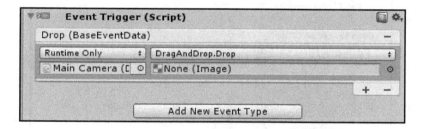

31. Now, drag the `Food` Image that this **Event Trigger** component is attached to in to the parameter slot:

32. Play the game and when you drag the orange into the slot over the banana, the `Drop()` function doesn't appear to trigger. This is because the orange being dragged is blocking the raycasting from reaching the banana, so the banana never thinks anything is dropped on it. This is an easy fix. Add the following line of code to the end of the `StartDrag()` function in the `DragAndDrop` script so that the raycast won't be blocked by the orange anymore:

```
dragItem.GetComponent<Image>().raycastTarget=false;
```

33. Play the game, and you should now be able to drag the orange from the first slot of the `Inventory Panel` to the second slot of `Bottom Right Panel`.

34. The functionality of drag and drop is now complete; we just need to add the functionality to the other slots. Let's add the drag events to the other `Inventory Panel` items first.

35. Copy the **Event Trigger** component of the `Food` Item in the `Inventory Panel` that we hook the events up to:

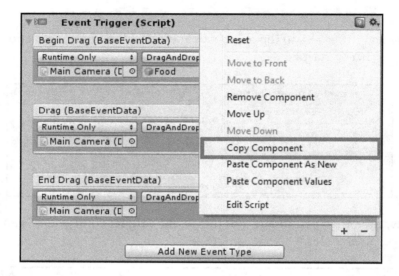

36. Select all the other `Food` Images in the `Inventory Panel` by clicking on them while holding *Ctrl*.

37. Now, with all eight `Food` Images still selected, click on the settings cog on the Image component and select **Paste Component as New**. Each of the `Food` Images should now have the **Event Trigger** component with all the appropriate events.

38. We're not done with these other inventory items yet. We need to select each one and drag it into the parameter of the `BeginDrag` event type. Otherwise, each of these other eight food items will drag out oranges instead of the appropriate food item.

39. Before continuing, play the game and ensure that each inventory item in `Inventory Panel` drags out the appropriate image.

40. Now we will copy the drop events from the second `Food` Image in the `Bottom Right Panel` to all the other `Food` Images within the Panel. Copy the **Event Trigger** component from the second `Food` Image in the `Bottom Right Panel`.

41. Select the other four Food Images in the Bottom Right Panel while holding down *Ctrl*.
42. With each of the Food Images shown in the preceding screenshot still selected, paste the component as new in the inspector.
43. Now, select each of the new Food Image and assign each to the parameter slot within their **Event Trigger** component.
44. Play the game and ensure that the correct image slot is changed when a food item is dropped to it.
45. Now that the drag and drop code is done, re-enable the ShowHidePanels script on the Main Camera and Pause Panel.

That's it for the drag and drop code. Currently, the Pause Panel blocks the raycast on the items within the Inventory Panel, so you don't have to worry about disabling these events when the game is paused. However, if you end up changing the layout, you will want to do so by checking whether the pauseUp variable is false before performing the tasks. You can do that by wrapping the code within each of the functions of the DragAndDrop script with the following if statement:

```
if(GetComponent<ShowHidePanels>().pauseUp==false){}
```

The provided example project has this change implemented in the each of the functions for reference.

If you want to allow the objects to go back and forth (drag from both panels and drop in both panels), all you have to do is copy the appropriate component to the opposite panels!

There're so many more examples I would love to cover in this chapter, but I can't make this chapter take up the entire page count of the book! You'll see more examples of using the **Event System** in the upcoming chapters, so don't worry, this isn't the last code example you will see.

Summary

Now that we know how to utilize the Event System and program for UI elements, we can start making interactive as well visual UI elements. We can also create UI that has its various properties change when events occur.

In this chapter, we discussed the following topics:

- How to access UI elements and their properties via code
- What the Event System is and how to work with it
- How to customize input axes with the Input Manager
- What an Input Module is and which ones are provided by Unity
- How to use the Event Trigger component to receive events on UI objects
- What Raycasters are and what types of Raycasters are provided by Unity
- How to show and hide pop-up panels using keyboard inputs
- How to pause the game
- How to create a drag and drop inventory system

In the next chapter, we will look at how to make and program UI Buttons.

5
Buttons

Buttons provided by Unity's UI system are graphical objects that preutilize the Event System we covered in the last chapter. When a Button is placed in a scene, it automatically has components added to it that allow the player to interact with it. This makes sense, because the whole point of a button is to interact with it.

In this chapter, we will discuss the following topics:

- Creating UI Buttons and setting their properties
- How to set button transitions that make the button change appearance when it is highlighted, pressed, or disabled
- Navigating button selection on screen with the keyboard or joystick
- How to create an onscreen button that looks like it is physically being pressed
- How to create buttons that swap images without using the built-in transitions, like a mute/unmute button
- Loading scenes with a button press
- Creating Button Transition Animations

All the examples shown in this section can be found within the Unity project provided in the code bundle. They can be found within the scene labeled Chapter5Text in the Assets/Scene/ExamplesInText/ folder.

Each example image has a caption stating the example number within the scene.

In the scene, each example is on its own Canvas and some of the Canvases are deactivated. To view an example on a deactivated Canvas, simply select the checkbox next to the Canvas' name in the **Inspector**:

UI Button

Buttons are UI objects that expect a click from the player. You can create a **Button** by selecting **Create | UI | Button**. When you make a button, a Button object with a Text child will be placed in the scene. As with all other UI objects, if no Canvas or Event System is in the scene when you create the **Button**, a **Canvas** and **Event System** will be created for you, with the Canvas being a parent of your new Button:

You can delete the child **Text** object if you do not want to have text displaying on your **Button**.

The Button object has three main components: The **Rect Transform** (like all other UI graphical objects), an **Image** component, and a **Button** component:

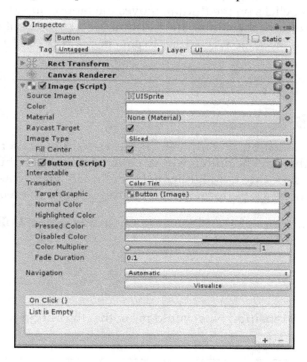

We'll discuss the **Image** component more thoroughly in the next chapter, but for now, just know that the **Image** component determines the look of the **Button** in its standard state.

Button component

The **Button** component provides all the properties that allow the player to interact with the button and determine what the **Button** will do when the player attempts to interact with it.

The first property of the **Button** component is the **Interactable** property. This property determines whether the **Button** can or cannot be interacted with by accepting input from the player. This is turned on by default, but can be turned off if you want to disable the button.

You'll see that the Button component already has an `On Click` Event attached to it. The `On Click` Event triggers when the player clicks and releases the mouse while hovering over the button. If the player clicks on the **Button**, moves the mouse outside of the Button's Rect Transform, and then releases the mouse, the Button's `On Click` Event will not register. You set the `On Click` Event the same way we set Events in `Chapter 4`, *The Event System and Programming for UI*.

Transitions

The second property of the Button component is the **Transition** property. The Transition property determines the way the button will visually react when the button is in different states. These different states are not-highlighted (or normal), highlighted, pressed, or disabled. These transitions are performed automatically and do not require coding.

There are four different types of Transitions you can assign: **None**, **Color Tint**, **Sprite Swap**, and **Animation**.

None

Selecting **None** for the **Transition** type would mean that the button will not visually change for the different states:

Color Tint

The **Color Tint** Transition type will make the button change color based on its state. You assign the **Normal Color**, **Highlighted Color**, **Pressed Color**, and **Disabled Color**.

In the following example, you can see that the button changes to the color green when the mouse is hovering over it (hence, highlighting it) and turns red as the mouse is being pressed down on it:

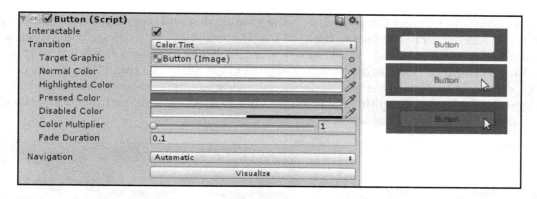

Color Swap Example in the Chapter5Text Scene

If you view the preceding example, you'll note that the button turns green after it is clicked on and when the button is no longer being hovered over. This is because a button is in the highlighted state when it is the last button clicked on, not just when it has hovered over. To return it to the normal state after clicking on it, you must click on an area outside of the button.

For a **Button** to enter the state that will give it its **Disabled Color**, the Button's **Interactable** property must be disabled. In the following screenshot, you will see how the button changes when the **Interactable** property is toggled on and off:

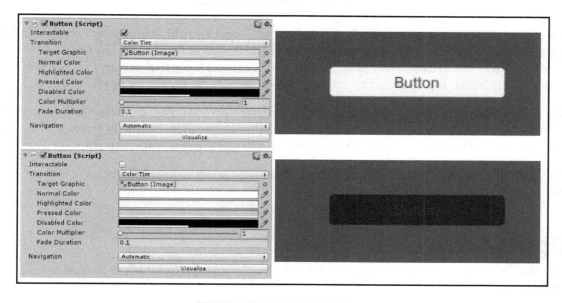

Disabled Button Example in the Chapter5Text Scene

You also can select **Target Graphic**. This is the graphic that will receive the transitions. By default, it is assigned to the **Button** itself, so the Button's Image will change color when it is highlighted, pressed, or disabled. However, you can choose to make a secondary graphic the **Target Graphic**. This means the item assigned to the **Target Graphic** will change color based on the interaction of the button. In the following example, a secondary image is assigned as the **Target Graphic**. You'll see the button does not undergo transition; instead, the star image undergoes transitions:

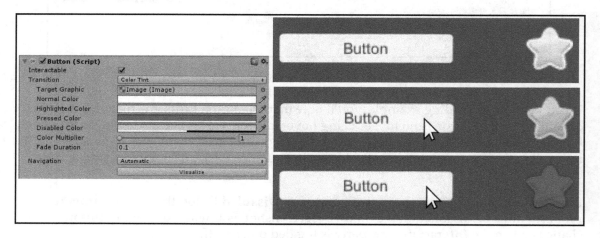

Target Graphic Example in the Chapter5Text Scene

It's important to note that these colors will tint the Target Graphic's image. So, it essentially puts a color overlay on top of **Target Graphic**. If the image of the **Target Graphic** is black, these tints will not appear to have any effect on the image. Note that the default **Normal Color** is white. Putting a white tint on an image does not change the color of the image.

The **Color Multiplier** property allows you to brighten up the colors or increase the alpha of the graphic. So, if the graphic has an alpha value that is less than 1, this property will increase the alpha of the graphic. This applies to all (including the normal) state.

The **Fade Duration** property is the time (in seconds) it takes to fade between the state colors.

Sprite Swap

The **Sprite Swap** Transition type will make the button change to different images for different states.

You'll note that there is no property to assign a sprite for the normal state. This is because the normal state will just use the sprite assigned to the Image component.

The sprite sheet we imported in `Chapter 2`, *Canvases, Panels, and Basic Layouts*, containing our UI images has four button images that will be helpful in demonstrating the Sprite Swap Transition: the images labeled **uiElement_39, uiElement_40, uiElement_41,** and **uiElement_42** (as shown in the following screenshot):

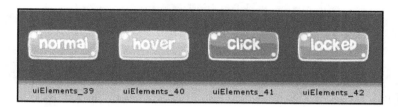

To have the button take on these images at the appropriate states, we simply need to assign `uiElement_39` to the **Source Image** on the **Image** component, `uiElement_40` to the **Highlighted Sprite**, `uiElement_41` to the **Pressed Sprite**, and `uiElement_42` to the **Disabled Sprite**. We also need to delete the child **Text** object from the button:

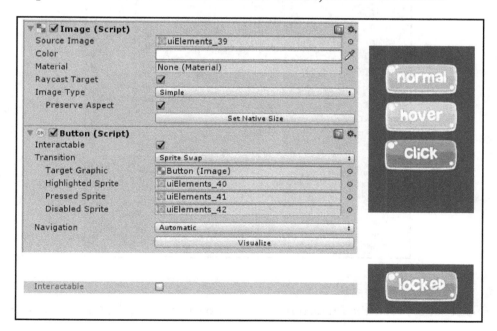

Sprite Swap Example in the Chapter5Text Scene

A nice sprite swap animation that I always find appealing is applying an image of a button that appears down-pressed to the pressed image. For example, I took the button on the left and slightly edited it to create the button on the right. The change is slight, but I changed it by down slightly moving down the top part of the button to make it look pressed:

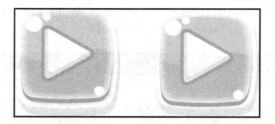

It doesn't look like much of a difference when viewed side by side. However, when the left-hand image is used as the **Source Image**, **Highlighted Sprite**, and **Disabled Sprite** and the right-hand Button is used as the **Pressed Sprite**, the button transitions to show a very nice button pressing animation:

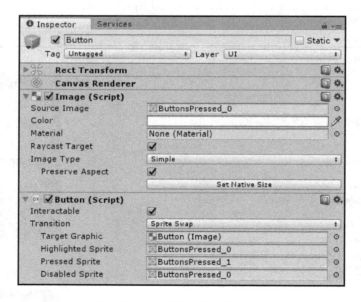

Pressed Button Example in the Chapter5Text Scene

To see this in action, view the Pressed Button Example Canvas in the `Chapter5Text` Scene.

Animation

The Animation Transition allows the button to animate in its various states.

Animation transition types require an Animator Component attached to the **Button**. It can add a preexisting set of animations to a **Button** by dragging it onto the Button's Inspector, or you can make a whole new Animator Controller by selecting **Auto Generate Animation**. If you use a preexisting Animator Controller, you can simply assign the Animations to the individual states. However, if you generate a new Animator Controller, you can select the state from the list of Clips in the Animation window and edit them from that window. An example of making a Button with animated transitions is provided in the examples section of the text.

Navigation

Buttons have a **Navigation** property that determines the order in which they will be highlighted via keyboard inputs:

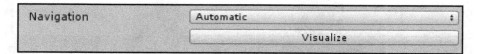

Each Button within the scene must have this property set if you want to navigate to all the Buttons. Recall from `Chapter 4`, *The Event System and Programming for UI*, we discussed the **First Selected** property of the Event System component. If you have a **Button** assigned to **First Selected**, that **Button** will be highlighted when you load the scene. If you then navigate throughout the Buttons with the keyboard, the navigation will begin at that Button. However, if you do not have a **Button** assigned as **First Selected**, navigation will not start until a button has been selected with the mouse. The next button selected is determined by the navigation option you have selected for the buttons.

There are five Navigation options: **None, Horizontal, Vertical, Automatic**, and **Explicit**.

Selecting **None** will disable all keyboard navigation to the specified Button. Remember that this is for the individual button, so if you want to disable all keyboard navigation, you must select **None** for all Buttons.

Horizontal and **Vertical** are pretty self-explanatory. If a **Button** has its **Navigation** property set to **Horizontal**, when it is selected the next button selected will be chosen horizontally, meaning with the right and left arrows. Vertical works similarly; this represents the navigation *away* from that button, not *to* that button. So, if a button that has Horizontal set has its navigation property, you can still access that button from another with a vertical button.

Automatic will allow the Button to navigate both Horizontally and Vertically, as determined automatically by its position relative to the other buttons.

The **Visualize** button allows you to see a visual representation of the navigation setup. Each Button will be connected with arrows demonstrating which Button will be selected after it. Each arrow begins on the side of the button to symbolize the directional arrow pressed, and it points at the next button that will be highlighted if that arrow is pressed. For example, if an arrow begins on a Button's right, that arrow symbolizes what Button will be selected next if the player presses right on the keyboard. The following example shows the Visualization of five Buttons all with their **Navigation** property set to **Automatic**:

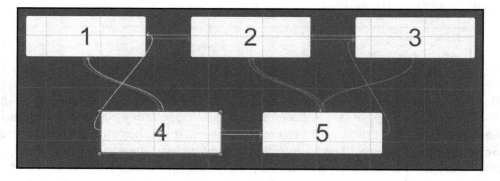

Navigation Example in the Chapter5Text Scene

In the preceding example, each Button has a **Color Tint Transition** property with the **Highlighted Color** assigned to green. The Button labeled 1 has been assigned as **First Selected** in the **Event System**:

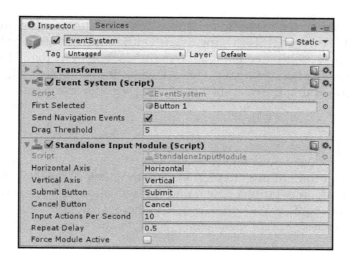

Therefore, when the scene begins playing, it will automatically be highlighted. Based on the Visualized graph, if the left arrow key is selected on the keyboard after the scene loads, the **Button** labeled 2 will be selected:

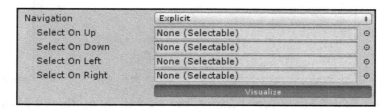

Navigation Example in the Chapter5Text Scene

The last **Navigation** type is **Explicit** and allows for significantly better control. With this, you can explicitly define which button will be accessed with each individual keyboard press.

Let's say that you wanted the player to cycle through the buttons in the order 1-2-3-4-5 and then loop back to 1. You want this to happen with either the up button or the right button. None of the previously mentioned navigation methods will allow that. However, you can achieve that with the **Explicit** Navigation type. Due to this example is slightly more complicated, it is covered in the next section as a step-by-step example.

Examples

For the first three examples in this chapter, we will momentarily step away from the scene we have been working on to build a new scene that will allow us to experiment with button navigation and scene loading. We'll then pick up where we left off with our scene from Chapter 4, *The Event System and Programming for UI*, to add some buttons to our scene.

Navigating through Buttons and using First Selected

We'll build out a faux start screen that appears as follows:

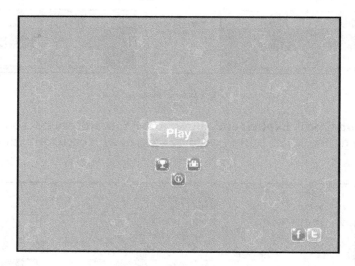

Most of these buttons will be dummy buttons, but we will set up the **Play** button in the next example to load the scene we have been working on.

To give us the ability to experiment with button navigation, we'll assign an **Explicit** navigation scheme to it so that we can cycle through the buttons with the following pattern:

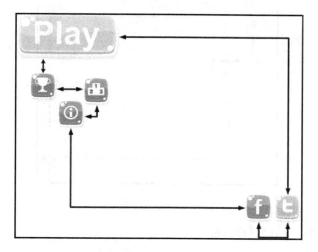

First, the **Play** button will be selected. Pressing the down key on the keyboard continuously will result in the following selection path:

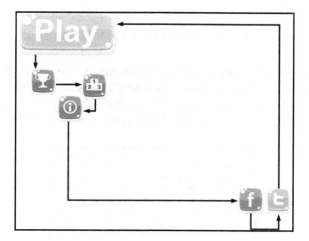

Pressing the up button continuously will result in the following path:

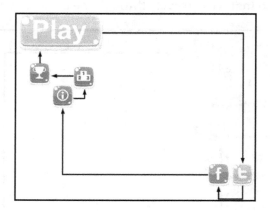

Laying out the Buttons

Let's start by creating a new scene and laying out the buttons.

To make a faux-start screen as shown in the image at the beginning of this example, complete the following steps:

1. Create a brand new empty scene and name it `Chapter5StartScreen`. Open the new scene.
2. To give it the same background as the scenes we've made in the last three chapters, we can create the **Background Canvas** afresh, but it will be easier to just copy it from one of the other scenes. We'll do this by having our new scene and one of our old scenes open in the **Hierarchy** at the same time:

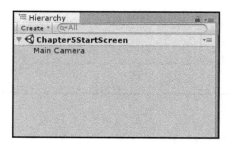

3. You will see the name of the current scene in the **Hierarchy**. From the `Project` folder view, drag the `Chapter2` scene to the **Hierarchy**. You should now see the following:

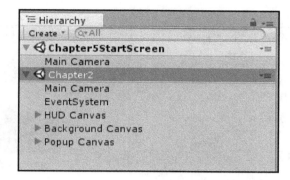

Select `Background Canvas` and press *Ctrl + D* to duplicate it. Now, drag the duplicate, labeled `Background Canvas (1)`, to the `Chapter5StartScreen` scene:

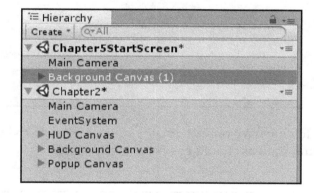

We can now close the Chapter2 scene, as we no longer need it. To do so, select the drop-down menu on the right of the Chapter2 scene, and select **Remove Scene**. Just in case you accidentally deleted something, select **Don't Save** when prompted:

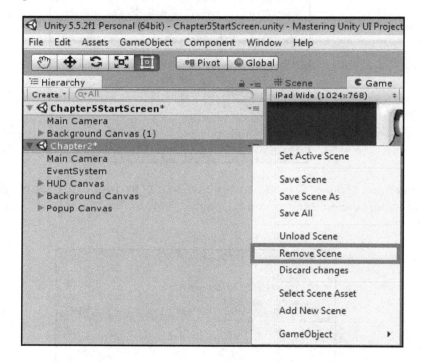

You should now have only Chapter5StartScreen in the **Hierarchy**, and the **Background Canvas** should be visible in the scene:

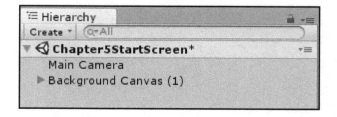

Rename Background Canvas (1) to Background Canvas and save the scene.

You'll note that by doing this, we have a **Canvas** in the scene without an **Event System**. That's okay, though, once we add new UI elements, the **Event System** will be added in for us.

4. Before we can proceed, we should take care of a warning message that is popping up. As we copied `Background Canvas` from another scene, it is trying to access the camera from the other scene.

5. A warning message will also appear on the Canvas component of the `Background Canvas`:

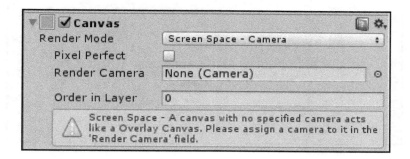

To fix this, simply drag the `Main Camera` from the current scene to the **Render Camera** slot.

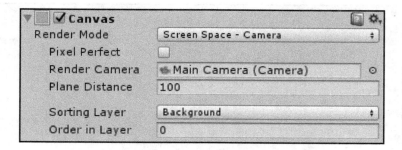

6. Now, let's add the **Play** button. Create a new UI Canvas to place our Buttons on named `Button Canvas`. Note that once we placed the `Button Canvas`, the **Event System** was created for us. Create a new UI Button (**Create | UI | Button**) as a child of the `Button Canvas` and give it the following **Rect Transform** and **Image** component properties:

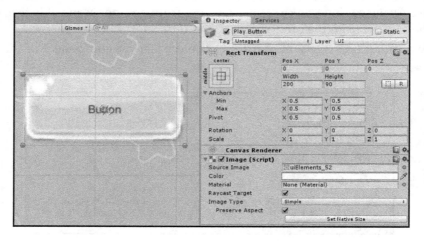

7. Now, select the child **Text** object of the **Play Button** and set its **Rect Transform** and **Text** component properties as such:

8. Now, let's create an `Achievement Button`, a `Leaderboard Button`, and an `Info Button` so they appear as follows:

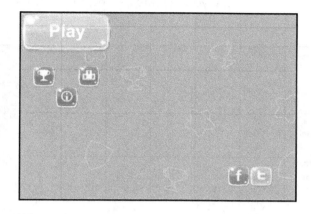

To achieve the preceding layout, use the following properties:

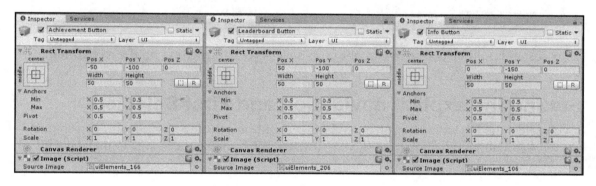

9. Now all that is left to do to set up our scene's layout is create the `Facebook Button` and `Twitter Button` in the bottom-right corner of the scene. To achieve the preceding layout, create two buttons with the following properties:

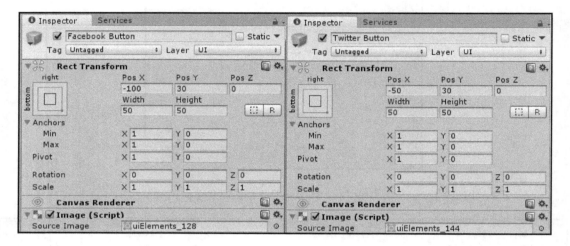

Your scene should be correctly laid out now, so let's work on setting up the navigation.

Setting the explicit navigation and First Selected

If you select the **Visualize** button on any of your Button's **Button** component, you should see the following navigation path (I have disabled the background image to make it a bit easier to view):

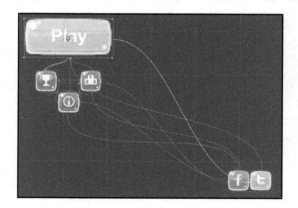

This navigation setup allows significantly more navigation range that the setup I described at the beginning of this example. This is because each button has its navigation set to **Automatic** by default, and **Automatic** allows multidirectional navigation. Let's make our navigation a bit more linear and make our `Play Button` the **First Selected** Button in our **Event System**.

To set up the navigation described at the beginning of this example, complete the following steps:

1. Select the **Event System** in the **Hierarchy** and assign the **Play Button** to the **First Selected** slot by drag and drop:

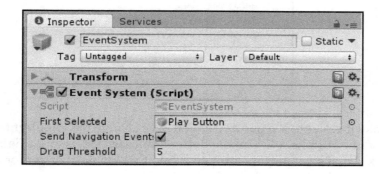

Now, when we start cycling through our buttons, our navigation will begin at the `Play Button`. Also, if we were to hit the *Enter* key when this scene loads, the `Play Button` will automatically be executed.

2. Now, let's set all the Buttons to have an **Explicit Navigation** type. Select all six of the buttons in the **Hierarchy** list:

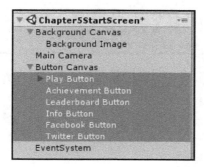

3. With all selected, change the Navigation type to Explicit from the drop-down menu. Now, each Button should have the following settings in their Button component:

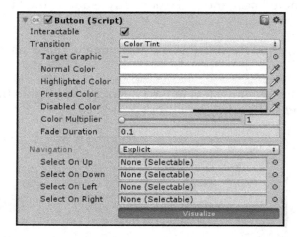

4. To make it easier to see our navigation, let's change the **Highlighted Colors** on each of our Buttons. With all the Buttons still selected, set the **Highlighted Color** to dark red. It's not terribly attractive, but it will make it easier for us to see whether our buttons are being highlighted:

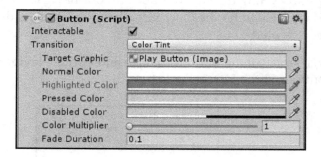

If you play the game, you should see the **Play Button** highlighted red, symbolizing that it is selected (since we set it as **First Selected** in Step 1):

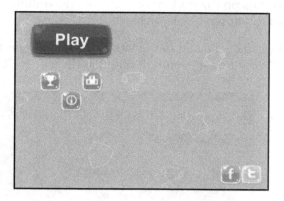

5. Now, we can explicitly (hence the name) set the Buttons that each individual Button is to navigate to by dragging and dropping them into the appropriate slots. Let's set the **Navigation** for the Play Button first, since it will be the first button selected. Select the Play Button.

   According to the diagrams, the Play Button should navigate to the Twitter Button when the up key is pressed and to the Achievements Button when the down key is pressed. So, drag and drop those buttons into the slots labeled **Select On Up** and **Select On Down**, respectively from the **Hierarchy**. If you have the **Visualize** button selected, as you are dragging the Buttons into their slots, you should see the navigation visualization starting to build out. In the following screenshot, I have disabled the background to make it a bit easier to see:

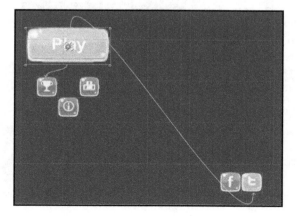

Remember that if an arrow begins on top of a Button, that arrow symbolizes where navigation will go if the up key is pressed, and if the arrow begins on the bottom of a Button, it symbolizes where navigation will go if the down key is pressed.

6. Play the game to check and see whether it works. Press the up key and you should see the following, symbolizing that the Twitter Button is selected:

To see the Achievement Button become selected, you actually have to stop playing the game and replay, because we have not set up the navigation for the Twitter Button to go back to the Play Button. So stop the game, press **Play** again, then press the down key, and you should see the following, symbolizing that Achievement Button is selected:

Instead of restarting the game, you can also highlight the `Play Button` with your mouse so that you can then navigate to the `Achievement Button`.

7. Once you set up the navigation for one Button, the rest aren't too difficult, albeit tedious. Use the following chart to help you set up the rest of the Buttons:

Button	Select On Up	Select On Down
Play Button	Twitter Button	Achievement Button
Achievement Button	Play Button	Leaderboard Button
Leaderboard Button	Achievement Button	Info Button
Info Button	LeaderBoard Button	Facebook Button
Facebook Button	Info Button	Twitter Button
Twitter Button	Facebook Button	Play Button

When you are done, your navigation visualization should look like the following:

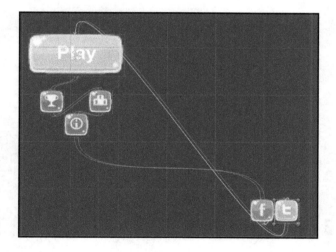

If you play your game, you should be able to easily cycle through the Buttons using the arrow keys. I recommend setting all the buttons to have Horizontal or Vertical Navigation patterns and seeing how it differs from what we have created so that you can see that this pattern is not attainable with a predefined pattern applied to all the Buttons.

Loading scenes with Button presses

Now that we have our start screen laid out, let's hook up the Play Button to play our "game". First, duplicate the scene you created in Chapter 4, *The Event System and Programming for UI*, called Chapter4, using *Ctrl + D*. The new scene should be called Chapter5. Our goal is to have the Play Button in Chapter5StartScreen load up the Chapter5 scene.

To make the Play Button in Chapter5StartScreen, load up the Chapter5 scene, complete the following steps:

1. To transition between scenes within Unity, you must first ensure that they are each listed within the **Scenes In Build** list in the **Build Settings**. Select **File | Build Settings** (or *Ctrl + Shift + B*). The following should be visible:

2. From the `Project` folder, drag and drop the `Chapter5StartScreen` and `Chapter5` scenes into the list:

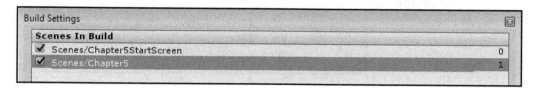

The order in which scenes appear in this list does not matter, except for the first scene (the one listed as scene 0). The first scene in the list should be the scene you want to load when the game loads. Therefore, it makes sense for us to put `Chapter5StartScreen` in position 0.

3. Now that our scenes are in the **Build** Settings, we can write a script that will allow us to navigate between them. Right-click on the `Scripts` folder in your **Project** view and select **Create | C# Script**. Name the new script `LevelLoader`. Open the new `LevelLoader` script, and replace the code with the following:

```csharp
using UnityEngine;
using System.Collections;
using UnityEngine.SceneManagement;

public class LevelLoader : MonoBehaviour {
 public string sceneToLoad="";
 public void LoadTheLevel(){
 SceneManager.LoadScene(sceneToLoad);
 }
}
```

The preceding code contains a single function—`LoadTheLevel()`. This function calls the `LoadScene` method in the `SceneManager` class. We will load the `sceneToLoad`, which is a string we will specify in the **Inspector**. Note that the `UnityEngine.SceneManagement` namespace must be included with the following line at the top of the script:

```csharp
using UnityEngine.SceneManagement;
```

4. If you still do not have the `Chapter5StartScreen` scene open, open it again. Select the `Play Button` and drag and drop the `LevelLoader` script onto its **Inspector**:

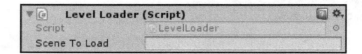

Now, within the **Scene To Load** slot, type `Chapter5`. You don't need to put it in quotes; since the `sceneToLoad` variable is a string, `Chapter5` is assumed to be a string without you needing to put it in quotes:

5. Now all that is left is to hook up the button. Select the + sign at the bottom of the **OnClick()** Event list of the **Button** component to add a new event. The script we want to access, `LevelLoader.cs`, is on the `Play Button`, so drag the `Play Button` into the object slot. Now, from the function drop-down menu, select **LevelLoader | LoadTheLevel**.

That's it! Your `Play Button` should now navigate to the `Chapter5` scene when clicked on or when you press enter when it is highlighted (as it is at the beginning or with your keyboard navigation).

Button Animation Transitions

In the first example, we set the highlighted state of the `Play Button` to a dark red color to make it easier for us to see when it was highlighted. It didn't look great, but it was helpful. Now, we'll give the Button an Animation Transition so that we don't have to worry about changing our **Highlighted Color** any longer. In this example, we will make the `Play Button` pulsate in its normal state, enticing you to click on it.

To create those button animation transitions, complete the following steps:

1. Select the Play Button and change its **Transition** type to **Animation**:

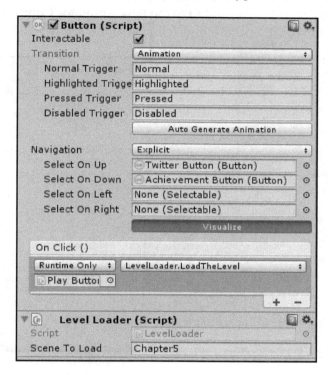

2. We do not have an Animator Controller prebuilt, so select **Auto Generate Animation** to create a new one. A window will pop up, asking you save the newly created Animator Controller. Create a new folder in the `Assets` folder, called `Animations`, and save the new Animator Controller as `Play Button` to the folder:

You should now see the new Animator Controller in the new `Animations` folder:

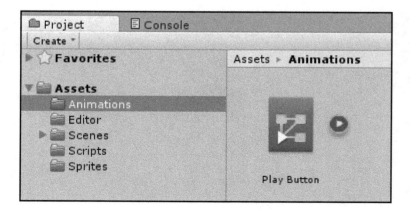

You will also see the new **Animator** component on the `Play Button`:

3. Open the Animation window by selecting **Window | Animation**. If you want to dock this new window, dock it somewhere so that you can still see the scene and game views when it is up. For example, I am currently using the following window set up:

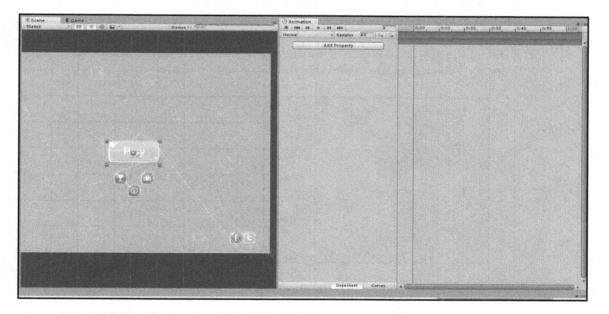

4. When you have the `Play Button` selected and open the **Animation** window, the various animation clips associated with the transition states will be visible in the animation clip drop-down menu:

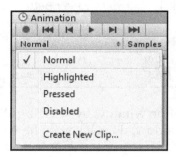

We want to edit the animation for the **Normal** transition state, so if you have selected a different animation clip, reselect the normal animation clip (**Normal** is the animation selected by default).

5. To make the button look like its pulsating, we want to affect its scale. Select **Add Property** | **Rect Transform** and then hit the + next to **Scale**:

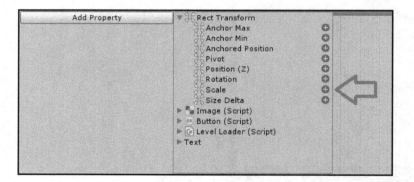

The **Scale** property should now be showing up in the Animation timeline:

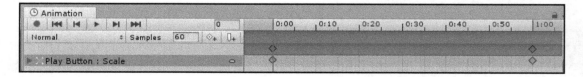

6. To achieve the pulsation with scaling, we want the button to start at its normal size, get big, and then go back to its normal size. The diamonds that appear on the timeline are known as keyframes. To do what I just described, we need one more keyframe, right in the center of the timeline. Click on the top of the timeline (where the numbers appear) to move the timeline to the **0:30** mark. Then, select the **Add keyframe** button to add in a new keyframe:

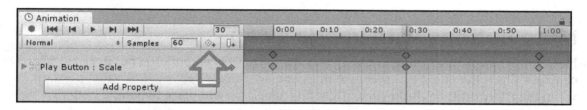

7. Expand the **Scale** property by selecting the arrow to its left. You will see that if you select any of the keyframes, the number 1 is next to all the three scaling directions. This indicates that the scale at that frame is 100% (or its normal scale):

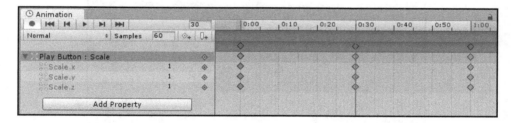

8. Select the **keyframe** in the center. Change the number **1** on **Scale.x** and **Scale.y** to 1.2 by clicking on the number **1** and typing. You can press the play button in the animation window to preview your animation. You will see that the button now pulsates:

That's it! Your button should now pulsate when you play the game (and will not turn red any longer). Note that it does not pulsate immediately, which is because the button will only pulsate when it is not highlighted, and since we have it set to **First Selected**, it is highlighted on start. To remove the highlight, simply click anywhere in your scene outside of the button or navigate away using your keyboard. Once the highlight is removed, it should begin pulsating.

Mute buttons with image swap

Now, let's go back to working in our UI scene that we've been building out over the last few chapters. Open the `Chapter5` scene. In the scene, we have a `Pause Panel` that pops up when the *P* key is hit on the keyboard. On this panel, we will place two mute buttons, one for music and one for sound that will toggle between muted and not unmuted states. The panel will appear, as shown:

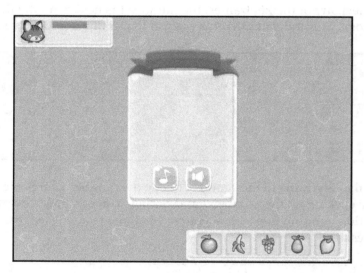

To add the music and sound buttons, as shown in the preceding image, complete the following steps:

1. First, we need to bring in a new art asset. The button images on the sprite sheet we imported previously are a bit too small and didn't contain a muted version. So, I edited them a bit and provided a new image for you. In the `Chapter5/Sprites` folder of the book's source files, you should find the image named `MuteUnmute.png`:

Import this image file into your project's `Assets/Sprites` folder.

2. Slice the image into multiple subimages by changing its **Sprite Mode** to **Multiple**, opening its **Sprite Editor**, and applying the automatic slice type. The multiple sprites should appear as follows:

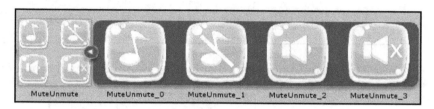

3. Create two new Buttons as children of the `Pause Panel` and name them `Music Button` and `Sound Button`:

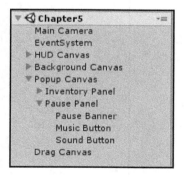

4. Give the two new buttons the following **Rect Transform** and **Image** properties:

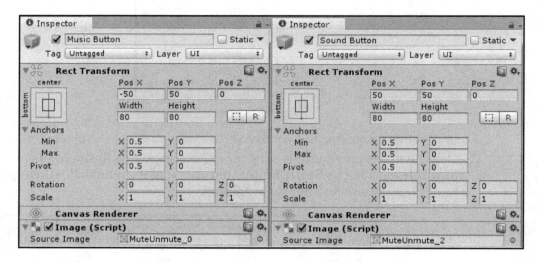

Your Panel should now look just like the one at the beginning of this example:

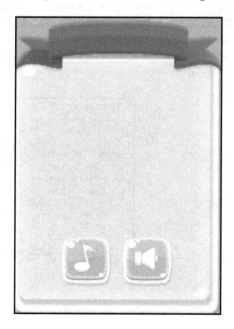

5. Now, let's write some code to make these buttons swap images that will represent the sound and music toggling on and off. Create a new script called MuteUnmute in your Assets/Scripts folder.
   Replace the code of MuteUnmute with the following:

```
using UnityEngine;
using UnityEngine;
using System.Collections;
using UnityEngine.UI;

public class MuteUnmute : MonoBehaviour {
    public Button musicButton;
    public Button soundButton;
    Image musicImage;
    Image soundImage;
    public Sprite MusicOn;
    public Sprite MusicOff;
    public Sprite SoundOn;
    public Sprite SoundOff;
    bool musicMuted;
    bool soundMuted;
    void Awake(){
        musicImage=musicButton.GetComponent<Image>();
        soundImage=soundButton.GetComponent<Image>();
    }
    public void MuteAndUnmuteMusic(){
        if (musicMuted==false) { //mute music
            musicImage.sprite=MusicOff;
            musicMuted=true;
        } else { //unmute music
            musicImage.sprite=MusicOn;
            musicMuted=false;
        }
    }

    public void MuteAndUnmuteSound(){
        if (soundMuted==false) { //mute sound
            soundImage.sprite=SoundOff;
            soundMuted=true;
        } else { //unmute sound
            soundImage.sprite=SoundOn;
            soundMuted=false;
        }
    }
}
```

As you can see, this code contains two main functions: `MuteAndUnmuteMusic()` and `MuteAndUnmuteSound()`. These two function identically, by simply swapping the image on the specified button based on the Boolean values `musicMuted` and `soundMuted`.

To swap the image, the script first finds the image component on the two buttons specified as `musicButton` and `soundButton`, within the `Awake()` function. These buttons will be assigned in the **Inspector**. It then swaps the sprite of the image component. It determines which sprite to select by checking whether it is currently considered muted or not. The images for the mute and unmute states are assigned in the inspector.

Sadly, this text does not cover adding sound and music to a Unity project; the code provided here doesn't actually mute and unmute audio, it simply swaps sprites. However, I have provided you with a more complete script in the book's code bundle that includes the code for turning audio on and off, along with toggling the buttons. You will simply need to include two audio sources: one for playing music and one for playing sounds that have the **Music** and **Sound** tags, respectively.

6. Go back to the Unity Editor and attach the `MuteUnmute.cs` script to the `Pause Panel` by dragging it into its **Inspector**:

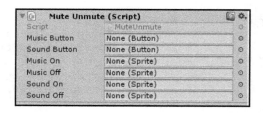

7. Now, we want to assign the appropriate Buttons and sprites to the slots. Drag the `Music Button` and `Sound Button` into their designated slots from the Hierarchy. Drag and drop the audio button sprites from the project view to their appropriate slots:

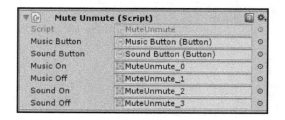

8. Now, we just need to hook up the buttons to call the appropriate functions. Select the `Music Button`. Select the **+** sign at the bottom of the `OnClick()` Event list of the Button component to add a new event. The script we want to access, `MuteUnmute.cs`, is on the `Pause Panel`, so drag the `Pause Panel` into the object slot. Now, from the function drop-down menu, select **MuteUnmute | MuteAndUnmuteMusic**.

9. Perform the same actions as you did in the previous step for the **Sound** Button, but this time select **MuteUnmute | MuteAndUnmuteMusic** from the function drop-down list.

Now, play the game, press *P* to bring up the `Pause Panel`, and you will see the buttons toggle back and forth between their two different images.

Summary

Once you learn how to work with the Event System, working with buttons is a very easy extension. Buttons are the most common interactive UI element, so having a good grasp on them is essential to effective UI development. Setting them up so that they function when clicked on is only half the process, though. You want to also ensure that you have your button navigation set up properly if you will be developing for PC, Mac, or console.

In this chapter, we discussed the following topics:

- Creating UI Buttons and setting their properties
- Setting button transitions that make the button change appearance when it is highlighted, pressed, or disabled
- Navigating button selection on screen with the keyboard or joystick
- Creating an onscreen button that looks like it is physically being pressed
- Creating buttons that swap images without using the built-in transitions, like a mute/unmute button
- Loading scenes with a button press
- Creating Button Transition Animations

Next, we will cover UI Text and Images.

6
Text, Images, and TextMesh Pro-Text

We've spent some time with UI Text and UI Images already, as they are the most basic graphical UI objects. We discussed them briefly in Chapter 2, *Canvases, Panels, and Basic Layouts* because it was pretty hard to start laying out UI without having anything to display visually. UI Text and UI Images are also subcomponents of the UI elements we covered in the previous chapters, so we've worked with them at their basic level. Now we will discuss these two UI objects more thoroughly so that we can have more control over our UI Text and UI Images. We will also discuss TextMesh Pro-Text objects and how they allow for even more control of the text in our game.

In this chapter, we will discuss the following topics:

- Creating UI Text objects and setting their properties
- Importing fonts into Unity
- Using markup format with UI Text objects
- Creating UI Images and setting their properties
- Using the various UI Effects components to further customize our graphical UI
- Creating TextMesh Pro-Text Objects and setting their properties
- Creating text that animates, as if, being typed out
- Creating a custom font to be used with UI Text objects
- Creating text that wraps along a curve and renders with a gradient
- Creating horizontal and circular progress bars

All the examples shown in this section can be found within the Unity project provided in the code bundle. They can be found within the scene labeled `Chapter6Text` in the `Assets/Scene/ExamplesInText/` folder.

Each example image has a caption stating the example number within the scene.

In the scene, each example is of its own Canvas and some of the Canvases are deactivated. To view an example on a deactivated Canvas, simply select the checkbox next to the Canva's name in the **Inspector**.

UI Text

You can create a new UI Text object using **Create** | **UI** | **Text**.

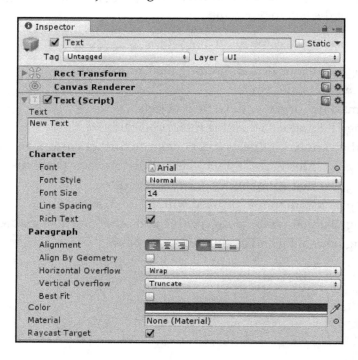

The UI Text object contains the **Rect Transform** and **Canvas Renderer** components as well as the **Text** component.

Text component

The UI Text component gives the object it is attached to a non-interactive text display. This component does not allow you to create all types of text you may be interested in, but it does allow for most basic text displays.

The Text and Character properties

The **Text** property changes the text that will be displayed. Whatever is typed within this box will be displayed within the text object.

Below the **Text** property are a group of **Character** properties. These properties allow you to change the properties of the individual characters within the **Text** property's field.

The **Font** property determines which font is used for the entire block of text. By default, the **Font** is set to **Arial**. However, if you happen to not have **Arial** installed on your computer, it will default the font included within Unity—**Liberation Sans**. To use any other font, you must import the font into your **Asset** folder. Refer to the *Importing Fonts* section to learn how to bring in additional fonts.

Font Style provides a drop-down list of available font styles that come with the provided font. Possible styles are **Normal, Bold, Italic,** or **Bold And Italic**:

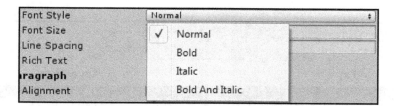

It's important to note that not all fonts will support all the listed font styles. For example, Liberation Sans, the font bundled within Unity, does not support a Bold or an Italic font style.

Font Size determines the size of the text, and **Line Spacing** represents the vertical spacing between each line of text.

If the **Rich Text** property is selected, you can include markup tags within the **Text** property field and they will appear with Rich Text styling rather than as typed. If this property is not selected, the text will display exactly as type. Refer to the *Markup Format* section for more information concerning writing with Rich Text.

Paragraph properties

The next set of properties, the **Paragraph** properties, allow you to determine how the text will display within (or outside of) the Rect Transform's bounds.

The **Alignment** property determines where the text will align based on the Rect Transform bounds. You can choose both Horizontal and Vertical alignment options. The buttons represent the position relative to the Rect Transform bounds, so the left horizontal alignment will have the text pushed up all the way to the edge of the Rect Transform's left bound.

The **Align by Geometry** property aligns the text as if the glyphs or characters are cropped down just to their opaque area rather than the area they cover based on their character map. This can give a tighter alignment but might also cause things to overlap.

The **Horizontal Overflow** property determines what happens to text if it is too wide for the Rect Transform area. There are two options: **Wrap** and **Overflow**. **Wrap** will cause the text to continue on the next line and **Overflow** will cause the text to expand past the rectangular area.

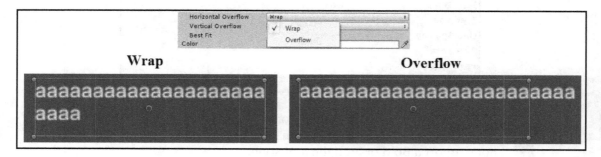

Horizontal Overflow Example in the Chapter6Text Scene

The **Vertical Overflow** property determines what happens to text if it is too long for the Rect Transform area. There are two options: **Truncate** and **Overflow**. **Truncate** will cut off all text outside of the rectangular area, and **Overflow** will cause the text to expand past the rectangular area. In the following example image, both textboxes have the same text, but the Truncate removes the last two lines of text due to them being outside of the rectangular area:

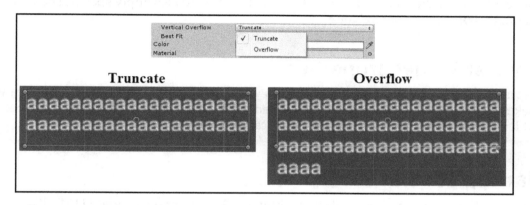

Vertical Overflow Example in the Chapter6Text Scene

The **Best Fit** property attempts to resize the text so that all of it fits within the rectangular area. When you select the **Best Fit** Property, two new Properties will become available: **Min Size** and **Max Size**. These properties allow you to specify the range the font size can maintain.

Keep in mind that depending on the text you have written, the **Horizontal Overflow** property may cause this to work slightly differently than you'd expect. For example, the following two textboxes have **Best Fit** selected, but the first has the **Horizontal Overflow** set to **Wrap**, and the second has it set to **Overflow**:

Best Fit Example in the Chapter6Text Scene

The Color and Material properties

The **Color** and **Material** properties both allow you to adjust the appearance of the text's font. The **Color** property will set the base rendering color of the text and is the quickest way to change the font's color. By default, this property is set to a very dark (not fully black) grey. The **Material** property allows you to assign a material to your font. This gives you more control over the look of the font and will allow you to also apply specific shaders. By default, this property is set to **None**.

Raycast Target properties

The last property, **Raycast Target**, determines whether the object's Rect Transform area will block raycasts or not. If this property is selected, clicks will not register on UI objects behind it. If it is not selected, items behind the object can be clicked.

Markup format

When the **Rich Text** property is selected within the **Text** component, and HTML-like markup language can be included within the text field of the **Text** component to format the text. This markup format is HTML-like, in that it uses angle bracket tags around the text that is to be formatted. The tags use the `<tag>the text you wish to format</tag>` format, where you replace tag with the appropriate tag. These tags can be nested, just as they can in HTML.

This formatting allows you to change the font style, font color, and font size. The following chart lists the tags necessary to perform the specified formatting:

Format	Tag
Bold	`b`
Italic	`i`
Color	`color`
Size	`size`

Font style

You can change the font style of the text using the bold and italic tags.

To add a bold font style to text, add the `<b></b>` tags around the text you wish to bold. To add an italic font style to text, add the `<i></i>` tags around the text you wish to italicize.

`<b>Bold Text</b>`	**Bold Text**
`<i>Italic Text</i>`	*Italic Text*
`<b><i>Nested Text</i></b>`	***Nested Text***

Font color

You can change the color of the font with either the hex value representation of a number or using the color name. To change the color of the text, add `<color=value></color>` around the text you wish to color, where you place either the hex value (following a #) or color name where the word value appears.

Only a limited set of colors have names that can replace the hex values. The color names that are recognized are `black`, `blue`, `brown`, `cyan`, `darkblue`, `green`, `grey`, `lightblue`, `lime`, `magenta`, `maroon`, `navy`, `olive`, `orange`, `purple`, `red`, `silver`, `teal`, `white`, and `yellow`. You can also use `aqua` in place of `cyan` and `fuchsia` in place of `magenta`.

When using the `color` tag, any text not surrounded by the `color` tag will be colored based on the **Color** property selected.

The following tables show how to use the `color` tag:

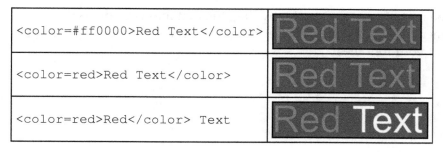

`<color=#ff0000>Red Text</color>`	Red Text
`<color=red>Red Text</color>`	Red Text
`<color=red>Red</color> Text`	Red Text

Font size

To change the font size, add the `<size=#></size>` tags around the text you wish to resize. Any text not within the tag will be sized based on the **Font Size** property setting. The following example shows how to use the **size** tag:

```
<size=30>Small</size> Normal <size=100>Big</size>
```

Importing new fonts

The only font that installs with Unity is `Liberation Sans`, but fonts default to `Arial` if you have `Arial` installed on your computer. If you have `Arial` installed on your computer, it will be the only font available in the initial list of fonts to choose from. If you want your text to render with a different font, you must import it into your project's `Assets` folder. The process is pretty simple and no more difficult than importing a sprite into your project.

The font file formats accepted by Unity are `.tff` (TrueType) and `.otf` (OpenType). You can get these files in multiple places. My favorite places to find fonts are as listed:

- Google Fonts: `https://fonts.google.com/`
- Font Squirrel: `https://www.fontsquirrel.com/`
- DaFont: `http://www.dafont.com/`

All the fonts on Google Fonts are open source and are free for personal or commercial use (at least at the time of writing this text), but the fonts on Font Squirrel and DaFont have varying licensing options. Ensure that you always make sure that any font you get has a licensing agreement that meets your needs before you use it.

After you download the font of your choice, simply drag the font into your project's `Asset` folder. I highly recommend that you create a folder called `Fonts` within your `Asset` folder in which you place all of your font files.

You can then adjust the font's import properties in the **Inspector**, if you so choose. The following screenshot shows the import settings of the **BungeeShade-Regular** font downloaded from Google Fonts:

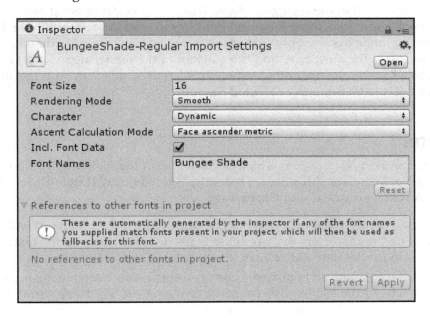

Here, you can adjust quite a few of the settings concerning how the font will be handled by the engine.

Font Size

The **Font Size** setting determines how large the font will appear on its Unity created texture atlas. Increase or decreasing the **Font Size** setting will change the size of the various glyphs on the texture atlas. If your font is appearing fuzzy in your game, adjusting this **Font Size** may improve its appearance.

Rendering Mode

The Rendering Mode settings tells Unity how the glyphs will be smoothed. The possible options are **Smooth**, **Hinted Smooth**, **Raster**, and **OS Default**.

The **Smooth** rendering mode is the fastest rendering mode. It uses anti-aliased rendering, which means it will smooth out jagged, pixelated edges. The **Hinted Smooth** rendering mode will also smooth out edges, but it will the "hints" contained within the font's data files to determine how to fill in those jagged edges. This is a slower rendering mode than **Smooth**, but will likely look more crisp and be easier to read than **Smooth**. The **Hinted Raster** rendering mode does not provide anti-aliasing and instead provides aliased or jagged edges. This is the most crisp and the quickest of the rendering modes. **OS Default** will default to whatever the operating system's preferences are set to on Windows or Mac OS. This will select from **Smooth** or **Hinted Smooth**.

Character

The **Character** property determines which character set of the font will be imported into the font texture atlas. There are six options: **Dynamic**, **Unicode**, **ASCII default set**, **ASCII upper case**, **ASCII lower case**, and **Custom set**:

- Setting the **Character** property to **Dynamic** (which is the default) will only include the characters that are actually needed. This reduces the texture size needed for the font and, in turn, the download size of the game.
- ASCII (or American Standard Code for Information Interchange) is a set of characters from the English-language character set. The three variations of ASCII character sets allow you to choose between the full set, only uppercase, or only lowercase characters. You can find a list of the ASCII characters at `http://ascii.cl/`.
- **Unicode** is used for languages that have characters that are not supported in an ASCII character set. So, for example, if you want to display text in Japanese, you will want to use Unicode.

If you'd like to include Unicode characters in your scripts, you need to save them with UTF-16 encoding. This will allow you to type Unicode characters directly in your code as strings so that they can display in your Text objects on screen.

The Noto fonts provided by Google Fonts have support for many languages and can be very helpful if you want to create a game that is translated into multiple languages. The Noto fonts can be found at `https://www.google.com/get/noto/`.

- A **Custom set** character will allow you to import your own texture atlas for your own custom font. I find this most commonly used when developers want beautified text with an extremely limited character set—like numbers only.

Ascent Calculation Mode

The **ascent** of a font is the distance between the font's baseline and the highest glyph point. There is no standard for how this supposed "highest glyph point" is determined, so there are different modes presented in Unity to choose from, each determining a different "highest glyph point". The **Ascent Calculation Mode** determines how the ascent will be calculated. There are three options for how this calculation will be chosen: **Legacy version 2 mode (glyph bounding boxes)**, **Face ascender metric**, and **Face bounding box metric**. The method chosen may have affect the vertical alignment of the font.

Legacy version 2 mode (glyph bounding boxes) measures the ascent using the highest point reached by any one of the font's glyphs listed within its character set as the height. This only uses those listed in the character set, and not all glyphs may be included within that set. The **Face ascender metric** uses the face ascender value that is defined to measure the ascent, and **Face bounding box metric** uses the face bounding box to measure the ascent.

 Typography is a lot more complicated than many people realize, and it's definitely too complicated to fully cover in this text—not to mention that I am no typography expert. If you'd like to learn more about glyph metrics, a good introduction can be found at `https://www.freetype.org/freetype2/docs/glyphs/glyphs-3.html`.

Dynamic font settings

When you import your font with a Dynamic character set, two new settings are made available: **Incl. Font Data** and **Font Names**.

Incl. Font Data (Include Font Data) builds the font file with the game. If this is not selected, the game will assume that the player has the font installed on their machine. If you are using a font you have downloaded from the web, it is a pretty safe bet that the end user will not have the font installed and you should leave **Incl. Font Data** selected.

Font Names is the list of names of fonts that Unity will fall back on if it cannot find the font. It will need to fall back on this font name if the font doesn't include the requested glyph or the **Incl. Font Data** property was deselected and the user does not have the font installed on the machine. If Unity cannot find the font, it will search the game's project folder or the user's machine for a font matching one of the names listed in **Font Names**. Once the fonts have been typed into **Font Names**, the appropriate fonts will then be listed in the **References to other fonts in project** section.

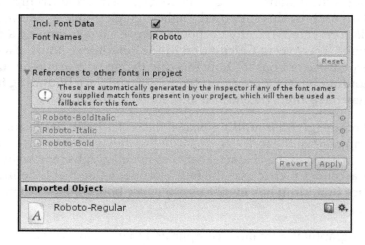

If Unity cannot find one of the fonts listed, it will use a font provided in a predefined list of fallback fonts hard-coded within Unity.

 Some platforms don't have built-in fonts in their system or can't access built-in fonts. These platforms include WebGL and some console systems. When building to these platforms, Unity will always include fonts, regardless of the setting chosen for **Incl. Font Data**.

Importing font styles

If you bring in a font that has multiple styles (that is, Bold, Italic, or Bold and Italic), you must bring in all the font styles for them to appear properly. Bringing the fonts into your project may not be sufficient for the font to recognize which fonts should be used when the Bold, Italic, and Bold and Italic fonts styles are selected, however. For example, the following screenshot shows the **Roboto-Regular** Google Font with the **Bold and Italic** Font Style on the top line of text and the **Roboto-BoldItalic** Google Font with the **Normal** Font Style on the bottom line:

If the **Font Style** property were working correctly, the two lines should match. However, as you can see, they do not. To make the fonts appear correctly, select the regular font and retype the **Font Name** to make all the appropriate ones appear in the font list (as shown in the second to last image) and hit **Apply**. After doing so, the two fonts should appear the same:

Custom fonts

You can create a custom font by selecting **Create | Custom Font** from the project window. To use a custom font, you will need a font material and font texture. How to do this is covered in the *Examples* section of this chapter. Once you create your custom font, you will be given the following properties to set:

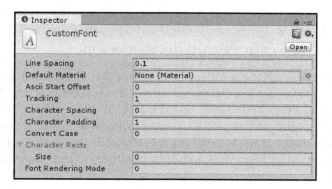

- The **Line Spacing** property specifies the distance between each line of text.
- The **Ascii Start Offset** property defines the first ASCII character in the font's character set. For example, if you created a font that only included numbers, your character set would start with the number 0, which is ASCII index 48. Therefore, you would set the **ASCII Start Offset** to 48, indicating the first character in this font's character set the character 0. You can determine the ASCII index number for individual characters at http://ascii.cl/.
- **Tracking** is spacing between characters for a full line of text. It allows the spacing between all characters to be uniform.

> The **Kerning** property has been replaced with the **Tracking** property. Tracking and Kerning are both properties related to spacing between characters, but they are different. For more information, check out http://www.practicalecommerce.com/Typography-101-The-Basics.

- **Character Spacing** is the amount of space between characters, and **Character Padding** is the amount of padding surrounding individual characters, before the spacing.
- The **Character Rects** property determines how many total characters are in your font. Changing the number from 0 to any positive number will provide a list of **Elements** that can be expanded.

Each element represents a character on your character set. The **Index** is the ASCII index of the specified character.

The **UV** values width (**W**) and height (**H**) values of your font represent the percentage of the width and height your characters occupy. For example, if you had a font file with five columns of characters and two rows of characters, the **UV W** would be one-fifth or .2 and the **UV H** would be one-half or .5. This should be consistent throughout all of your characters. The **UV X** and **Y** values are determined by multiplying the **UV W** and **UV H** values by the column or row that the character is located in.

The **Vert** properties represent the width and height of the character in pixels. The **H** property is *always* negative. So, if a character's pixel dimension is 50 by 50, the **Vert W** and **Vert H** properties would be 50 and –50, respectively. To be perfectly honest, I am not exactly sure why the height property is always negative and I can't seem to find the answer. I suspect that it has something to do with the fact that this uses texture coordinates. The **Vert X** and **Vert Y** properties represent a shift in position, where these numbers can be negative or positive.

The **Advance** setting represents the pixel distance between the specific character and the next character.

Refer to the *Examples* section for an example of calculating **UV**, **Vert**, and **Advance** on a custom font.

As of writing this text, not all the properties for Custom Fonts are fully defined within Unity's documentation and a few of these properties are a bit ambiguous. For example, **Convert Case** used to be a drop-down menu, and it is unclear to me how it is now used, since it accepts only a number input. Perhaps, in the future, these properties will be more fully described and the manual will be updated to reflect the new changes made, at https://docs.unity3d.com/Manual/class-Font.html.

UI Image

You can create a new UI Image object using **Create** | **UI** | **Image**:

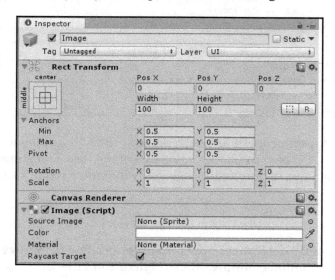

The UI Image object contains the **Rect Transform** and **Canvas Renderer** components as well as the Image component.

Image component

The first setting on the Image component is the **Source Image** property, which represents the sprite that will be rendered. The **Color** property represents the base color of the sprite being rendered. Leaving the color at white will make the image appear exactly as the sprite, but changing the color will add a tinted color overlay to the image. You can also change the transparency of the image by reducing the alpha value. The **Material** property allows you to add a material to the image. The **Raycast Target** property works the same way as it does on the Text component, by specifying whether the image will block clicks on UI objects behind it or not.

Chapter 5 contains an example that demonstrates how to swap the **Source Image** via code.

When a sprite is assigned to the **Source Image** slot, new options appear in the Image component, as shown:

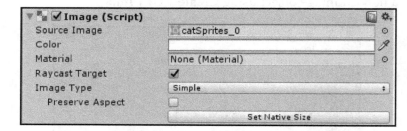

When the **Preserve Aspect** property is checked, the sprite will display with its portions preserved and may not appear to fill the entire area of the Rect Transform. Selecting this property ensures that your sprites look as originally intended and not stretched out.

Image Type

The **Image Type** property determines how the sprite specified by **Source Image** will appear. There are four options: **Simple**, **Sliced**, **Tiled**, and **Filled**.

Simple

An Image with its **Image Type** set to **Simple** scales evenly across the sprite. This is the default type. When **Simple** is selected as the **Image Type**, a button labeled **Set Native Size** becomes available.

Selecting the **Set Native Size** button sets the dimensions of the image to the pixel dimensions of the sprite.

Sliced

Sliced Images are split into nine areas. When a **Sliced** image is scaled, all areas of the image are scaled, except the corners. This allows you to scale an image without distorting its corners. This works particularly well with sprites that have rounded corners that you want to be able to stretch into rounded rectangles. In the following image, the first shape represents the original image's proportions, the second shows the shape scaled horizontally with an **Image Type** of **Simple**, and the bottom shape is set to **Sliced**. The **Sliced** rounded rectangle has maintained its rounded edges, whereas the **Simple** one has become distorted. Note that **Preserve Aspect Ratio** is not selected on either of the scaled images.

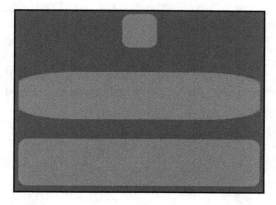

Sliced Image Type Example in the Chapter6Text Scene

You must specify where the nine areas will be, within the Sprite Editor of the image or the Image's sprite sheet. If you have not specified the regions, a message will appear within the Image component.

To specify the area in the Sprite Editor, you drag the green boxes on the edges of the sprite to the desired position. As you can see from the following screenshot, you want to drag the green lines so that they stop surrounding the curves of the edges.

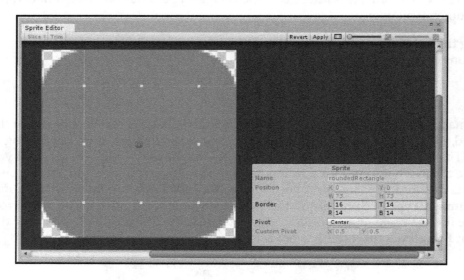

Tiled

Selecting **Tiled** for **Image Type** will cause the Image to repeat to fill the stretched area. The following screenshot demonstrates how selecting **Simple** and **Tiled** for **Image Type** affects the scaled Images:

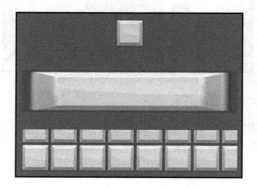

Tiled Image Type Example in the Chapter6Text Scene

Filled

Images with **Filled** selected for their **Image Type** will "fill in" a percentage of the sprite, starting at an origin in a specified direction. Any part of the sprite past the designated percentage will not be rendered. When **Filled** is selected, new properties are displayed:

The **Fill Method** determines whether the sprite will be filled horizontally, vertically, or radially. There are five options: **Horizontal, Vertical, Radial 90, Radial 180,** and **Radial 360**. Each of these **Fill Methods** will begin drawing the sprite at the **Fill Origin** up to the **Fill Amount**. When one of the radial methods are selected, you can also select the option to have the fill progress **Clockwise**; if you choose not to select it, the image will fill counterclockwise. The following image demonstrates the three **Fill Methods**, all with **Fill Amounts** of 0.75 or 75 percent:

Filled Image Type Example in the Chapter6Text Scene

The **Horizontal** and **Vertical Fill Methods** are somewhat self-explanatory when you see them in action, but it's a little more difficult to determine exactly how the three radial methods work just from looking at them. **Radial 90** places the center of the radial at one of the corners, **Radial 180** places the center of the radial at one of the edges, and **Radial 360** places the center of the radial in the center of the sprite.

The **Filled Image Type** also has the **Set Native Size** option.

UI effect components

There are three effects components that allow you to add special effects to your **Text** and **Image** objects: **Shadow**, **Outline**, and **Position as UV1**.

Shadow

The **Shadow** component adds a simple shadow to your **Text** or **Image** object.

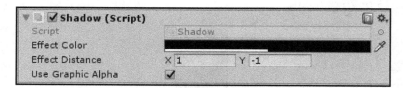

You can change the color and transparency of the shadow with the **Effect Color** property. The **Effect Distance** property determines its position relative to the graphic to which it is attached. The **Use Graphic Alpha** property will multiply the color of the shadow with the color of the graphic on which the shadow is attached. So, if this property is checked and the alpha (opacity) of the original graphic is reduced, the alpha of shadow will reduce as well, with the resulting shadow being a product of the two alpha values. However, if the **Use Graphic Alpha** property is unchecked, the shadow will maintain its alpha value regardless of the alpha of the original graphic. So, if you turned the alpha of the original graphics all the way down to 0, rendering it invisible, the shadow would remain visible based on the alpha specified on the **Effect Color**.

The following image shows a few examples of the **Shadow** component in action:

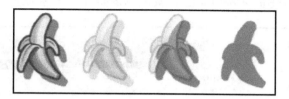

Shadow Component Example in the Chapter6Text Scene

All four bananas have the same alpha value set on their **Shadow** component's **Effect Color**. The Image **Color** of the first banana has the alpha set to full opacity. The second, third, and fourth bananas have the opacity of their Image reduced. The second and third banana have identical properties, except that the second banana is using the **Use Graphic Alpha** property and the third is not. So, you can see that the shadow of the third banana has not been dimmed by the dimming of the banana's image. The fourth and final banana has its Image opacity set to 0, but since **Use Graphic Alpha** is selected on the Shadow component, the shadow did not dim with the banana and remains at its designated alpha value.

Outline

The **Outline** component simulates an outline around the graphic by creating four shadows around it at specified distances.

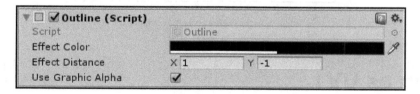

The **Outline** will create two shadows to the left and right of the original graphic based on **Effect Distance X** and two shadows to the top and bottom of the original graphic based on **Effect Distance Y**. Unlike the **Shadow** component, there is no difference in a negative or positive value for these two distances, because the two shadows created for each axis are mirrored.

Setting the **Effect Distance X** to −3 essentially just switches the positions of the two horizontal shadows, but the effect looks exactly the same, as shown in the following image:

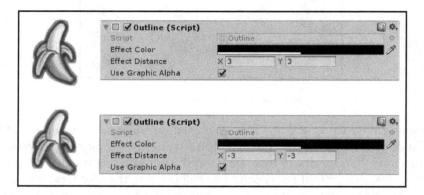

Outline Component Example 1 in the Chapter6Text Scene

The **Use Graphic Alpha** property works identically on this component as it does on the **Shadow** component, as shown:

Outline Component Example 2 in the Chapter6Text Scene

Position as UV1

The **Position as UV1** component allows you to change the UV channel that the canvas renders on. This is used if you want to create custom shaders that utilized baked light maps.

Sadly, custom shaders are a pretty heavy topic and go past the scope of this text.

TextMesh Pro-Text

There is a bit of limitation to what you can do with UI Text. Luckily, there is TextMeshPro. TextMesh Pro is a Unity asset that allows for significantly more text control. Additionally, its rendering allows text to appear crisp at more resolutions and point sizes than possible with the standard UI Text. TextMesh Pro used to be a paid asset in the Unity Asset Store, but it was adopted by Unity around March 2017 and is available for free now. Unity has stated that they will be implementing TextMesh Pro in Unity 2017, but at the time of writing this chapter, has not done so yet. However, it is a safe bet to assume that it will be implemented in Unity soon and will not need to be downloaded as a separate asset. It may eventually replace UI Text entirely, but it is not entirely clear at this time whether that will happen.

You can download the TextMesh Pro asset for free on the Unity Asset store at `https://www.assetstore.unity3d.com/en/#!/content/84126`. If you're just experimenting with TextMesh Pro, I recommend downloading the entire package into an empty project. However, if you are looking to implement it in an existing project, don't just select **All** on the import settings! All the example scenes that come along with the package will greatly increase your project size.

 Due to the robustness of TextMesh Pro, I sadly can't cover everything you can possibly do with it within this chapter. A full run-down on what you can do with TextMesh Pro could probably take up an entire book alone! In this chapter, I am providing a broad overview of its functionality. Luckily, the TextMesh Pro asset comes with many examples and good documentation, which can be found at `http://digitalnativestudios.com/textmeshpro/docs/`.

Once you download TextMesh Pro, selecting **Create** | **UI** will have a few more objects to choose from:

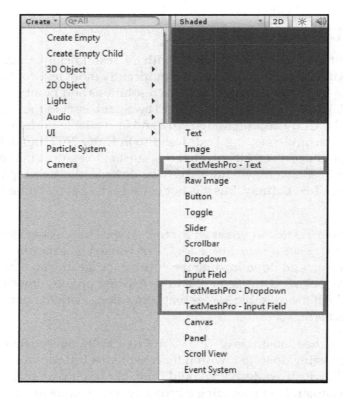

As you can see in the preceding screenshot, three new UI objects have been added: **TextMeshPro-Text**, **TextMeshPro-Dropdown**, and **TextMesh Pro-Input Field**.

When you create a new **TextMesh Pro-Text** GameObject, you will see a GameObject with the following components:

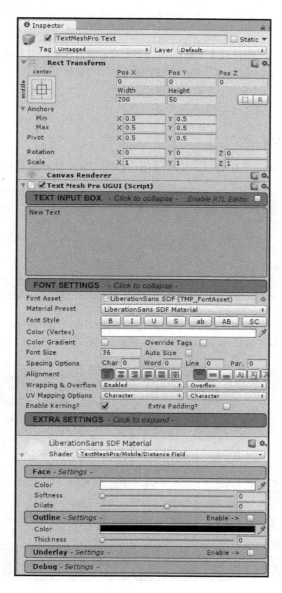

As with all other UI objects, a **Rect Transform** and **Canvas Renderer** component are attached. The graphic display of **TextMeshPro-Text** GameObject is controlled by the **Text Mesh Pro UGUI** component, where UGUI stands for Unity Graphic User Input.

 You can also create TextMeshPro-Text outside of Unity's UI system with **Create | 3D Object | TextMeshPro-Text**. This will render the text independent of the UI and without a Canvas.

Text Input Box

You can enter the text you wish to display within the **Text Input Box** menu:

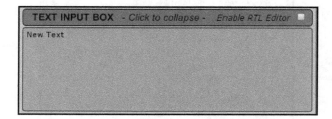

The **Enable RTL Editor** property allows you to create text that will display from right to left. When you select it, the text will appear in a second area in its right to left order:

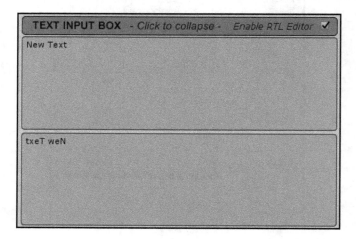

Font Settings

The **Font Settings** menu allows you to adjust all the properties of the text:

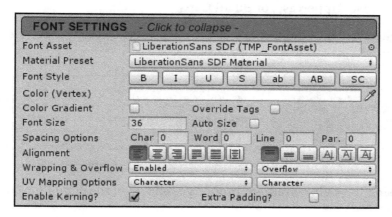

Font Asset represents the font that will be used. By default, the **Font Asset** is Liberation Sans SDF (TMP_FontAsset). To use a different font in a TextMesh Pro GameObject, you cannot simply drag in a new font to the **Font Asset** slot as you can with a **UI Text** GameObject. To change the font, you must create a **Font Asset** via the **Font Asset Creator**. To access the **Font Asset Creator**, select **Window | TextMeshPro - Font Asset Creator**. This will allow you to convert a font file to one usable by TextMesh Pro.

There are quite a few settings that can be controlled via the Font Asset Creator. You can find a breakdown of the settings at http://digitalnativestudios.com/textmeshpro/docs/font/.

The **Font Asset** needs a material to render. Any material that contains the name of the Font Asset will appear in the **Material Preset** list. You can create your own material, but when you create a new Font Asset, it comes with a default material. Whichever material is selected here will also appear below **Extra Settings**. From this area, you can also select the material's shader.

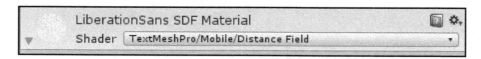

The **Font Style** property allows you to create basic formatting for your text. You can select from **Bold**, **Italic**, **Underline**, **Strikethrough**, **Lowercased**, **Uppercased**, or **Small Caps**. You can chose any combination of the first four settings; however, you can only choose between one of the **Lowercase**, **Uppercase**, or **Small Caps**.

You can change the color of the text using either the **Vertex Color** property or the **Color Gradient** property:

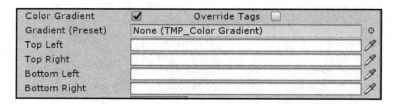

An example using the **Color Gradient** property is shown at the end of the chapter in the *Examples* section.

The **Font Size** works as you would expect, but you also have the option to select **Auto Size**. The **Auto Size** property will attempt to fit the text within the bounding box of the Rect Transform as best as it can based on the properties you specify:

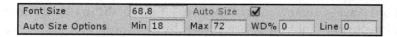

You can specify the minimum (**Min**) and maximum (**Max**) font size along with the **WD%** and **Line** properties. The **WD%** property allows you to squeeze text horizontally to make the characters taller, and the **Line** property allows you to specify line height.

You can set the spacing between characters, words, lines, and paragraphs in the **Spacing Options**.

You also have significantly more **Alignment** options available to you in TextMeshPro-Text than you did with the standard UI Text. You also have more **Wrapping & Overflow** options.

The **UV Mapping** property allows you to affect the way a texture is displayed across the text. The first drop-down menu affects the *x*-direction, and the second drop-down menu affects the *y*-direction:

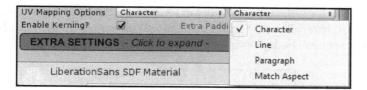

Lastly, you have the ability to specify whether or not you want to **Enable Kerning** or allow **Extra Padding**. Selecting **Enable Kerning?** will use the kerning data provided by the font file. Selecting **Extra Padding** will add a little padding around the glyphs of the sprite on its sprite atlas.

Extra Settings

The **Extra Settings** menu allows you to adjust "extra" settings of the font.

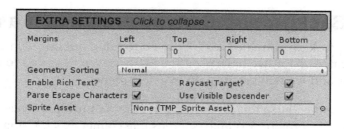

The most notable properties in this menu are the ability to add **Margins** and the ability to enable **Raycast Target**.

Examples

In this chapter, we'll expand on the scene we've been building further and also add in a new scene that occurs between our start screen and our main game screen.

Animated text

First, we will create a new scene that acts like a "cut scene" between our start screen and our gameplay scene. It will include our cat, introducing itself. The text will animate in as if it is being typed, and the user will have the option to speed it up by pressing a button. Once the text is fully displayed, pressing that same button will either show the next block of text or go to the gameplay scene. The text windows will appear as follows:

Creating a Background Canvas prefab and a new scene

Before we can start making animated text, we need to build out our scene. In both the scenes we have created so far, we have used the `Background Canvas` to display the background image, and we will use it again in a new scene.

Since it's likely that we will use this `Background Canvas` multiple times, we should create a `Background Canvas` prefab. A prefab is a reusable GameObject. Using a prefab in a scene creates an instance of the prefab within the scene. If you make a change to the saved prefab, the change will be reflected to all prefab unbroken instances across all scenes.

To create a reusable `Background Canvas` prefab GameObject, complete the following steps:

1. Create a new folder named `Prefabs` within your `Assets` folder. We'll use this folder to store any prefabs we create in the future.
2. Drag the `Background Canvas` GameObject from the **Hierarchy** into the `Prefabs` folder within the **Project** view. The name `Background Canvas` should now be blue in the **Hierarchy** (symbolizing that it is a prefab).
3. Let's create a new scene in which we will use this `Background Canvas` prefab. Create a new scene called `Chapter6AnimatedText`.

4. Drag the `Background Canvas.prefab` into the new scene from the **Project** view.

5. Assign the `Main Camera` to the **Render Camera** slot of the **Canvas** component on the `Background Canvas`.

Now we can start setting up the windows that will hold our animated text.

Laying out the Text Box Windows

To create the textbox windows that will display our text, complete the following steps:

1. Create a new UI Canvas and name it `Text Canvas`. Set its **Canvas** and **Canvas Scalar** properties, as shown:

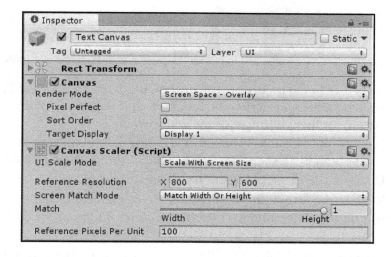

2. Create a new UI Image and name it `TextHolder1`. Set its anchor and pivot to **middle center**. Assign `uiElements_10` to the **Source Image**, and then select **Set Native Size** to cause the image's size to be set to `223 x 158`.

3. This panel will hold an image of our cat, some text, and a continue button. Utilizing anchors, pivots, and stretching, lay out the UI objects as children of `TextHolder1` so that they appear as illustrated:

Note that in the preceding screenshot, the `Text` child's Rect Transform does not stretch all the way across the image of `TextHolder1`. That way, the text won't cross over the white area of the window.

4. We'll want to be able to turn this window on and off, so add a **Canvas Group** component to `TextHolder1`. Leave the settings at their default values.

5. Duplicate `TextHolder1` and name the duplicate `TextHolder2`.

6. Replace the text on the Text child of `TextHolder1` with `Hello there!` and the text on the `Text` child of `TextHolder2` with `I'm a cat and, for some reason, I'm collecting food!`.

7. Let's hide and disable `TextHolder2` by disabling **Interactable**, disabling **Blocks Raycasts**, and setting the **Alpha** value to `0` on the **Canvas Group** component.

Now we're ready to start animating our text!

Animating the Text Box text

Now that we have our layout set up, we can animate our text. To do this, we will need to create a new script. This script will control the animation of the text as well as load the next scene when all text has displayed.

To create animated text that looks like it's typing out, complete the following steps:

1. Create a new C# script called `AnimateText.cs`.

2. We will be writing code that accesses UI elements as well as code that implements scene loading. Therefore, we need to include the following namespaces at the top of our new script:

```
using UnityEngine.UI;
using UnityEngine.SceneManagement;
```

3. Now, let's begin our variable declaration. We'll create three lists that hold our Canvas Groups, Text display objects, and the strings of dialogue that we want to display. Declare the following three public variables within your `AnimateText` class:

```
public List<CanvasGroup> textHolder=new List<CanvasGroup>();
public List<Text> textDisplayBox=new List<Text>();
public List<string> dialogue=new List<string>();
```

4. Create one more public variable that will hold the name of the scene that loads after the text is done animating:

```
public string nextScene; //name of the next scene
```

5. Before we proceed, let's assign these variables in the Unity Editor. Attach the `AnimateText.cs` script to the `Main Camera`. Now, drag `TextHolder1` from the **Hierarchy** and hover over the words **Text Holder** within the **Animate Text** component until you see the square with the plus sign, as shown:

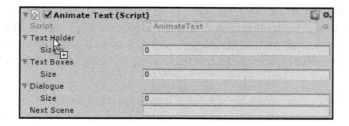

Once you release your mouse, you should see that **TextHolder1 (Canvas Group)** has been added to the **Element 0** slot. It's important to note that if `TextHolder1` did not have a Canvas Group component attached to it, we would not have been able to add it to this list.

6. Add `TextHolder2` to the list in the same way you added `TextHolder1`. Also, add the `Text` children of `TextHolder1` and `TextHolder2` to the **Text Boxes** list. Once completed, you should see the following:

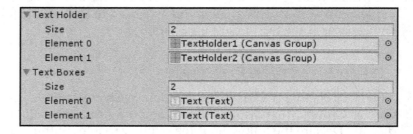

Ensure that you drag the `Text` objects in the correct order.

7. Now change the **Size** of the **Dialogue** list to 2. Then, add the following text to **Element 0** and **Element 1**, respectively: `Hello there!` and `I'm a cat and, for some reason, I'm collecting food!`. We will be generating the text within the textboxes via code using this list. In the last subsection, we added the text to the textboxes that we placed in the scene. However, due to the code we will write, that step will be rendered unnecessary. It was helpful adding the text to those textboxes, though, because we were able to see exactly how it will display.

8. The last thing we need to do in the Editor, for now, is assigned the scene that the game will navigate to once the dialogue has completed. We'll create a scene called `Chapter6` later, but, for now, let's just assign the `Chapter5` scene to the **Next Scene** slot by typing `Chapter5`.

9. Now we can go back to our `AnimateText.cs` script. We aren't quite done with our variable declaration. We need two variables that will track string in our dialogue we wish to display as well as which character within that specific string we are displaying. Add the following variable declaration to your script:

```
int whichText=0; //which string will be read
int positionInString=0; //which letter is being typed
```

10. Note that these two variables are not public and thus cannot be adjusted in the Inspector. Their values will be adjusted by the script. The `whichText` variable will allow us to switch between displaying the first string in the dialogue list and the second. The code we will write will easily be extendable to more strings. The `positionInString` variable will keep track of which character is being typed out by the animation. We want to keep track of this so that we can tell whether the text is being sped up by the user or if they have already read the whole text and just want to proceed to the next part.

11. We will use a coroutine to animate our text one letter at a time. Coroutines work very well for timed and scheduled events. The last variable we need to declare will allow us to reference our coroutine so that we can easily stop it. Declare the following variable:

```
Coroutine textPusher; //so we can stop the coroutine
```

12. The coroutine that will control the text animation is as follows:

```
IEnumerator WriteTheText(){
    for(int i=0; i<=dialogue[whichText].Length; i++){
        textDisplayBox[whichText].text=dialogue[whichText].Substring(0,i);
        positionInString++;
        yield return new WaitForSeconds(0.1f);
    }
}
```

13. This code finds the current string in the `dialogue` list using the `whichText` variable and loops through all of its characters. With each step of the loop, the text property of the UI Text object is updated to display the first `i` characters of the string, where `i` represents the current step of the loop. It then increases the `positionInString` variable and waits a tenth of a second to display the next character by proceeding to the next step in the loop.

14. Before the preceding code will do anything, we need to start our coroutine. In the process of starting it, I also want to assign the `textPusher` variable. Add the following to the `Start()` function:

```
void Start () {
textPusher=StartCoroutine(WriteTheText());
}
```

15. If you play your game now, you should see the "Hello there!" text type out within your scene.

16. The coroutine currently only loops through the first string in the dialogue list. We need to now make it proceed to the next string in the list by increasing the `whichText` variable. We also need to add functionality to allow players to show all the text so that they don't have to wait for it to fully animate, if they're impatient. Let's create a function that will be called by the press of our buttons:

```
public void ProceedText(){
    //haven't made it to the end of the string
    if(positionInString<dialogue[whichText].Length){
        //stop typing the text
        StopCoroutine(textPusher);
        //show the full string
        textDisplayBox[whichText].text=dialogue[whichText];
        positionInString=dialogue[whichText].Length;

    //have completed the whole string
    }else{
        //hide the text holder
        textHolder[whichText].alpha=0;
        textHolder[whichText].interactable=false;
        textHolder[whichText].blocksRaycasts=false;

        //proceed to next string
        whichText++;

        //there's no more text, go to the next scene
        if(whichText>=textDisplayBox.Count){
            SceneManager.LoadScene(nextScene);

        //there are more text boxes, show them
        }else{
            positionInString=0;
            textHolder[whichText].alpha=1;
            textHolder[whichText].interactable=true;
            textHolder[whichText].blocksRaycasts=true;
            textPusher=StartCoroutine(WriteTheText());
        }
    }
}
```

17. When a button is pressed, the code first determines whether the whole string has been displayed using the `positionInString` variable. If the `positionInString` variable is smaller than the total characters in the current string, it displays the complete string; otherwise, it proceeds.
    When the `positionInString` variable is less than the total characters in the current string, the coroutine is stopped early with `StopCoroutine(textPusher)`. The text property of the `textDisplayBox` is updated to display the full string, and the `positionInString` is set to the length of the string; that way, if the button is clicked on again, this function will know that it can proceed to the next step.
    When the `positionInString` variable is not less than the total characters in the current string, the current Canvas Group is deactivated, and then the `whichText` variable is increased. Once this variable is increased, the code checks whether there are any more textboxes that need animating. If there are not, the next scene loads. If there are more textboxes that need animating, the `positionInString` variable is reset to 0, so the very first character in the string needs to be displayed first. The new Canvas Group is now activated, and the `textPusher` variable is reassigned so that the coroutine loop will play again.

18. Now that our code is done, we just need to hook up our buttons to perform the function described in the previous step. For both buttons on both `TextHolders`, set the **On Click()** event to run the `ProceedText()` function in the `AnimateText` script attached to the `Main Camera`. Now, when you play the game, clicking on the button when the text isn't finished yet will cause it to finish, and clicking on it when it is done will cause it to go to the next dialogue or the next scene.

To improve on this script, you might want to put a checker that ensures that your three lists are all of the same length. You can also create a prefab of the `TextHolder` object and generate a set amount in code based on the text you enter. I would recommend implementing this change if you will be making a more complicated dialogue system.

Custom font

Let's take a step away from building out our scenes for a moment to explore making a custom font. We won't be using this custom font in the scenes we've been working on, but the process of creating a custom font is still important to cover. We'll create a custom font that displays the number 0 through 9 using the following sprites:

The sprites used to create the font are modified from the free art asset found at `https://opengameart.org/content/shooting-gallery`.

> To create an evenly spaced sprite sheet for this font, I used the TexturePacker program along with Photoshop. The process can be done entirely with a photo editing software such as Photoshop, but TexturePacker simplifies the process. TexturePacker can be found at `https://www.codeandweb.com/texturepacker`.

The process of creating a custom font is time-consuming and kind of a pain. To create a custom font, you have to put in coordinate location for each character you plan on rendering with the font, so I don't really recommend it for anything other than numbers or a very limited character set.

> If you want a custom font with a more robust character set, check out the Unity asset store for various options on streamlining the bitmap font process.

To create the custom font displayed in the preceding image, complete the following steps:

1. Create a new folder called `Custom Font` within your `Assets/Fonts` folder.
2. Find the `customFontSpriteSheet.png` file within the code bundle and drag the file into the folder you created in step 1. The sprite sheet appears as follows:

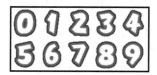

When manually creating a custom font, it is important that your individual characters be spaced evenly. This will make your life significantly easier while entering the settings of the individual characters. You can leave the sprite sheet's import settings at the default **Sprite (2D and UI) Texture Type** and **Single Sprite Mode**.

3. A custom font requires a material to render. Create a new material by right-clicking in your **Custom Font** folder and selecting **Create | Material**. Rename the new material to **CustomFontMaterial**.

4. Select **CustomFontMaterial** to bring up its **Inspector**. Drag `customFontSpriteSheet` into the square next to **Albedo** in **Main Maps**. Once you do so, the material's preview image should update:

5. Now we need to change the material's shader. There are a few different options you can use for the Shader. You can use **UI | Default** or any of the unlit or unlit UI options. My preference is to use **GUI | Text Shader**, as I tend to have the best luck with it rendering correctly, and I prefer the way it displays in the **Project** view.

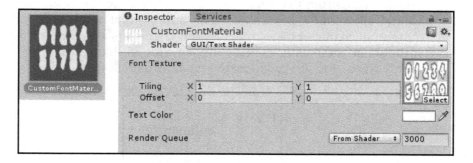

6. Now we can create our Custom Font. Within the `Custom Font` folder, right-click and select **Create | Custom Font**. Name the new font `CustomFont`.

7. Select `CustomFont` and assign `CustomFontMaterial` to the **Default Material** slot.

8. The properties under **Character Rects** will specify the coordinates of the individual characters on the sprite sheet. The **Size** property specifies how many total characters are there in our sprite sheet. Many of these properties are repeated for each character. To save time, I like to set the properties of **Element 0** before I increase my **Character Rects' Size** to the amount of characters I wish to display. This way, the properties I specify in **Element 0** will be duplicated to all subsequent Elements. So, set the **Size** property to 1 for now. We will change it to 10 once we have the properties that will repeat for all characters entered. When you set the **Size** to 1, you should see the properties of **Element 0** appear.

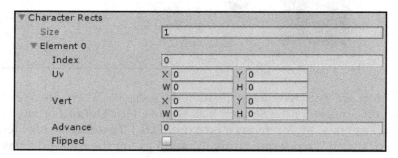

9. The first properties that repeat for all characters are **UV W** and **UV H**. These values represent the percentage of the sprite's total width and total height that the individual character takes up. Since our characters are all evenly spaced in our sprite sheet, these values will be the same for all characters. If your characters are evenly sized, you can calculate these values as follows:

$$UV\ W = \frac{1}{columnCount}$$
$$UV\ H = \frac{1}{rowCount}$$

There are a total of five columns of characters. Therefore, each sprite takes up one-fifth of the width of the sprite. One-fifth is equal to 20 percent or 0.2 as a decimal. We need to put 0.2 in the **UV W** slot. If you're not great with percentages, that's fine. Unity will perform the calculation for you! Typing 1/5 in the **UV W** slot and pressing *Enter* will automatically compute the 0.2 decimal.

There are total two rows of characters. Therefore, each sprite takes up 1/2 of the height of the sprite; one-fifth is equal to 50 percent or 0.5 as a decimal. Typing 1/2 in the **UV H** slot and pressing *Enter* will automatically compute the correct decimal of 0.5 in the slot.

10. The next values that repeat for each character are the **Vert W** and **Vert H** values. When the sprite sheet was created, each individual sprite was made from a 50x57 pixel image. So, type 50 in the W slot and −57 in the **H** slot. Remember that the **H** property will always be negative!

11. The last property that remains consistent throughout all the characters is the **Advance** property. This property is the space between the characters. Since our sprites are a width of 50, we should make this property 50 or larger. You can fiddle with this property to see what looks best to you, but I think it looks nice at 51.

After completing steps 9 through 11, your Element 0 character should have the following properties:

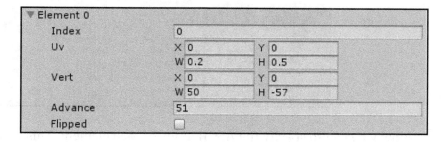

12. Now that we have placed all the repeated properties, we can increase the **Size** or our **Character Rects** set. There are a total of 10 character in our sprite sheet, so change the **Size** property to 10. You'll see that once we do this, the properties of **Element 0** are repeated in **Element 1** through **Element 9**.

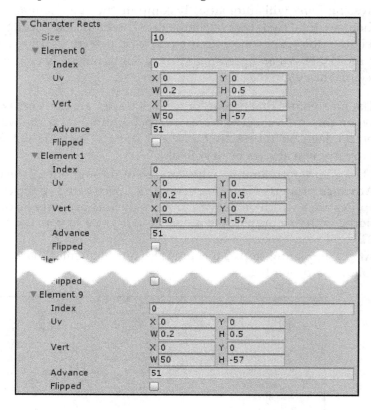

13. Now we need to specify the ASCII index of each element. This will tie the typed text to the correct sprite. Without this, the font would not know that typing the number 0 should show the first sprite in the sheet. The following table indicates that the numbers 0-9 are the ASCII numbers 48-57: http://www.ascii.cl/. Therefore, we should enter the Index values of 48 through 57 in **Element 0** through **Element 9**:

Element	0	1	2	3	4	5	6	7	8	9
Index	48	49	50	51	52	53	54	55	56	57

14. The next step is to specify the **UV X** and **Y** values. This is the part of creating custom fonts that takes up the most time. These values represent the UV coordinate position of the characters in the sprite sheet. These numbers are calculated based on the row and column numbers that the character lies in. The row and column numbers start at 0 and start in the bottom-left corner.

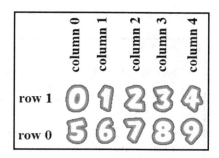

To calculate the **UV X** and **UV Y** values, use the following formulas:

$$UV\ X = columnNumber \times UV\ W$$
$$UV\ Y = rowNumber \times UV\ H$$

Remember that since our characters are evenly spaced, our **UV W** and **UV H** values are the same for each character.

So, if we look at **Element 0**, its **UV X** value can be found by multiplying 0 (for column 0) by 0.2 (the **UV W** value) to get 0. Its **UV Y** value can be found by multiplying 1 (for row 1) by 0.5 (the **UV H** value) to get 0.5.

The following chart represents the **UV X** and **UV Y** values that should be entered for each character:

Element	UV X	UV Y
0	0	0.5
1	0.2	0.5
2	0.4	0.5
3	0.6	0.5
4	0.8	0.5
5	0	0
6	0.2	0

7	0.4	0
8	0.6	0
9	0.8	0

The following image gives a more visual representation of the coordinate pattern:

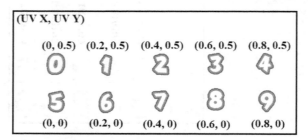

15. Now, we can test our font to see whether it works. Within any of your scenes, create a new **UI Text** object. I have created a new scene called `Chapter6CustomFont` on which I have my test fonts. Change the **Text** to `0123456789` and drag the `CustomFont` into the `Font` slot. The text should appear as it did at the beginning of this example.

Adjusting the character spacing and changing the font size

In our example, all the numbers are evenly spaced and the font size cannot be changed. It's very likely that you will want your numbers to be closer together or of a different font size. Let's alter our custom font so that the sprites are closer together. The following image shows our font after the adjustments versus the original created in the last part of this example:

To change the spacing of the characters, complete the following steps:

1. Duplicate the CustomFont with *Ctrl + D* and rename the duplicate to `CustomFontTight`. Open the **Inspector** of `CustomFontTight`.

2. If you'd like the numbers to be closer together, you have to simply change the **Advance** property for the specific elements. The **Advance** property represents the pixels from the start of the sprite to the start of the next sprite. So, if we wanted the number 2 to appear closer to the number 1, we could change the **Advance** on **Element 1** to something smaller, as shown here:

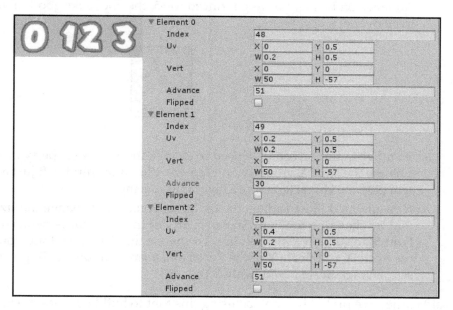

 You can change the settings on your custom font while previewing the results in the Scene. To get the text to refresh in the scene after making a change to your custom font, you have to first save the scene.

3. Adjust the **Advance** properties of each element based on the following chart:

Element	0	1	2	3	4	5	6	7	8	9
Advance	39	30	35	35	35	35	35	35	38	35

4. The font should now appear as follows:

5. There is still a bit too much spacing between the 0 and the 1; however, if you try to reduce the **Advance** on the 0 to bring 1 closer, other numbers will overlap the 0 if they follow the 0. The following example shows what will happen if the Advance on Element 0 were reduced to 35; the one looks good following 0, but the 0 overlaps it.

6. To move in the 1 closer, we need to change the **Vert X** property on **Element 1**. Change the **Vert X** property on **Element 1** to –3 to shift it left just a smidge. This will give the character a more favorable spacing.

7. Now, if you'd like to adjust the font size, you cannot change the size of a custom font by changing the **Font Size** property of the Text component; changing the **Font Size** value will do nothing. To change the size of the font, you must change the **Scale X** and **Scale Y** of the Rect Transform component. To get the font half the size, change **Scale X** and **Scale Y** to 0.5.

As I said earlier, we probably won't be using this font to build our master example scene, but the process of creating a custom font is still a useful exercise. Now, let's move on to creating some other common UI assets—health/progress pars.

Horizontal and circular health/progress meters

Let's get back to our main scene. Duplicate the Chapter5 scene to create a Chapter6 scene.

In this section, we'll cover how to create two types of progress meters, a horizontal one and a vertical one, as shown:

We'll hook up the circular and horizontal progress meters so that they both display the progress of the same variable and we can watch them both change at the same time.

The circular progress meter doesn't really fit in the master scene that we've been building and we'll hide it after this chapter, but circular progress bars are common game elements, and it's hard to find information on how to do them, so I thought it was important to include an example of how to do them in the text.

Remember when we created the scene `Chapter6AnimatedText`, I stated that we'd change the scene that loads after it once we created `Chapter6`. Now that we have a `Chapter6` scene, let's change the scene navigation before we begin working on the progress bars.

To hook up the correct scene navigation, complete the following steps:

1. Open the `Chapter6AnimatedText` scene and select the `Main Camera`.
2. In the **Animated Text** component, change the text in the **Next Scene** slot to `Chapter6`.
3. Open the `Chapter5StartScreen` scene and select the `Play Button` in the `Button Canvas`.
4. In the **Level Loader** component, change the text in the **Scene To Load** slot to `Chapter6AnimatedText`.
5. Open the **Build Settings**. Remove the `Chapter5` scene, and add the `Chapter6AnimatedText` and `Chapter6` scenes.

Now when you play the game from the start screen, Chapter5StartScreen, the game will play through the animated text and load the main game screen.

Horizontal health bar

There are a few different ways that a horizontal health bar can be created, but the quickest and easiest way is to scale a single axis based on percentage. When setting up a horizontal health bar in this way, it is important to ensure that the anchor is set at the position that represents a completely depleted bar.

Remember that back in Chapter 2, *Canvases, Panels, and Basic Layouts*, we set the anchor of the health bar to the left, so we have already set the anchor correctly. We also scaled the health bar in the *x* direction to show what the bar would look like as it depleted.

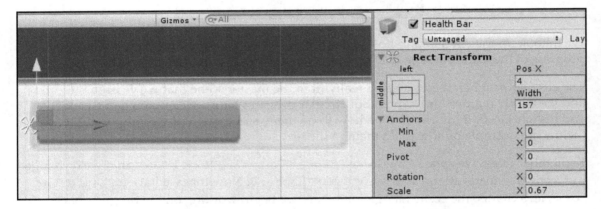

Now, all we need to do is tie the percentage to the **X Scale** of the health bar.

To tie the fill of the health bar to an actual value, complete the following steps:

1. Create a new C# script in your Scripts folder and name it ProgressMeters.cs.

2. In the ProgressMeters script, initialize the following four variables.

```
public uint health;
public uint totalHealth;
public float percentHealth;
public RectTransform healthBar;
```

The `health` variable represents the current health of the player, and the `totalHealth` variable represents the total health the player can obtain. As it doesn't make sense for these values to be negative, they have been initialized at the `uint` type or a positive integer. I have made these two variables public so that they can easily be edited in the inspector. The `percentHealth` variable will be calculated based on the quotient of the health and `totalHealth` variables. I made this value public, not so that we can edit it in the Inspector but so that we can easily see its values change in the **Inspector**. The `healthBar` variable stores the `RectTransform` component of the **Health Bar UI** Image within our scene.

> Since `RectTransform` inherits from `Transform`, we could have declared `healthBar` as a `Transform` and the following code would still work.

3. Return to the Unity Editor and drag the `ProgessMeters` script onto the `Main Camera`. Assign the value 500 to both the **Health** and **Total Health** slots. Drag the `Health Bar` UI Image into the **Health Bar** slot. Any value you try to type in to the **Percent Health** slot will be overridden by the code we write in the next step.

4. We want any changes made to our health value to automatically update the `percentHealth` value and the scale of our `healthBar`. Therefore, we need to put the following code in the `Update()` function:

```
void Update () {
    //cap health
    if(health>totalHealth){
      health=totalHealth;
    }

    //calculate health percentage
    percentHealth=(float)health/totalHealth;

    //horizontal health bar
    healthBar.localScale=new Vector2(percentHealth, 1f);
  }
```

Declaring our health and `totalHealth` variables with the `uint` type stopped them from becoming negative, but we still need to put a cap on our health variable. It doesn't make sense for it to exceed the `totalHealth` variable. While `percentHealth` is a float variable, performing a division between two `uint` variables will result in a `uint`, so adding `(float)` at the beginning of the integer division provides a float result from the division.

The last part of the code sets the `localScale` of the `healthBar`. When you scale a UI object, you have to use `localScale`. This scales the object locally, meaning relative to its parent object.

5. Now we can test the code easily in the Editor. Play the game and hover your mouse over the word **Health** in the **Progress Meter** component of the `Main Camera` until the mouse displays two arrows around it, as shown in the following screenshot:

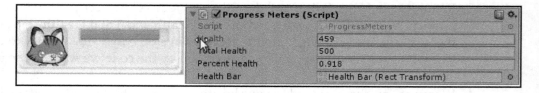

When these arrows appear, clicking and dragging will manipulate the values of the variable based on your mouse position. You'll see, as you do this, that the **Health** value decreases, the **Percent Health** value decreases, and the `Health Bar` in the scene changes size. You'll note that you cannot set the value of Health below 0 or above 500.

As you can see, setting up a horizontal health bar isn't terribly difficult. Duplicating this process in a game where the health reduces by events won't require a lot of steps to achieve. Just ensure that you set the anchor of the health bar correctly. This process will work similarly for a vertical health bar.

Circular progress meter

Horizontal health bars didn't take a lot of work to set up. The work to make a circular progress meter is just about as easy and can be completed with only two more lines of code. Since we don't already have a circular progress bar in our scene, we will have to start with a bit of setup first.

To create a circular progress bar, complete the following steps:

1. From the code bundle, drag the `circular meter.png` image into the `Sprites` folder of your project.
2. Set the **Sprite Mode** of the `circular meter.png` to **Multiple** and automatically slice it in the Sprite Editor.
3. Select the `Top Left Panel` within the **Hierarchy** and give it a new UI Image child. Name the image `Progress Holder`.
4. Similar to how we set up the health bar, there will be a holder and a fill. Drag the `circular meter_0` subimage into the **Source Image** slot of the Image component of `Progress Holder`.
5. It's important that we get the right proportions on our holder and fill images. So, to ensure that holder image is correctly proportioned, hit the **Set Native Size** button on the **Image** component.
6. Now, add a child UI image to `Progress Holder` called `Progress Meter`.
7. Set the anchor preset of `Progress Meter` to middle center. Do not stretch it.
8. Add `circular meter_1` to the **Source Image** of the **Image** component on the `Progress Meter`.
9. Hit the **Set Native Size** button for the `Progress Meter` **Image** component as well. After completing this step, you should see the following:

If the pink fill is not perfectly nestled inside the blue holder, you may have forgotten to hit the **Set Native Size** button on one of the images or the `Progress Meter` does not have its anchor preset set to middle center.

10. Let's move this meter and scale it a bit. Select `Progress Holder` and move it below the `Character Holder`. Set the **Scale X** and **Scale Y** of the `Progress Holder` to `0.8` to make it a little smaller.

11. The last thing to do before we code to the code is change the **Image Type** of the `Progress Meter`. Change the **Image Type** to **Filled** with a **Radial 360 Fill Method**. Change the **Fill Origin** to **Top**. Adjust the scroll bar on the **Fill Amount** to preview the meter filling:

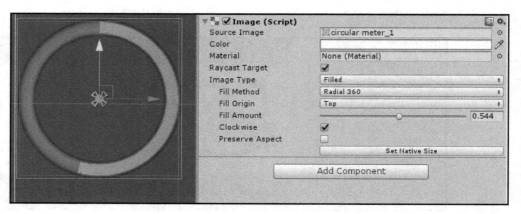

12. Now we're ready to write some code. As you have probably guessed from adjusting the **Fill Amount**, we'll want to tie the **Fill Amount** to the percentHealth variable in our code. First, we need to create a public variable with which we can access the Image component of our Progress Meter. Declare the following variable at the top of your code:

```
public Image progressMeter;
```

13. Now, add the following at the end of the Update() function:

```
//circular progress meter
progressMeter.fillAmount=percentHealth;
```

14. The last thing we need to do is hook the Progress Meter UI Image to the progressMeter variable. Drag the Progress Meter into the **Progress Meter** slot.

15. Play the game and Adjust the **Health** value in the Inspector as you did earlier and watch the two meters move in unison:

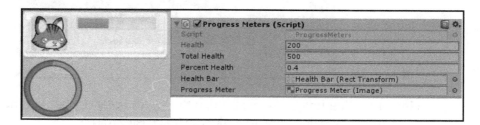

As you can see, making a circular progress meter is really not more difficult than making a horizontal one!

Wrapped text with Gradient

The banner of our Pause Panel has been looking a bit bare so far. Now that we've covered using TextMesh Pro-Text, we can create a nice curved text with a gradient that lines up well with our banner.

To create the curved text shown in the preceding screenshot, complete the following steps:

1. If you have not done so already, download the TextMesh Pro asset for free on the Unity Asset store at `https://www.assetstore.unity3d.com/en/#!/content/84126`. Import all the provided files.

2. Select the `Pause Banner` UI Image and give it a child TextMeshPro-Text object by right-clicking on it in the Hierarchy and selecting **UI | TextMeshPro-Text**. Rename the child object `Paused Text-Pro`.

3. In the **Text Mesh Pro UGUI** component, change the **Text Input Box** setting to `Paused`.

4. Set the **Font Style** to bold and center align the text in both the horizontal and vertical axes. Set the Font Size to 43.

5. Adjust the Rect Transform so that the text is centered more within the banner. Your text should appear as follows:

In the preceding image, I have hidden the `Inventory Panel` behind the `Pause Panel` from my scene view to make the text easier to see.

6. Now, let's give the text a gradient fill. Select the checkbox next to **Color Gradient**.

7. To achieve the desired look, we will leave the **Top Left** and **Top Right** colors white. Select the white rectangle next to **Bottom Left** to bring up the Color picker. Select the eye dropper at the top of the Color picker and then move your mouse over the tan area of the `Pause Panel` image. When you close the Color picker window, the tan color should now be in the **Bottom Left** slot.

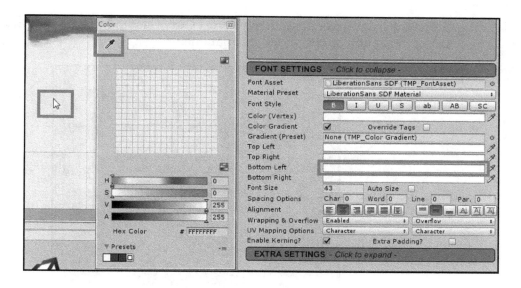

8. Right-click on the color in the **Bottom Left** slot and select **Copy**.

9. Right-click on the color in the **Bottom Right** slot and select **Paste**. Now, the two **Top** colors should be white and two **Bottom** colors should be tan.

10. In the **Outline Settings**, select **Enable**. Set the **Color** to white (if it is not already) and change the **Thickness** to 0.25.

11. The last thing to do is curve the text. TextMeshPro has made this pretty easy for us by providing an example script that curves text at runtime. To view the changes, you have to play the game, and they are not represented in the Scene view. Select the **Add Component** button and choose **Scripts** | **TMPro.Examples** | **Warp Text Example**.

12. Select the wavy green lines in the **Vertex Curve** slot to bring up the curve editor. Select the option on the far left, the flat line:

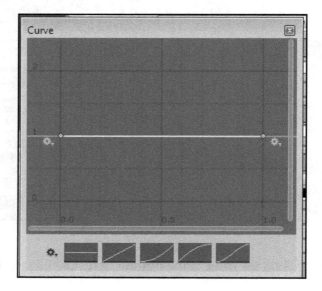

13. Right-click on the green line at the **0.5** mark and select **Add Key**.
14. Select that new key and drag it upward to a little below **1.3**.

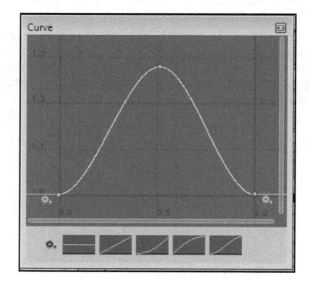

15. Now, select the keys at the **0.0** mark and **1.0** mark and grab the handles that appear. Drag the handles upward until they are at approximately 45 and -45 degree angles.

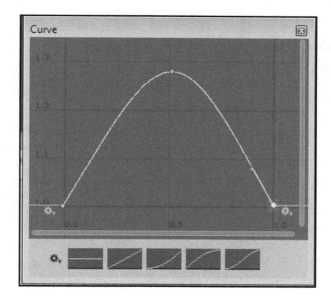

16. Play the game and press the *P* key to view the `Pause Panel`. The text should now appear as it did at the beginning of this example.

Summary

UI Images and Text make up the vast majority of graphical user interfaces.

In this chapter, we discussed the following topics:

- Creating UI Text objects and setting their properties
- Importing fonts into Unity
- Using markup format with UI Text objects
- Creating UI Images and setting their properties
- Using the various UI Effects components to further customize our graphical UI
- Creating TextMesh Pro-Text Objects and setting their properties

- Creating text that animates, as if being typed out
- Creating a custom font to be used with UI Text objects
- Creating text that wraps along a curve and renders with a gradient
- Creating horizontal and circular progress bars

Next, we will cover other input types as well as masks.

Masks and Other Inputs

7

The most popular UI objects are Buttons, Text, and Images, but there are a few other interactable UI objects available.

In this chapter, we will discuss the following topics:

- Appropriate use all the UI objects available
- Creating a settings menu with a mask, scrolling text, an input text field, checkbox, and toggle
- Attaching code to each of the inputs

All the examples shown in this section can be found within the Unity project provided in the code bundle. They can be found within the scene labeled Chapter7Text in the Assets/Scene/ExamplesInText/Chapter7Text folder.

Each example image has a caption stating the example number within the scene.

In the scene, each example is on its own Canvas and some of the Canvases are deactivated. To view an example on a deactivated Canvas, simply select the checkbox next to the Canvas' name in the Inspector:

Masks

Masks affect the visibility of objects within their shape. If an object is affected by a mask, any part of it outside the mask's restricted area will be invisible. The restriction area of a mask can either be determined by an image with the Mask component or a Rect Transform with the Rect Mask 2D component.

With UI, masking is primarily used for scrolling menus, so items that exist outside of the menu's area will not be visible. However, it is also used to *cut out* images. For example, the following image shows a cat's image being cut out by a circular mask:

With Mask   **Without Mask**

Circular Mask Example in the Chapter7Text Scene

You may note that the edges on the cat with mask don't look great. To avoid this, ensure that you use sprites with appropriate image resolutions and try different Filtering modes on the Sprite's **Import Settings**.

Mask component

The **Mask** component can be added to any UI object with an Image component. If its added to a UI object that doesn't have an **Image** component, it won't function, since it needs an Image to determine the restricted area.

The **Mask** component can be added to a UI Object by selecting **Add Component** | **UI** | **Mask** within the **Inspector**:

Any children of the UI Object containing the **Mask** component will then have their visibility restricted to only the area within the opaque area of the **Source Image** on its Image component.

In the following image, the object named `Mask` is a UI Image with a **Mask** component added to it. As you can see, the purple triangle on the left of the panel is only partially visible, while the green triangle on the right is fully visible. The green triangle is fully visible, because it is not a child of the UI Image that contains a **Mask** component:

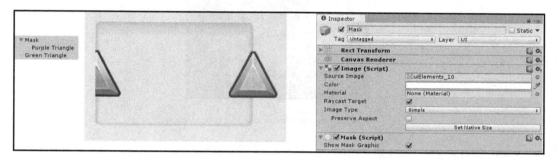

Mask Component Example in the Chapter7Text Scene

You have the option to hide the **Source Image** that is defining the Mask component's visibility area. If you deselect **Show Mask Graphic**, the parent's source image will not be visible. It's important to note that changing the opacity on the **Source Image** does not affect the Mask's functionality.

Rect Mask 2D component

Using the **Mask** component allows you to restrict the visible area to a non-rectangular shape. However, if you want to restrict the visible area to a rectangular shape and don't want to use an image to restrict the visible area, you can use a Rect Mask 2D component.

The Rect Mask 2D component can be added to a UI Object by selecting **Add Component | UI | Rect Mask 2D** within the **Inspector**, as shown:

When a Rect Mask 2D component is added to a `GameObject`, the visibility of its children will be affected by the shape of its Rect Transform. An **Image** component is not required on the parent object for the Rect Mask 2D to function properly.

In the following image, an Empty UI GameObject is created and a Rect Mask 2D is added to it. It is then given a child UI Image. As you can see, the triangle is masked by the Rect transform area:

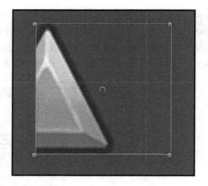

Rect Mask 2D Component Example in the Chapter7Text Scene

If you want to apply a mask to a rectangular shape, I highly recommend that you use the Rect Mask 2D component rather than the stand **Mask** component, as it is more performant.

 It's important to note that, as implied by the name Rect Mask 2D, this mask will only work on 2D objects. You can read more about its limitations at `https://docs.unity3d.com/Manual/script-RectMask2D.html`.

UI Toggle

The UI Toggle object is an interactable checkbox with a label.

To create a UI Toggle, select **Create** | **UI** | **Toggle**. By default, a UI Toggle has two children: a `Background` and a `Label`. The `Background` also has a child, a `Checkmark`.

The `Background` child is a UI Image that represents the "box" in which the `Checkmark` UI Image appears. The `Label` is a UI Text object.

If you want to change the appearance of the box and checkmark, you change the source images of the Image components on the `Background` and `Checkmark` children, respectively.

Toggle component

The parent `Toggle` object has a Toggle component. The Toggle component looks very similar to the Button component and has many of the same properties. As you'll see in this chapter, the first few properties of all interactable UI objects are the same. The properties at the bottom of the component are the ones that are exclusive to the UI Toggle object:

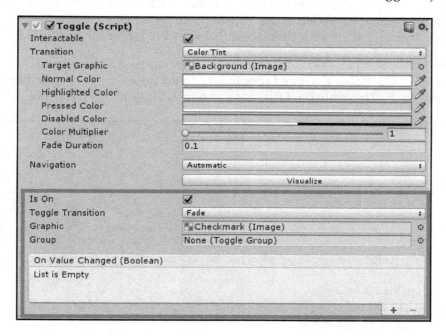

The **Is On** property determines whether the Toggle is checked or not when it is initialized in the scene.

The **Toggle Transition** property determines what happens when the toggle transitions between on and off or checked and not checked. The two options are **None** and **Fade**. The **None** transition will instantaneously toggle between the checkmark Image being visible and not visible while the **Fade** transition will have the checkmark Image fade in and out.

The **Graphic** property assigns the **Image** component that will display the checkmark. The Checkmark child's Image component is automatically assigned to this property, but you can change it if you so desire.

The last property, **Group**, assigns the **Toggle Group** component that will define which Toggle Group the Toggle belongs to (if any).

The **Toggle** component's default Event is the `On Value Changed` Event, as seen in the **On Value Changed (Boolean)** section.

Toggle default event – On Value Changed (Boolean)

The **Toggle** component's default event is the **On Value Changed** Event, as seen in the **On Value Changed (Boolean)** section of the Toggle component. This event will trigger whenever the toggle is selected or deselected. It can accept a Boolean argument.

When a public function has a Boolean parameter, it will appear twice within the function's drop-down list of **On Value Changed (Boolean)** events: once within a **Static Parameter** list and again within the **Dynamic bool** list, as shown in the following screenshot:

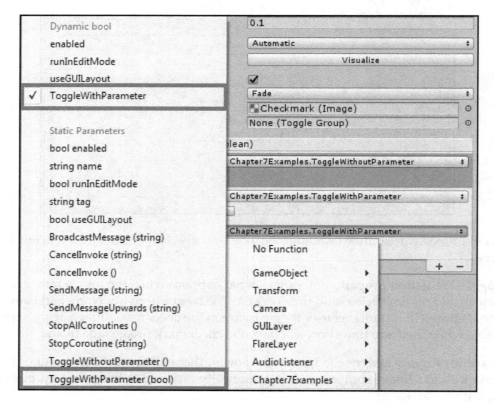

If the function is selected from the **Static Parameters** list, a checkbox will appear as an argument within the Event. The event will then only send the value of that checkmark. In the example shown in the preceding screenshot, the only value that will ever be sent to the `ToggleWithParameter()` function will be `false` (since the checkbox is deselected).

If you want to pass the `.isOn` value of the Toggle to the script, the function must be chosen from the **Dynamic bool** (not **Static Parameters**) list in the function dropdown of the event.

To demonstrate how **On Value Changed (Boolean)** events work, let's see how the following two functions will respond when called:

```
public void ToggleWithoutParameter(){
    Debug.Log("changed");
}

public void ToggleWithParameter(bool value){
Debug.Log(value);
}
```

The following events are added to a Toggle in the `Chapter7Text` scene:

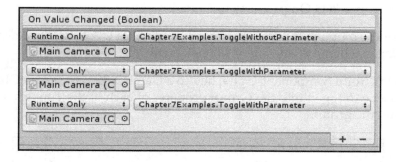

Events on Toggle Event Example in the Chapter7Text Scene

When the **Toggle** within the scene is deselected, the following will print in the **Console**:

```
changed
False
False
```

When the **Toggle** is selected, the following will print in the **Console**:

```
changed
False
True
```

Since the function called from the first event does not have a parameter, it will always execute when the value of the Toggle changes, regardless of what the value of the Toggle is when executed.

The second event will always print the value of `False`, because the function has a parameter and, since the event was chosen from the **Static Parameters** list, the argument being sent is represented by the checkbox, which is set to `False`. So, the value `False` is always sent to the function.

The third event's function was chosen from the **Dynamic bool** list, so the argument sent to the function will be the `.isOn` value to which the Toggle changes.

Toggle Group component

The **Toggle Group** component allows you to have many UI Toggles that work together, where only one can be selected or *on* at a time. When Toggles are in the same Toggle Group, selecting one Toggle will turn off all others. For the Toggle Group to work properly at start, you should either set all the Toggles within the Toggle group's **Is On** property to **False** or set only a single Toggle's **Is On** property to **True**.

The **Toggle Group** component does not create a renderable UI object, so attaching it to an empty GameObject will not create any visible element.

Once the **Toggle Group** component is attached to a GameObject, the GameObject it is attached to must be dragged into the **Group** property of each of the Toggles that will be contained within the group:

There is only one property on the **Toggle Group** component: **Allow Switch Off**. The **Allow Switch Off** property allows the Toggles to be turned off if they are selected when already in the on state. Remember that the Toggle Group component forces at most one Toggle on at a time. So, the **Allow Switch Off** property being turned off forces there to be at least one Toggle selected at all times.

My suggestion when using this component is to use an empty GameObject that acts as the parent for all the Toggles you wish to group together. This empty GameObject will then contain the Toggle Group component (as demonstrated in the **Toggle Group** example in the Chapter7Text Scene). The object containing the Toggle Group component must then be assigned to the **Group** property on the **Toggle** component of each of the Toggle children.

UI Slider

The UI Slider object allows the user to drag a handle along a path. The position on the path corresponds to a range of values.

To create a UI Slider, select **Create | UI | Slider**. By default, a UI Slider has three children: a Background, a Fill Area, and a Handle Slide Area. The Fill Area also has a child, Fill, and the Handle Slide Area has a child, Handle.

The Background child is a UI Image that represents the full area that the Slider's Handle can traverse. In the default Slider example, this is the darker gray background area that gets filled.

The Fill Area child is an empty GameObject. Its main purpose is to ensure that its child, the Fill, is correctly aligned. The Fill is a UI Image that stretches across the Fill Area based on the Slider's value. In the default Slider example, this is the light gray area that trails behind the handle and fills in the Background.

The Handle Slide Area child is also an empty GameObject. Its purpose is to ensure that its child, the Handle, is correctly positioned and aligned. The Handle is also a UI Image. The Handle represents the interactable area of the Slider.

If you want to change the appearance of the Slider, you change the **Source Image** of the **Image** components on the Background, Fill, and Handle children.

Slider component

The parent `Slider` object has a **Slider** component. It has all the properties common to the interactable UI objects along with a few that are exclusive to Sliders:

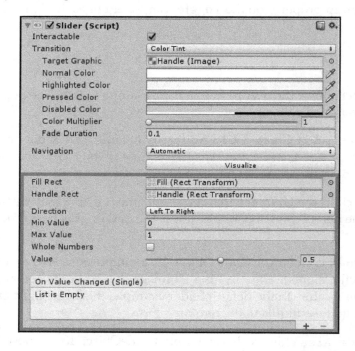

The **Fill Rect** property assigns the Rect Transform of the object that displays the Image of the filled area. By default, this is the `Fill` GameObject's Transform component. You'll note that on the Rect Transform component of the Fill, a message stating **Some values driven by Slider** is displayed. This is indicating that the values are changed based on the **Slider** component. While playing the scene, if you move the `Handle` of the `Slider`, you will not see the Rect Transform properties of `Fill` update. However, if you make the Scene view visible while moving the `Handle` in the **Game** view, you will see the Rect Transform area of the `Fill` change as you affect the slider.

The **Handle Rect** property assigns the Rect Transform of the object that displays the handle's image. By default, the Rect Transform of `Handle` is assigned to this property. You'll note that the Rect Transform component on the `Handle` GameObject also has the **Some values driven by Slider** message, since the position of the `Handle` is affected by the Slider.

The range of values that the Slider represents is determined by the **Min Value** and **Max Value** properties. You can assign any value to the **Min Value** and **Max Value** properties, even negative numbers. While the **Inspector** will allow you to define the **Min Value** as a number larger than the **Max Value**, the Slider will not work properly if you do so.

The **Direction** property allows you to select the orientation of the Slider. The available options are **Left To Right, Right To Left, Bottom To Top,** and **Top to Bottom**. The order of the positions in each direction represent the first position (or **Min Value**) and then the last position (or **Max Value**) of the Slider's value range.

If the **Whole Numbers** property is selected, the range of values the Slider can represent will be restricted to integer (non-decimal) values.

As I am a math teacher, I feel the need to point this out. In math, the term Whole Numbers represents all non-negative Integers. Here, in the Slider component, the term Whole Numbers represents all Integers, even negative ones. So, if you're a math nerd like me, don't let this imply to you that the Slider cannot hold negative values if the **Whole Numbers** property is selected.

The **Value** property is the value of the `Slider`. The position of the Slider's `Handle` is tied to this property. The slider in the **Inspector** next to the **Value** property is a one-to-one representation of the Slider in the scene.

Slider default event – On Value Changed (Single)

The Slider component's default event is the `On Value Changed` event, as seen in the **On Value Changed (Single)** section of the Slider component. This event will trigger whenever the Slider's Handle is moved. It can accept a float argument.

If you want the Slider's value to be sent as an argument to a function that has a parameter, you must select the function from the `Dynamic float` list (similar to selecting functions from the Toggle's `Dynamic bool` list).

The following functions and image represent a Slider example found in the `Chapter7Text` scene that triggers events that call functions with and without parameters:

```
public void SliderWithoutParameter(){
    Debug.Log("changed");
}

public void SliderWithParameter(float value){
    Debug.Log(value);
}
```

In the following screenshot, the third option shows the function chosen from the **Dynamic float** list and will send the value of the **Value** property as an argument to the function:

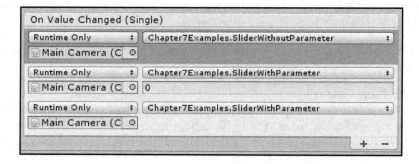

Events on Slider Example in the Chapter7Text Scene

 It's important to note that if the **Whole Numbers** property is selected and the Slider can only hold integer values, the functions called by this event will receive those integers as `float` values.

UI Scrollbar

The UI Scrollbar object allows the user to drag a handle along a path. The position of the handle on the path affects the position of an image or objects within a usable area.

If you're having trouble seeing what a scroll bar is from the preceding description, it is most commonly used in video games with menus that have a lot of information within a viewable area that is smaller than the area that all the information takes up.

To create a UI Scrollbar, select **Create | UI | Scrollbar**. By default, a UI Scrollbar has a child named `Sliding Area`. The `Sliding Area` also has a child named `Handle`.

The `Sliding Area` child is an empty GameObject. Its purpose is to ensure that its child, the `Handle`, is correctly positioned and aligned. The `Handle` is a UI Image. The `Handle` represents the interactable area of the `Scrollbar`.

Unlike the Toggle and Slider GameObjects, the background image of the Scrollbar is actually on the main `Scrollbar` parent object and not on a child named `Background`. Therefore, if you want to change the appearance of the Scrollbar's background and Handle, you change the **Source Images** of the **Image** components on the `Scrollbar` parent and `Handle` child, respectively.

The Scrollbar component

The parent `Scrollbar` object has a **Scrollbar** component. It has all the properties common to the interactable UI objects, along with a few that are exclusive to Scrollbars:

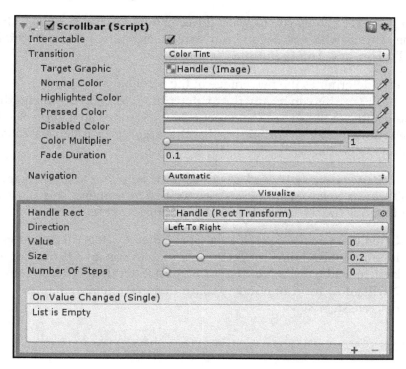

The Scrollbar works (and looks) just like the Slider. However, you'll note that you do not have the ability to select the range of values for the **Scrollbar** as you do with a **Slider**. A Scrollbar's values are always restricted to be between 0 and 1. This difference in properties has to do with a difference in intent for the two types of objects. Sliders are used, generally, to allow the player to select values that can vary greatly based on the slider. However, Scrollbars are used to move objects that take up more room than the viewable space. Due to this, the Scrollbar's position should easily translate to a percentage, or value between 0 and 1.

The **Handle Rect** property assigns the Rect Transform of the object that displays the handle's image. By default, the Rect Transform of Handle is assigned to this property. You'll note that the Rect Transform component on the Handle GameObject has the **Some values driven by Scrollbar** message, since the position of Handle is affected by the Scrollbar.

As with Sliders, the **Value** property is the value of the Scrollbar. The position of the Scrollbar's Handle is tied to this property. The slider in the **Inspector** next to the **Value** property mirrors the position of the Scrollbar's Handle.

The **Direction** property allows you to select the orientation of the Scrollbar. The available options are the same as with a Slider and translate accordingly: **Left To Right**, **Right To Left**, **Bottom To Top**, and **Top to Bottom**.

The **Size** property determines the percentage of the Scrollbar's Sliding Area taken up by the Scrollbar's Handle. This can be any float value from 0 to 1. I recommend that you choose a value relative to the size of the object(s) being scrolled so that the Scrollbar's movement feels more intuitive. This means that the larger the scrollable area is, the smaller the Scrollbar Handle becomes.

The **Number of Steps** property is used if you want the Scrollbar to have staggered, discrete steps and don't want it to have continuously controlled movement. This is used if you want your scrollbar to move the scrolling object(s) to specific locations.

Often you will see a scroll area represented by dots (like the dots that identify which home screen you are viewing on an iOS device). This can be achieved using a **Number of Steps** greater than 0. Setting this value to 0 will allow for continuously controlled movement rather than staggered discrete steps.

Examples of creating continuous and discrete Scrollbars are provided in the *Examples* section at the end of this chapter.

Scrollbar default event – On Value Changed (Single)

The Scrollbar component's default event is the **On Value Changed** Event, as seen in the **On Value Changed (Single)** section of the Scrollbar component. This event will trigger whenever the Scrollbar's Handle is moved. It can accept a float argument. It works identically to that of the Slider.

UI Scroll View

The UI Scroll View object creates a scrollable area along with two child UI Scrollbars. The scrollable area can be scrolled using the scrollbars, by dragging the area within the Scroll View, or using the scroll wheel on the mouse.

To create a UI Scroll View, select **Create | UI | Scroll View**. By default, a UI Scroll View has three children: Viewport, Scrollbar Horizontal, and Scrollbar Vertical. The Viewport object also has a child named Content. The Scrollbar Horizontal and Scrollbar Vertical children have the same parent/child relationship as default UI Scrollbars, as discussed in the previous section.

Even though the UI Scroll View comes with two Scrollbar children by default, you don't have to use both Scrollbars with your Scroll View. In fact, you don't have to use Scrollbars at all! Refer to the Scroll Rect Component section for further details.

The Viewport child object is a UI Image with a **Mask** component. The **Mask** component of Viewport has the **Show Mask Graphic** property turned off, by default. As you can see from the Rect Transform (look for the blue handles) in the following screenshot, the Viewport applies a mask to an area within the Scroll View:

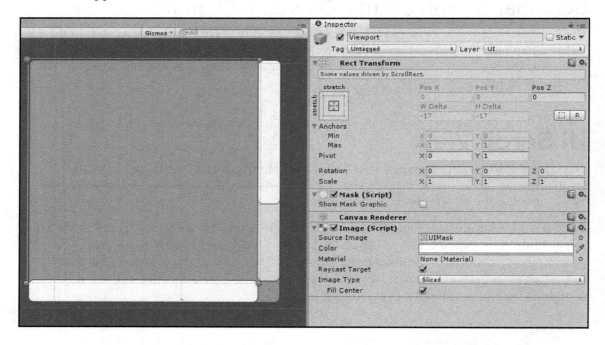

This will make the items within the Scroll View only viewable within the defined area (between the Scrollbars). You cannot change most of the **Rect Transform** properties of the Viewport, because this area is set based on how you have the settings of your Scroll View set in its **Scroll Rect** component (refer to the *Properties of the Scrollbars* section for more details).

The child of Viewport is an empty Rect Transform named Content. This will act as the *holder* of all the items you wish to place within the Scroll View. You can think of the Content as the things that will be moving around within the Scroll View. As you can see from the following image, the Rect Transform of Content is larger than the viewable area defined by Viewport, since the objective of a Scroll View is to have items outside of the viewable area.

To add items to the `Scroll View`, you simply add children to the `Content` object. Since `Content` is a child of `Viewport`, any of its children will also be affected by the Mask component on the `Viewport`.

The following example shows four images added as children of `Content`. `Content` has also been given a **Vertical Layout Group** component:

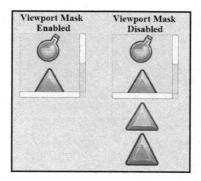

Scroll View Example in the Chapter7Text Scene

You can see that when the **Mask** component is disabled from the `Viewport`, all items are visible. When you are setting up your Scroll View, I highly recommend that you disable the Mask on the `Viewport` so that you can see the general layout of the items you are placing and re-enable it when you are done laying out all the items.

You should also adjust the Rect Transform area of `Content` to enclose all of its child items or use a **Content Size Fitter** component so that you can more easily predict the behavior of `Scroll View`. If the area of the Rect Transform `Content` does not fully encompass all the items, scrolling the Scroll View may not show the items outside of its viewable area.

`Scroll View` contains an **Image** component. If you want to change the background of the `Scroll View` (the gray rectangle that encapsulates everything), change the **Source Image** of the Image component on the `Scroll View`. You can change the appearance of the Scrollbars by adjusting the appearance of the `Scrollbar Horizontal` and `Scrollbar Vertical` children, as described in the UI Scrollbar section.

Scroll Rect component

The behavior of the Scroll View is determined by the Scroll Rect component on the `Scroll View` parent object:

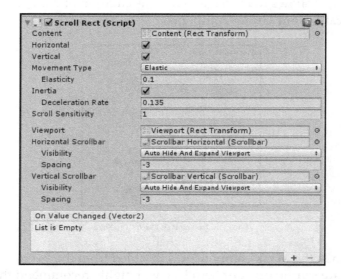

 Note that the Scroll Rect component doesn't have the **Interactable**, **Transition**, or **Navigation** properties that all the other UI components in this chapter (and previous chapters) have!

I'll discuss the properties slightly out of order to make them easier to discuss.

The **Content** property is assigned the Rect Transform of the UI element that will scroll. When using the UI Scroll View object, this is set to the Rect Transform component of `Content` by default. The **Viewport** property is assigned the Rect Transform that is the parent of item assigned to the **Content** property. When using the UI Scroll View object, this is set to the Rect Transform component of `Viewport` by default.

 If you are creating a scrollable area without using the UI Scroll View, the **Viewport** and **Content** properties must be assigned and the Rect Transform assigned to **Viewport** must be a parent of the Rect Transform assigned to **Content**, for the **Scroll Rect** component to function property.

Movement properties

There are three properties related to how the `Content` in the Scroll View will move. The **Horizontal** and **Vertical** properties enable and disable scrolling in the horizontal and vertical directions, respectively. By default, they are both enabled. The **Movement Type** property determines how the Scroll View moves at its boundaries.

There are three **Movement Type** options: **Unrestricted, Elastic,** and **Clamped.** These **Movement Types** only affect the way the scrollable area reacts to being dragged by the scrollable area and to the scroll wheel on the mouse. You will not note a difference between these three **Movement Types** when you are using the Scrollbars. All **Movement Types** will behave exactly like the **Clamped Movement Type** when the Scrollbars are used to move the `Content`.

When **Unrestricted** is selected as the **Movement Type** the player can drag the scrollable area endlessly without restriction to the Rect Transform of `Content`. The **Elastic** and **Clamped Movement Types** will stop moving the `Content` once the edges of Rect Transform of `Content` have been reached. However, when **Unrestricted** is selected as a **Movement Type**, the player can continue to drag or use the scroll wheel. If there is a Mask on the **Viewport**, this can result in the player dragging all content outside of the viewable space. If the player moves the content with the scrollbars, however, they will be restricted to the bounds of `Content`.

When **Elastic** is selected as the **Movement Type**, if the `Content` is dragged past its boundary, it will bounce *into place* once the player stops dragging. This will also bounce if the scroll wheel is used. When **Elastic** is selected, the subproperty **Elasticity** becomes accessible. The **Elasticity** property determines the intensity of the bounce.

When **Clamped** is selected as the **Movement Type**, the `Content` will not be draggable past its boundary and no bounce will occur.

Properties concerning scrolling speed

Selecting the **Inertia** property will make the Content continue to move after the player has stopped dragging. **Inertia** is only apparent when the scroll area is dragged and doesn't affect `Content` movement initialized by the Scrollbars or mouse scroll wheel. When **Inertia** is selected, the **Deceleration Rate** subproperty becomes accessible. The **Deceleration Rate** property determines when the `Content` will stop moving after the player has ceased dragging. A **Deceleration Rate** of 0 will stop the `Content` the instant the player stops dragging, and a **Deceleration Rate** of 1 will never stop. By default, **Deceleration Rate** is set to 0.135.

The **Scroll Sensitivity** property determines how far the Content will move with each turn of the scroll wheel. The higher the number, the further the content will move with a turn, making it appear to move more quickly.

> If you want to disable the use of the mouse scroll wheel for the Scroll View, set **Scroll Sensitivity** to 0.

Properties of the Scrollbars

You can set properties for the way your horizontal and vertical scrollbars react separately. The **Horizontal Scrollbar** and **Vertical Scrollbar** properties assign the **Scrollbar** components of the UI Scrollbars you wish to use for each. By default, these are assigned the Scrollbar Horizontal child and Scrollbar Vertical child, respectively.

> If you only want to use drag on the Scroll View area and don't want scrollbars, you can simply set the **Horizontal** and **Vertical Scrollbar** properties to None or delete the Scrollbar Horizontal and Scrollbar Vertical objects from the scene.

Under each Scrollbar assignment, you can set the **Visibility** and **Spacing** properties of the respective scrollbar.

The **Scrollbar Visibility** property has three options: **Permanent, Auto Hide**, and **Auto Hide And Expand Viewport**.

When **Permanent** is selected for the **Visibility** property, the respective scrollbar will remain visible, even if it is not needed, if its corresponding movement is allowed. For example, as shown in the following screenshot, if **Horizontal** movement is allowed, and the Horizontal Scrollbar's **Visibility** is set to **Permanent**, the respective scrollbar will be visible, even though it is not necessary (no horizontal movement can be achieved):

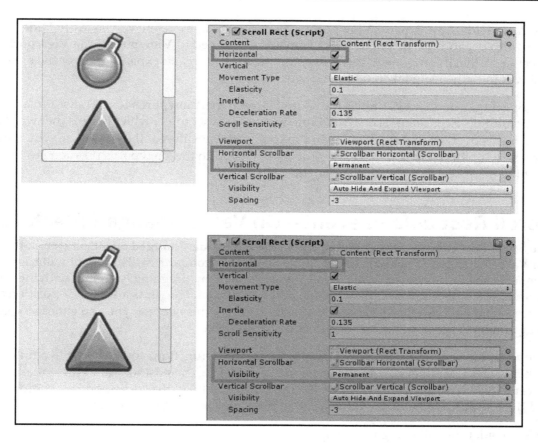

However, referencing the same image, you can see that if Horizontal movement is deactivated, setting the Horizontal Scrollbar's **Visibility** to **Permanent**, removes it from the Scroll View entirely. It is also deactivated in the **Hierarchy**.

When **Auto Hide** is selected for the **Visibility** property, the respective Scrollbar will become invisible and deactivate in the **Hierarchy** when the game is played if it is not needed (meaning that there is no movement in that direction required) or if the respective axis movement is disabled.

The **Auto Hide And Expand Viewport** property works in the same way as **Auto Hide**, but it will also expand the area of the Rect Transform assigned to **Viewport**. If the **Viewport** object has a Mask component, this will cause the Mask's area to expand to cover the area that was initially being taken up by the Scrollbar.

The **Spacing** property determines the space between the **Viewport**'s Rect Transform and the **Scrollbar**'s Rect Transform. By default, this value is set to −3, which means the two Rect Transforms overlap slightly. If you want to change the position of the Viewport, you have to do so with this property, since the properties related to the Viewport's position are disabled in its Rect Transform component.

Scroll Rect default event – On Value Changed (Vector2)

The Scroll Rect component's default event is the **On Value Changed** event, as seen in the **On Value Changed (Vector2)** section of the Scroll Rect component. This event will trigger whenever the Content area of the Scroll View is moved by dragging, scrolling with the mouse scroll wheel, or scrolling with one of the scrollbars. It accepts a Vector2 position as an argument and, as with the other events discussed in this chapter, you can choose to pass no argument, a static argument, or a dynamic argument.

If you want to send the Vector2 position of Content to a function, you'd send it to a function with a Vector2 parameter from the Dynamic Vector2 list. The position sent is essentially a percentage, with the starting position having a value of 1.0 in the corresponding coordinate and the last position having a value of 0.0 in the corresponding coordinate.

Let's consider the following function:

```
public void ScrollViewWithParameter(Vector2 value){
    Debug.Log(value);
}
```

If the previous function is selected from the Dynamic Vector2 list, the following image shows the Vector2 values printed in the **Console**:

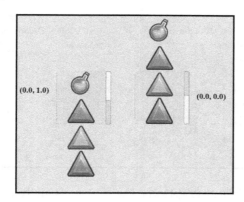

UI Dropdown and TextMeshPro – Dropdown

There are two Dropdown UI objects available, the UI Dropdown object packaged in Unity and the TextMeshPro—Dropdown object that comes with the TextMeshPro asset we discussed in Chapter 6, *Text, Images, and TextMesh Pro-Text*. Both the Dropdown objects allow the user to select from a list of options. The list becomes visible when the Dropdown is clicked on. Once an object is selected from the list, the list will collapse, making the chosen option visible within the Dropdown (if desired).

The two Dropdown options are pretty much identical in the way they work. The only difference between the two is the UI Dropdown uses UI Text objects to display text while the TextMeshPro - Dropdown uses TextMeshPro - Text objects. Due to this, I will discuss the two objects at the same time in this section. Additionally, because the two objects are identical in function, you will need to use TextMeshPro - Dropdown over the UI Dropdown if you want to include "fancy" text.

To create a UI Dropdown, select **Create | UI | Dropdown**. To create a TextMeshPro - Dropdown, select **Create | UI | TextMeshPro - Dropdown**. As you can see in the following screenshot, the two Dropdown objects have identical parent/child object relationships and names. By default, the Dropdown objects have three children: a Label, an Arrow, and a Template. The Template child is disabled by default (hence, it appears grayed out in the Hierarchy) and has multiple children.

The `Template` child and all of its children are discussed in the *Dropdown Template* section of this chapter:

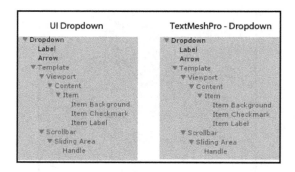

 In the following descriptions, I will discuss all Text objects as if they are UI Text objects. However, remember that the TextMeshPro - Dropdown uses TextMeshPro - Text objects.

The `Label` child is a UI Text object. By default, it displays the text within the Dropdown object that represents the selected option. As the player changes the selected option, the **Text** property of the **Text** component of `Label` changes to the appropriate option. To change the properties of the text that displays within the boxed area of the Dropdown, change the properties of the **Text** component on the `Label`. When new text replaces the text within the `Label`, it will automatically display based on the properties set by the Text component of the `Label`.

The `Arrow` child is a UI Image. Its only function is to hold the image for the arrow that (by default) appears at the right of the Dropdown. This arrow doesn't actually do anything and is simply an image. It doesn't accept inputs or change with the properties of the Dropdown component.

The background image of the Dropdown is on the main `Dropdown` parent object and not on a child named `Background`. Therefore, if you want to change the appearance of the Dropdown's background and Arrow, you change the **Source Images** of the Image components on the `Dropdown` parent and `Arrow` child, respectively. The image of the `Dropdown` only affects the rectangle that can be selected to display the drop-down menu. The background to the menu that expands outward when the player interacts with the drop-down is handled by the `Template` (discussed in the *Dropdown Template* section).

Dropdown Template

Before we discuss the various properties of the Dropdown component, let's look more closely at the Dropdown's **Template**.

The child of Dropdown named Template allows you to set the properties of the "items" that will appear as options in the drop-down menu. It also allows you to set the properties of the background of the menu and the Scrollbar that will appear if the list expands past the viewable area of the drop-down menu.

Remember that the Template child is disabled by default. Enabling the Template (by selecting the checkbox in its **Inspector**) will display the Template in the scene.

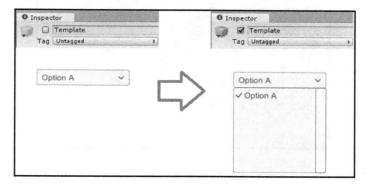

 You can actually leave this permanently enabled in your Editor, because once you enter **Play** mode, it will hide as it is supposed to.

If you look closely at the parent/child relationships of the Template within the **Hierarchy**, you'll note that it is simply a UI Scroll View object with a one Scrollbar:

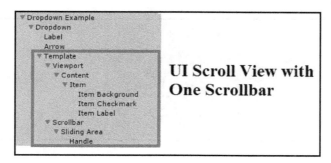

Viewing the **Inspector** of the `Template` GameObject, shows that it, in fact, is just a UI `Scroll View` object, as it has a **Scroll Rect** component attached to it with no **Horizontal Scrollbar** assigned:

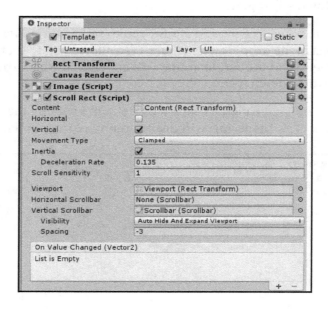

The `Content` of the `Template` Scroll View object has a single child named `Item`. `Item` has three children: `Item Background`, `Item Checkmark`, and `Item Label`. If you look at the **Inspector** of `Item`, you'll see that it is a just a UI Toggle and has the same children and properties as the UI Toggles discussed at the beginning of this chapter.

So, all `Template` is a Scroll View with a single Scrollbar and with a single Toggle as its `Content`! It looks way more complicated initially, but after you break down what the individual pieces are, you'll realize that it's just a combination of a few of the UI items we have already discussed!

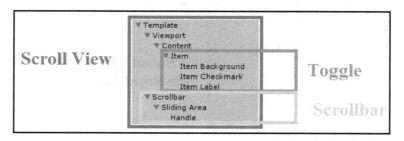

When working with the Dropdown `Template`, if you want to change the visual properties and the settings, just remember the breakdown shown in the preceding image, and the prospect of editing it will seem a lot less daunting.

Every item option you set to appear within the Dropdown will follow the exact same visual properties of those you set for the `Item` Toggle.

The Dropdown component

Now that we've broken down the `Template`, we can look at the properties of the **Dropdown** component.

The parent `Dropdown` object has a **Dropdown** (TMP_Dropdown for TextMeshPro - Dropdown) component. It has all the properties common to the other interactable UI objects, along with a few that are exclusive to Dropdowns:

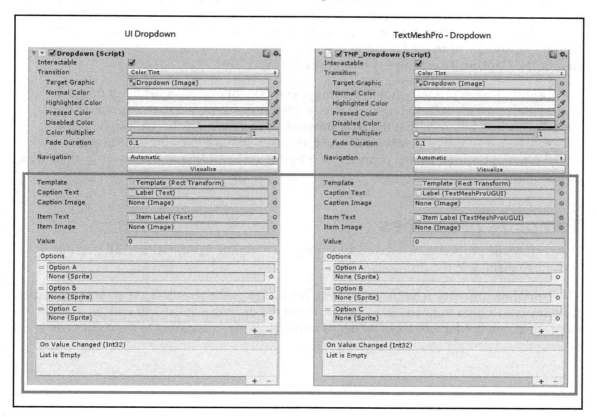

As you can see from the preceding image, the properties on the UI Dropdown and TextMeshPro - Dropdown are nearly identical. The only difference is the Text objects in are standard UI Text objects in the UI Dropdown and are TextMeshPro - Text objects in the TextMeshPro - Dropdown.

The Dropdown component is actually super powerful. It handles all interactions with the Dropdown menu and will switch text displays, open and close the dropdown, and move around the checkbox within the dropdown. It even adds a scrollbar and handle to allow the dropdown menu to have a really long list. The only thing that has to be coded by you is how to interpret the property the player selected.

Caption properties

There are two properties related to the **caption** or the option that is currently selected.

The **Caption Text** property references the Text component of the GameObject that will display the currently selected option's text. By default, this is the Text component of the `Label` child. The **Caption Text** is optional, so if you do not want the currently selected option displayed within the Dropdown area (and only within the Dropdown list), simply change the **Caption Text** property to `None (Text)`.

The **Caption Image** property holds the Image component of the GameObject that will display the currently selected option's image. Nothing is assigned to this property by default and, you will note that the **Dropdown** does not have a child that can hold the Image. To have an image display with the text, you will have to create a UI Image and assign it to the **Caption Image** property. It is best that the UI Image you create is created as a child of the Dropdown.

Template properties

There are three properties related to assigning the template's properties to all possible options to display in the drop-down list.

The **Template** property references the Rect Transform of the template. As stated previously, the template defines the way each option within the drop-down list will look as well as how the drop-down holder will look. By default, this property is assigned to the child `Template` object.

The **Item Text** property references the **Text** component of the GameObject that holds the text of the item template. By default, the **Text** component on the `Item Label` (child of the `Item`) is assigned to this property.

The **Item Image** property references the **Image** component of the GameObject that holds the image of the item template. By default, this property is unassigned, similar to the **Caption Image**. Just as with the **Caption Image**, to use this property, a UI Image will need to be created and assigned to this property. If you create one, ensure that you add it as a child of `Item` within the `Template` child to avoid confusion.

Option properties

The **Value** property represents which option is currently selected. The options are in a list, and the number in the **Value** property represents the currently selected option's index within the list. Since the options are represented by their indices, the first option has a **Value** of 0 (not 1).

The **Options** property lists out all the options within the **Dropdown** menu. Within the list, each option has a text string and sprite (optional). All strings and sprites within this list will automatically swap into the correct component properties of the children of `Dropdown`, based on the properties of the **Dropdown** component. So, you will not have to write any code to ensure that these items display appropriately when the player interacts with the Dropdown.

By default, the **Options** list contains three options. However, you can add or subtract options by selecting the plus and minus sign at the bottom of the list. You can also rearrange the options within the list by dragging and dropping the options' handles (two horizontal lines). Note that rearranging the options in the list will change their indices within the list and then change the **Value** they send to the **Dropdown** component.

Dropdown default event – On Value Changed (Int32)

The Dropdown component handles all interactions with the Dropdown menu itself. The only thing that has to be coded by you is how to interpret the option the player selected.

The Dropdown component's default event is the **On Value Changed** Event, as seen in the **On Value Changed (Int32)** section of the **Dropdown** component. This event will trigger whenever a new option is selected by the player. It accepts an integer as an argument and, as with the other events discussed in this chapter, you can choose to pass no argument, a static argument, or a dynamic argument.

If you want to send the index of the option selected (or the value of the **Value** property) to a function, you'd send it to a function with a `Int32` parameter from the **Dynamic int** list. Refer to the *Creating a Dropdown Menu with Images* example at the end of the text for an implementation of this.

UI Input Field

The UI Input Field provides a space in which the player can enter text.

To create a UI Input Field, select **Create | UI | Input Field**. By default, the `InputField` GameObject has two children: a `Placeholder` and a `Text` object.

The `Placeholder` child is a UI Text object that represents the text displayed before the player has input any text. Once the player begins entering text, the Text component on the `Placeholder` GameObject deactivates, making the text no longer visible. By default, the text displayed by the `Placeholder` is **Enter text...**, but the text being displayed as well as its properties are easily changed by affecting the properties on the **Text** component of the `Placeholder`.

The `Text` child is a UI Text object that displays the text the player inputs. Setting the properties on the `Text` object's **Text** component will change the display of the text entered by the player.

`InputField` contains an **Image** component. If you want to change the appearance of the input box, change the **Source Image** of the **Image** component on the `InputField`.

Input Field component

The parent `InputField` object has a **Input Field** component. It has all the properties common to the interactable UI objects along with a few that are exclusive to Input Fields:

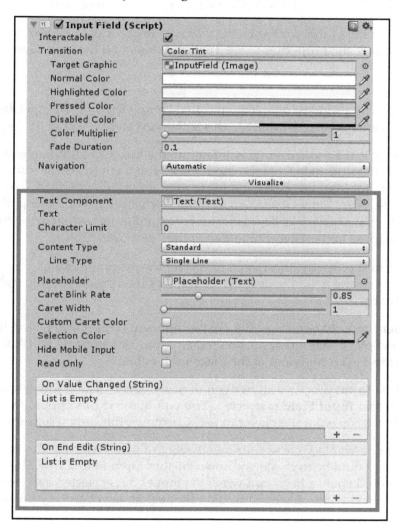

Properties of entered text and onscreen keyboards

Many of the properties within the **Input Field** component affect the text that displays within the Input Field. Due to some of the properties having a lot of options and information pertaining to them, I will discuss them slightly out of order.

Remember that to change the visual style of the entered text, you need to change the properties of the **Text** component on the Text GameObject.

The **Text** Component property references the Text component of the GameObject that will displays player's entered text. By default, this is the **Text** component of the Text child.

The **Text** property is the text currently entered into the Input Field. When you are attempting to retrieve the data from the Input Field, you want to get the information from this property and not from the **Text** component on the Text GameObject. The Text component on the Text GameObject will only store what is currently being displayed. So, if the text is displaying as asterisks because it's a password or has scrolled, the full and correct text will not be stored in the **Text** component of the Text GameObject.

The **Character Limit** property allows you to specify the maximum number of characters the player can enter into the field. Leaving the **Character Limit** property set to 0 allows unlimited text entry.

The **Placeholder** property references the **Text** component of the GameObject that displays the text when the player has either not entered anything or has cleared all entered text. By default, this is the **Text** component of the **Placeholder** child.

The **Hide Mobile Input** property allows you to override the default mobile keyboard that pops up when a text **Input Field** is selected. You would select this option if you have your own keyboard that you want the player to use. Currently, this only works for iOS devices.

If you wanted to use your own keyboard on an Android device, your best bet would be to create your own custom input field script. The script would show a keyboard when the input box is selected and then change the text within the box based on the custom keyboard key presses.

The **Read Only** property makes the text within the **Input Field** static and uneditable by the player. The player can still select the text to copy and paste it when this property is activated.

When the **Read Only** property is selected, the text displayed by the Input Field can still be edited via code by accessing the **Text** property on the Input Field component. However, changing the **Text** property on the **Text** component of the Text GameObject, will not change the displayed text.

Content Types

The **Content Type** property determines the types of characters that will be accepted by the Input Field. On devices that display keyboards on screen, it also affects the keyboard that the display by the device when the input field is selected. If the desired keyboard is not available, the default keyboard will be displayed. For example, if the device does not have a numbers-only keyboard, it will display the default keyboard. For more detailed explanations of each keyboard and character validations that come with these Content Types, refer to the *Keyboard Types* and *Character Validation Options* sections.

The possible options are **Standard, Autocorrected, Integer Number, Decimal Number, Alphanumeric, Name, Email Address, Password, Pin,** and **Custom**.

The **Standard** option allows any character to be entered. Note, however, that characters not available for the entered text's font will not display.

The **Autocorrected** option works like the **Standard** option, but on devices with onscreen keyboards (particularly touchscreen keyboards), it allows the device's autocorrect functionality to automatically override words based on its own autocorrecting algorithms.

The **Integer Number** option allows only integer values (positive and negative numbers without decimals). The player will be restricted from entering more than one negative symbol. The **Decimal Number** option works similarly, except that it also accepts decimal points. The player will be restricted from entering more than one decimal point. On devices with onscreen keyboards (particularly mobile devices), the numeric keyboard will appear rather than the standard keyboard with these two options.

The **Alphanumeric** option only allows letters (uppercase and lowercase) along with numbers and input. Mathematical symbols and punctuation, including negative numbers and decimal points (periods), are not accepted.

The **Name** option will automatically capitalize each new word entered within the field. The player has the option to lowercase the first letter of a word by deleting the letter and re-entering it lowercased.

The **Email Address** option will allow the player to enter an email address. It will also restrict the player from entering more than one @ symbol or two consecutive periods (dots/decimals).

The **Password** option allows letters, numbers, spaces, and symbols entered in the field. When the player enters text into a Password Input Field, the entered text will be hidden from view and displayed as asterisks (*).

The **Pin** option allows only integer numbers (no decimals) to be entered. Negative numbers are accepted. The text entered by the player in a field with the **Pin Content Type** will be hidden in the same way the **Password** option hides the player input. On an onscreen keyboard device, the numeric keyboard will be displayed with the **Pin** option.

The final option, **Custom**, gives you the most control of the type of input. When selected new properties appear in the **Inspector** allowing you to select the **Line Type**, **Input Type**, **Keyboard Type**, and **Character Validation**.

Line Types

The **Line Type** option is available with the **Standard**, **Autocorrect**, and **Custom** options for **Content Type**. There are three **Line Type** options: **Single Line**, **Multi Line Submit**, and **Multi Line New Line**. All other **Content Types** are automatically restricted to **Single Line** types. If the player is allowed to enter more text than the Input Field's visible area can display (meaning the **Character Limit** property does not restrict it to the visible space), the text will scroll based on the **Line Type** selected.

The **Single Line** option only allows the entered text to be displayed on one line. If the text exceeds the visible horizontal space, the text will scroll horizontally. If the player hits the *Enter* key, the Input Field acts as if the text has been "submitted".

The **Multi Line Submit** and **Multi Line New Line** options allow the text to overflow vertically if it exceeds the visible horizontal space and scroll vertically if the text exceeds the visible vertical space. The difference between the two options is what happens when the *Enter* key is hit: **Multi Line Submit** will "submit" the text and **Multi Line New Line** will start a new line.

Input Types

When the **Custom Content Type** is selected, you have the option to select from three Input Types: **Standard, Autocorrect**, and **Password**.

 Selecting these various **Input Types** does not change the keyboard or provide any validation, like the similarly named **Content Types**. For example, the **Password Input Type** will accept the Enter key as a new line with **Multi Line New Line** and display it as an asterisk in the field, but accept it as a new line in the actual data stored in the **Text** property.

The **Standard** option does not put any special circumstances on the type of input.

The **Autocorrect** option applies platforms with onscreen keyboards that have built-in autocorrect functionality. This option allows the device's autocorrect to change the text as it sees fit.

The **Password** option will display the text as asterisks.

Keyboard Types

When the **Custom Content Type** is selected, you have the option to select from the **Keyboard Types**. On devices with on-screen keyboards, this property allows you to select which keyboard will display when the Input Field is selected.

The possible options are **Default, ASCII Capable, Numbers And Punctuation, URL, Number Pad, Phone Pad, Name Phone Pad, Email Address, Nintendo Network Account, Social, and Search**.

If the keyboard selected is not available on the target device, the device's default keyboard will display.

The **Default** option displays the device's default (letters) keyboard. On most devices, this keyboard only displays letters, the *Space* key, *Backspace* key, and *Return* (Enter) key. When this option is selected, the player will have the ability to switch to the keyboard with numbers and punctuation keys.

For example, the iOS English default keyboard and numbers and punctuation keyboard can easily be switched between, as shown:

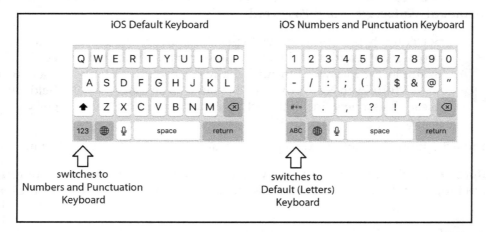

The **ASCII Capable** option displays the device's keyboard with standard ASCII keys. This option is available to restrict the keyboard to those of English and similar language keyboards. This keyboard is also a letters keyboard, and the option to switch to the numbers and punctuation keyboard is available. For example, the iOS ASCII keyboard is shown in the preceding diagram, as it is the same as the default English keyboard.

The **Numbers And Punctuation** option opens the device's numbers and punctuation keyboard with the option to switch to the "letters" keyboard. For example, the iOS numbers and punctuation keyboard is shown in the preceding diagram.

The **URL Keyboard** option brings up the device's URL keyboard. This keyboard has a *Period* key, *Forward Slash* key, and *.com* key in place of the *Space* Key. For example, the following image shows the iOS URL keyboard and its numbers/punctuation form. Note that the URL keyboard's numbers/punctuation form is not the same as the numbers and punctuation form that accompanies the default/ASCII keyboard:

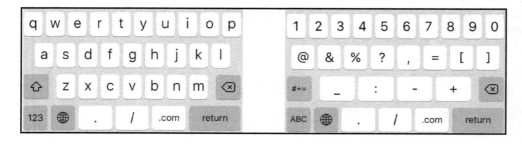

The **Number Pad** option displays the device's keyboard with numbers (*0-9*) and (usually) a *Backspace* key. This keyboard is used for pin numbers, so it does not allow alternate characters. For example, the following image shows the iOS number pad keyboard:

The **Phone Pad** option displays the device's keyboard with the same keys as the number pad keyboard, but it will also include keys for the asterisk and hash sign (pound sign). For example, the following image shows the iOS phone pad keyboard and its symbol display:

The **Name Phone Pad** option displays the device's "letters" keyboard and can switch to the phone pad keyboard. For example, the following image shows the iOS name phone pad keyboard's two views:

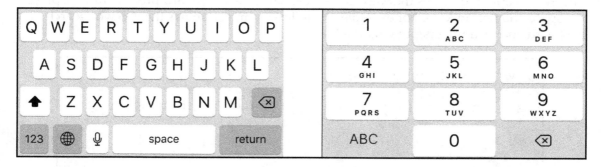

The **Email Address** option shows the device's email keyboard. The email keyboard has prominently displays the @ key and the period key as well as other common email address symbols. For example, the following image shows the iOS email keyboard and its numbers/punctuation form:

The **Social Keyboard** option displays the device's social keyboard. This keyboard prominently displays common social networking keys such as the @ key and the # key. For example, the following image shows the iOS "Twitter" keyboard and its numbers/punctuation form. On the iOS device, this keyboard is specifically called the twitter keyboard, but it displays on other social networking apps such as Instagram:

The **Search** option displays the web search keyboard. This keyboard prominently displays the space and period keys. For example, the following image shows the iOS web search keyboard and its numbers/punctuation form:

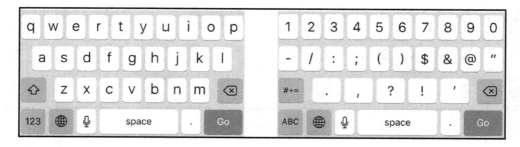

You can view a list of all the keyboard types available on iOS at `https://developer.apple.com/documentation/uikit/uikeyboardtype`.

You can view a list of all input types (not just keyboard, but they are included in the list) available on Android at `https://developer.android.com/reference/android/widget/TextView.html#attr_android:inputType`.

The **Nintendo Network Account** option displays the keyboard specific to the Nintendo Network Account. This keyboard is specific to the Wii U.

Unity's documentation states that this option is explicitly for the WiiU and no other Nintendo device; however, this option was added to Unity 2017, and I personally find it odd that the functionality would be added for a device that was essentially obsolete when implemented. Due to this, I think it may be possible that this option may eventually work with the Nintendo Switch as well. I do not have any way to verify this hunch at the time, though, so it's very likely that you will never use this option.

Character Validation options

When the **Custom Content Type** is selected, you have the option to select which type of **Character Validation** you would like to use. This option will restrict the type of characters that can be entered in the Input Field. If the player attempts to enter a character that does not meet the restrictions, no character will be inserted in the Input Field.

The possible options are **None, Integer, Decimal, URL, Alphanumeric, Name**, and **Email Address**.

Character Validation only checks each individual character being entered to see whether it is allowed within the field. It does not check the entire string to see whether the string itself is valid. For example, if **Email Address** is selected, it will not check whether it is actually in the format of an email address. That type of validation will have to be accomplished via code.

The **None** option does not perform any character validations, allowing any character to be entered into the Input Field with any formatting.

The **Integer** option allows any positive or negative integer value to be entered. This restricts the input to only allowing the digits 0 through **9** and the dash (negative symbol). The input is further restricted to allowing the negative symbol only as the first character entered.

The **Decimal** option has the same restriction as the **Integer** option, but it also allows a single decimal point to be entered.

The **Alphanumeric** option only allows English letters (a through z) and the digits 0 through 9. Capital and lowercase letters are permitted; the negative symbol and decimal point are not accepted.

The **Name** option allows characters typically found in names and provides formatting. It allows letters, spaces, and an apostrophe ('). It also enforces capitalization of the first character in the string and every character that comes after a space. A space cannot follow an apostrophe, and a space cannot follow another space. Only one apostrophe is allowed in the string. The letters are not restricted to just a-z as with the **Alphanumeric** option. Any Unicode letter is permitted.

 For a list of all allowable Unicode letters, check out the remarks on the `Char.IsLetter` method in .Net at https://msdn.microsoft.com/en-us/library/system.char.isletter(v=vs.110).aspx.

The **Email Address** option allows characters that are allowed within an email address and enforces a few formatting rules. It is significantly less restrictive in the types of characters that can be entered that the other validation options. The following characters are allowed:

- Lowercase and capital English letters (a through z)
- Digits 0-9
- The following punctuation marks and special symbols:

Symbol name	Character
at sign	@
dot/period	.
question mark	?
exclamation point	!
hyphen	-
underscore	_

apostrophe	'
backtick	`
tilde	~
open and close braces	{ and }
vertical bar	|
caret	^
asterisk	*
plus sign	+
equal sign	+
forward slash	/
hash sign/pound sign	#
dollar sign	$
percent	%
ampersand	&

Spaces are not allowed, only one @ symbol is allowed in the string, and a dot cannot follow another dot.

 Even though a dot as the first character of an email address is not valid, the **Email Address Character Validation** option does not restrict it from being the first character entered in the Input Field.

Properties of the caret and selection

A **caret** (also known as a **text insertion cursor**) is a vertical bar used to represent where text will be inserted when typed. When the game is playing, a third child is automatically added to InputField named InputField Input Caret. When the Input Field is selected, the caret becomes visible.

The properties discussed in this section affect the look of the caret as well as the look of text if it is selected (or highlighted) using the caret.

The **Caret Blink Rate** property determines how quickly the caret will blink. The number assigned to this property represents how many times the caret will blink per second. The default value is 0.85.

The **Caret Width** property determines how thick the caret is in pixels. The default value is 1.

When the **Custom Caret Color** property is selected, a secondary property, **Caret Color**, becomes available. You then have the option to change the color of the caret. Unless **Custom Caret Color** is selected and the **Caret Color** is changed, the caret will be a dark grey color.

When the caret is dragged across characters within the Input Field, the characters will be selected (or highlighted). The **Selection Color** property determines the color of the selected text.

Input field default events – On Value Changed (String) and On End Edit (String)

The Input Field component has two default events. The first default event is the **On Value Changed** Event, as seen in the **On Value Changed (String)** section of the Input Field component. This event will trigger whenever the text within the Input Field is changed. It accepts a string as an argument, and its use of the argument works in the same way as the **On Value Changed** events from UI components discussed earlier in this chapter. If you want to pass a parameter to the function, you can select the function from either the **Static Parameters** list or from the **Dynamic string** list, depending on how or if you want an argument passed to the function:

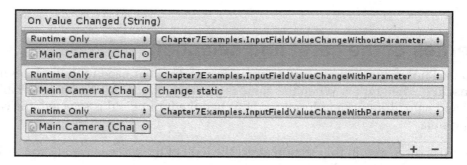

On Value Changed Events on Input Field Example in the Chapter7Text Scene

If you want to constantly check what the player is entering in the Input Field, you would use the third setup shown in the preceding image, which selected a function with a parameter from the **Dynamic string** list.

The second default event is the `On End Edit` event, as seen in the **On End Edit (String)** section of the Input Field component. This event fires whenever the player completes editing the text. This completion is confirmed by the player either clicking outside of the Input Field (so that the Input is no longer selected) or by submitting the text.

It accepts a `string` as argument and, as with the other events discussed in this chapter, you can choose to pass no argument, a static argument, or a dynamic argument. The following image shows the setup for all three options:

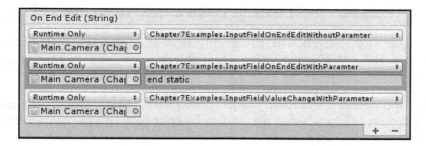

On End Edit Events on Input Field Example in the Chapter7Text Scene

If you want to have the `On End Edit` event called when the *Enter* key is hit, use either the **Single Line** or **Multi Line Submit** options for the **Line Type**.

TextMeshPro – Input Field

The TextMeshPro - Input Field is very similar to the UI Input Field. When added to the scene, you'll see it looks nearly identical, except that the placeholder text has a different font. The UI Input Field uses an Arial font by default, while the TextMeshPro - Input Field uses Liberation Sans.

To create a UI Input Field, select **Create | UI | TextMeshPro - Input Field**. By default, `TextMeshPro - InputField GameObject` has a child named `Text Area`, which has two children: a `Placeholder` and a `Text` object. You will observe that it is slightly different in setup than the UI Input Field.

The `Text Area` GameObject contains a Rect Transform component and a Rect Mask 2D component. The `Text Area` ensures that the text does not appear outside of a specified area, as shown by the highlighted area in the following image. If you wanted to change the size of this area, you would change the properties on the Rect Transform component:

The `Placeholder` and `Text` children are simply TextMeshPro - Text objects. You can find more information about the TextMeshPro - Text objects in `Chapter 6`, *Text, Images, and TextMesh Pro-Text*.

TextMeshPro - InputField contains an Image component. If you want to change the appearance of the input box, change the **Source Image** of the **Image** component on the `TextMeshPro - InputField` parent.

TMP_Input Field component

The parent `TextMeshPro - InputField` object has a **TMP_Input Field** component. It has all the properties common to the interactable UI objects, many of the same properties of the standard UI Input Field, and a few that are exclusive to TextMeshPro - Input Fields. This section will not discuss the properties that TextMeshPro - Input Fields share with UI Input Fields since they were discussed in the previous section, and we will only discuss those that are exclusive to it, as follows:

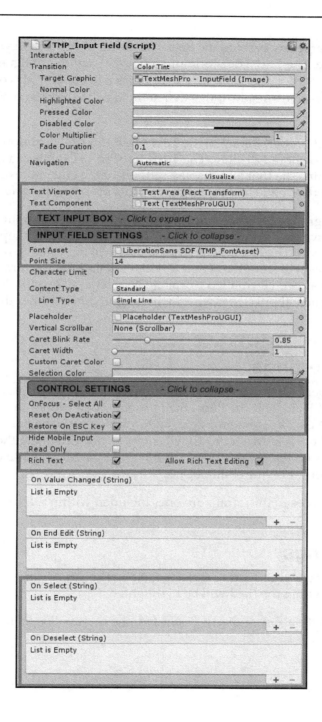

The **Text Viewport** property is set to the Rect Transform of the area in which the entered text should be visible. The Rect Transform of `Text Area` child is assigned to this property, by default. As stated earlier, the `Text Area` child has a Rect Mask 2D component that stops text from becoming visible outside of the area defined by the Rect Transform component of the `Text Area`.

The **Text Component** property is set to the Text Mesh Pro UGUI component of the object in which the entered text should display. The TextMeshPro - Text object assigned to this property will determine the font and display settings of the entered text. The Text Mesh Pro UGUI component of the `Text` child is assigned to this property, by default.

The **Text Input Box** group can be expanded to display a large text input area. The **Text Input Box** property works the same way as the **Text** property on the Input Field component of UI Input Field objects. The text entered by the user will be stored here and can be accessed by code. This will store the actual text entered and not the formatted text. For example, if the text has been formatted to appear as asterisks (as with **Pin** and **Password Content Types**), the actual pin or password will be stored here rather than a string of asterisks.

Input Field settings

The **Font Asset** property determines the font of the various texts displayed within the TextMeshPro - Input Field, and the **Point Size** property determines the size of the text. You'll note that the `Placeholder` and `Text` children also have the **Font Asset** and **Point Size** properties on their Text Mesh Pro UGUI components. Changing the **Font Asset** and **Point Size** properties on the TextMeshPro - Input Field parent will also change the corresponding properties on the child objects.

The rest of the properties in this group are ones included within the UI Input Field.

Control settings

If the **OnFocus - Select All** property is selected, when the TextMeshPro - Input Field is selected all the text within the field will be highlighted.

If the **Reset On DeActivation** property is selected, the caret will reset to the default position at the front of the text.

If the **Restore on ESC Key** property is selected, the text will reset back to the default when the escape key is hit. The default will be either an empty string or whatever is entered in the **Text Input Box** when the scene starts.

The **Rich Text** property means that any rich text tags to be accepted, and the **Allow Rich Text Editing** property allows the user to enter rich text tags within the field.

TextMeshPro - Input Field default events – On Select (String) and On Deselect (String)

The TextMeshPro - Input Field has four default events: the **On Value Changed** Event, the **On End Edit** Event, the **On Select** Event, and the **On Deselect** Event, as shown in the **On Value Changed (String)**, **On End Edit (String)**, **On Select (String)**, and **On Deselect (String)** sections.

The first two events, the **On Value Changed** Event and the **On End Edit** Event, are the same as those presented in the UI Input Field.

The third event is the **On Select** Event. This event fires whenever the TextMeshPro - Input Field is selected. The fourth event is the **On Deselect** Event. As you would expect, the event fires whenever the TextMeshPro - Input Field is deselected. It works similar to the **On End Edit** event, except that it does not fire when the text is submitted.

As with the other events discussed in this chapter, you can choose to pass no argument, a static argument, or a dynamic argument to the **On Select** and **On Deselect** events.

Examples

This chapter has so many new items in it that I could spend the rest of this book just showing you examples! Sadly, I can't do that, so I will show you examples that I hope will be the most useful.

Making a scroll view from a pre-existing menu

The first example we'll cover will build on the UI we have been working on. To help organize the project, duplicate the Chapter6 scene that you created in the last chapter; it will automatically be named Chapter7. Open Chapter7 and complete the following example within that scene.

I want to be able to add more items to my Inventory Panel and allow the player to scroll through the items. I could create a new UI Scroll View item and update it to look like my current Inventory Panel, but that would be more hassle than it's worth. So, instead, I will convert the current Inventory Panel to a scrollable view. After it is complete, it will look as follows:

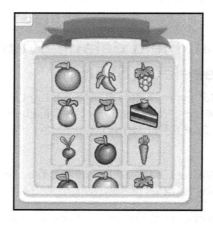

This panel can have its view adjusted by dragging the area beside the food items. I could have added a vertical scrollbar to control the movement, but I wanted to show you how simple it is to make a draggable area without one. It also just looks a little nicer without a scrollbar.

To have make the Inventory Panel scrollable, complete the following steps:

1. Right now, the Pause Panel is in the way. Let's disable it by deselecting the checkbox in its **Inspector** so that we can see the Inventory Panel more easily.

2. For the scrollable view to really work, we need more items in our inventory. Select all the children of Inventory Holder named ItemHolder and duplicate them with *Ctrl + D*. Now, with all the duplicates selected, rename them ItemHolder, so we don't have the numbered suffix added to each of them. You should now have twice as many items and in your Inventory Holder, and you should see the following:

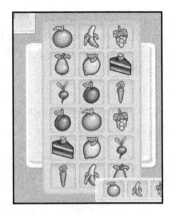

3. To get a scrollable view, we need to add a few more items to the scene that can be parents of the content we want to scroll. There is a very specific parent/child relationship you want to follow with each item having specific components on them to create a scrollable view, as demonstrated in the following diagram:

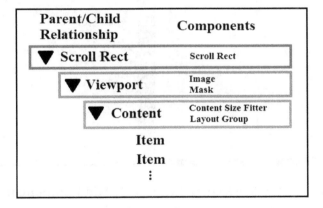

Let's start with the object that will hold the **Scroll Rect** component. Select `Inventory Panel`, right-click, and select **Create Empty**. This will create an empty object that is a child of our `Inventory Panel`. Rename the new item as `Scroll Rect` and reposition it in the **Hierarchy** so that it is below `Inventory Banner`.

4. Give `Scroll Rect` the Scroll Rect component, with **Add Component | UI | Scroll Rect**.

5. Now, let's create the item that will hold the Mask. Remember that the Mask component must be on an object that also has an **Image** component, so let's create a UI Image. Right-click on Scroll Rect and select **UI | Image** to create a child of Scroll Rect. Rename the new Image to Viewport.

6. Inventory Holder is in the way right now, so disable it momentarily.

7. Add the uiElements_38 image to the **Image** component of Viewport.

8. Adjust the Rect Transform properties of Viewport, as follows:

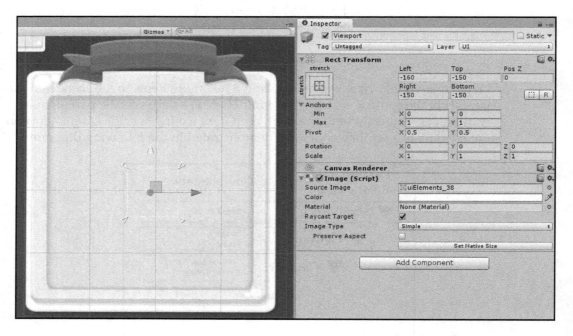

9. Give Viewport the Mask component, with **Add Component | UI | Mask**.

10. Re-enable Inventory Holder and rename it to Content.

11. Set the alpha of the **Color** property on Content to 0 so that the background is invisible. You should see the following:

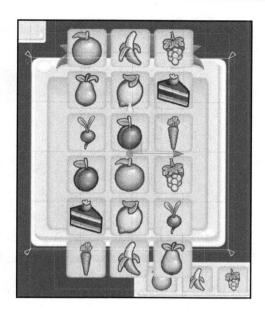

12. Now, drag `Content` in the **Hierarchy** so that it is a child of `Viewport`. Doing so should make the Mask instantly apply to the all the children of `Content`:

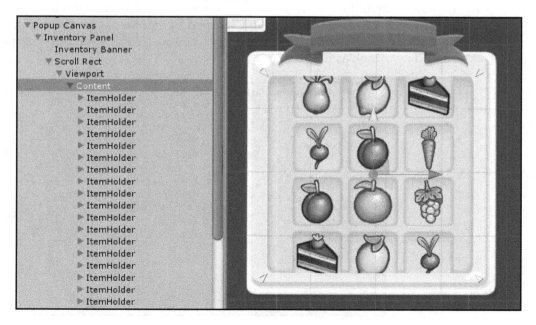

13. Position `Content` so that the food at the top of of the list appears fully within the Mask area:

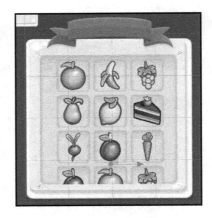

14. Now all that is left to do to have a properly functioning scrollable area is to set up the properties on the Scroll Rect component. Select `Scroll Rect` and drag `Content` and `Viewport` into their appropriate slots on the Scroll Rect component.

15. Disable **Horizontal** movement, because we only want the menu to move vertically. Set **Movement Type** to **Clamped** so that the menu doesn't "stretch and bounce" and stays within the appropriate bounds. Your Scroll Rect component should now look as follows:

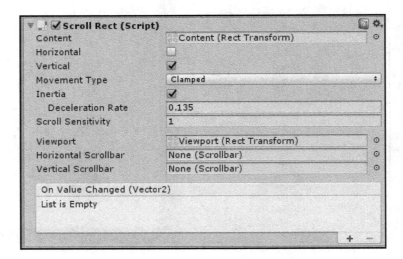

16. Re-enable the `Pause Menu` object so that our `Pause Menu` will function in the game.

If you play the game, the `Inventory Panel` should now have items that scroll when you drag beside them. Remember that you bring up the `Inventory Panel` by pressing the I key on your keyboard. As we have drag and drop functionality on our individual items, to scroll, we have to drag the area of `Content` that does not have a food item on it.

Creating a dropdown menu with images

Let's continue working in our scene and create a drop-down menu that will allow us to swap our player character between a cat and a dog. The final version will appear as follows:

Changing our selection will then change the image of the character that appears at the top of the screen.

The spritesheet containing the dog image is an asset that I've modified from free art assets found at the following:

`https://opengameart.org/content/cat-dog-free-sprites`

This is the same asset that provided us with the cat sprites.

When you want to see your UI Dropdown menu in play mode, you have to press P to bring up the `Pause Panel`. This can be kind of annoying when you just want to quickly check the layout. You can disable the automatic hiding of the `Pause Panel` momentarily by disabling the `ShowHidePanels.cs` script on the `Main Camera`. Just remember to turn it back on when you are done!

Laying out the dropdown with caption and item images

To create a UI Dropdown menu like the one shown in the previous image, complete the following steps:

1. Locate the `dogSprites.png` image provided in the `Chapter7/Sprites` folder of the source files of the text and bring it in to the `Assets/Sprites` folder of your project.

2. Slice the spritesheet by setting its **Sprite Mode** to **Multiple** and utilizing **Automatic** slicing. When you perform the **Automatic** slice, set the **Pivot** to **Bottom**.

3. Now, let's add a `UI Dropdown` to our `Pause Panel`. Right-click on the `Pause Panel` in the **Heirarchy** and select **UI | Dropdown**. Move the `Dropdown` upward in the **Hierarchy** so that it is listed right below `Pause Banner`.

4. Adjust the size and position of the `Dropdown` by settings its Rect Transform properties, as follows:

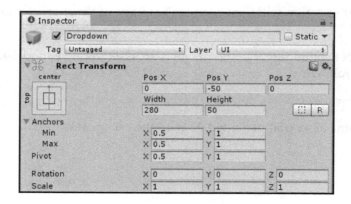

5. Your Dropdown should now appear as follows:

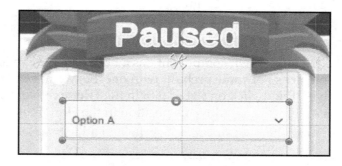

6. To change the `Dropdown` background, we need to change the **Source Image** on the Image component of the `Dropdown`. Assign the `uiElements_12` subsprite into the **Source Image**.

7. Expanding the `Dropdown` in the **Hierarchy** to view its children will reveal a child named `Arrow`. You can adjust the properties of `Arrow` to change its look and general position.

   Give the `Arrow` the `uiElements_132` sprite and adjust the Rect Transform, as illustrated:

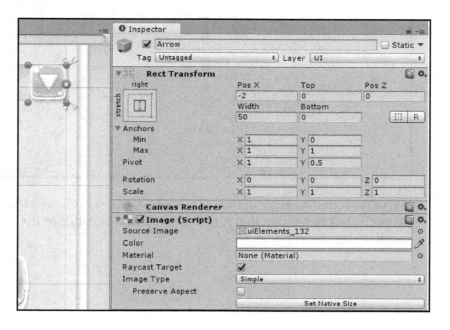

Typing 132 in the search bar of the Project view is a quick way to find the uiElements_132 image.

8. While the Dropdown component has a hookup for a caption, the UI Dropdown template does not come prebuilt with one. So, we have to manually add one in ourselves. Right-click on Dropdown in the **Hierarchy** and select **UI | Image**, to give it a child Image. Move its position in the **Hierarchy** so that it is above Label.

9. Give Image the catSprites_0 sprite and adjust its Rect Transform, as follows:

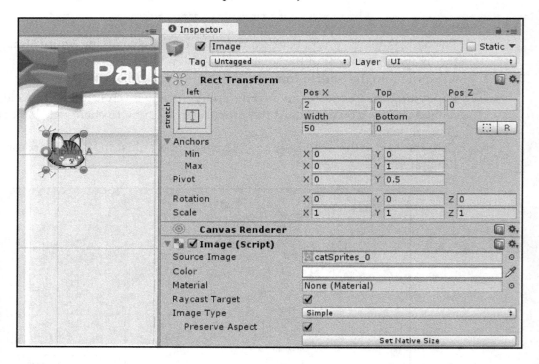

We've set it to the image of the cat so that we can see whether it is displaying properly, but remember that it will automatically change to the appropriate sprite based on the selection.

10. Now, select `Label` and adjust its Rect Transform and Text component as shown:

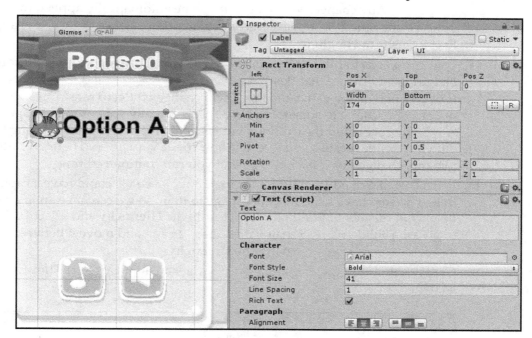

If you try to adjust the **Text**, it will revert to `Option A`, since this is driven by the Dropdown component.

11. Now that we have our caption set up the way we want it, let's work on the `Template`. Enable the `Template` object so that you can see it in the Scene and expand it in the **Hierarchy** to view all of its children.
    We won't use the `Scrollbar`, so we can leave it as it is. It will show up in the Scene view but will not be visible in Play mode, because its **Visibility** is set to **Auto Hide And Expand Viewport** in the Scroll Rect component of `Template`.

12. To change the background of the window that drops down, change the **Source Image** on Image component of `Template` to `uiElements_11`.

13. The `Item` child shows the general format to all options that will be listed in our `Dropdown`. Any changes we make to it will be automatically applied to all options when the Dropdown script populates them. Select `Item` and change its Rect Transform **Height** to 50.

14. `Content` needs to fully encapsulate the `Item`. So, change its Rect Transform **Height** to 52. Ensure that **Pos Y** is at 0.
    If you've played the game, the **Pos Y** will change on Rect Transform of `Content` from 0 to something else. This is actually supposed to happen (option A is being set behind the caption), but it's annoying when you are trying to lay out your `Item`, because you won't be able to see your `Item`. Therefore, after playing, change **Pos Y** back to 0 so that you can continue editing.

15. Just as we had to add a child Image to `Dropdown` so we could have a caption image, we too have to add a child Image to Item, so we can have an image display in the menu. Right-click on `Item` in the **Hierarchy** and select **UI | Image**, to give it a child `Image`. Rename it as `Item Image` and move it between `Item Checkmark` and `Item Label` in the **Hierarchy**.

16. Give `Item Image` the `catSprites_0` sprite and adjust its Rect Transform, as shown:

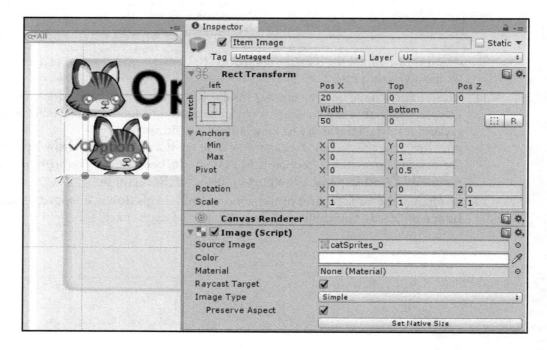

17. Select `Item Label` and adjust its Rect Transform and Text component, as follows:

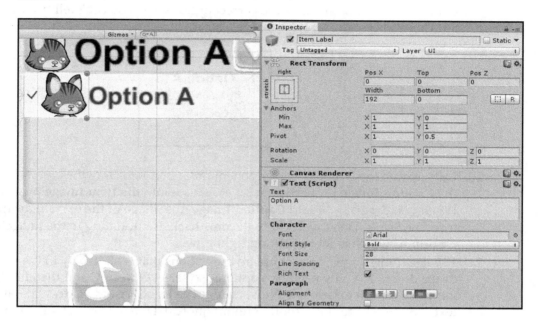

18. The last thing to do to `Item` is to remove the white background. Select `Item Background` and change the alpha on the **Color** property of the Image component to 0. Your Dropdown menu should now look as follows:

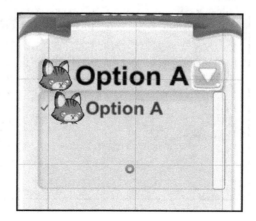

19. Now that we have set up our Dropdown visually, we need to set up the properties of the Dropdown component. If you play the game, you will see that our Dropdown doesn't have the correct options yet. You can't tell from playing it, but **Caption Image** and **Item Image** also aren't hooked up:

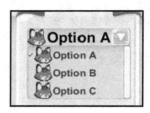

20. Let's update the Dropdown component on `Dropdown`. Drag the `Image` child into the **Caption Image** property and `Item Image` into the **Item Image** property. When you drag `Image` into **Caption Image**, the image of the cat will disappear from the Scene. Don't worry! It will come back. It's updating to the image of **Option A**, which is set to nothing right now.

21. The last thing we need to set up are the options that will display in the menu that drops down. We only need two options, so select **Option C** and then hit the minus (-) button to delete it. Now, change the text "`Option A`" to "`Cat`" and the text "`Option B`" to "`Dog`" (both without quotes). Drag `catSprites_0` in to the sprite slot under `Cat` and `dogSprites_0` into the sprite slot under `Dog`. Your Dropdown component should appear, as follows:

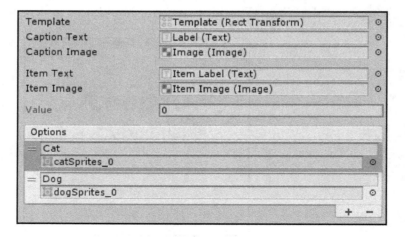

If you play the game, you will see that the dropdown now shows the appropriate list of options and the caption image and sprite update based on your selection:

Using the information from the dropdown selection

Now that our Dropdown looks the way we want it and is functioning properly, we can access the player's selection with code. We'll use the player's selection to update the player character image in the top-left corner of the screen.

To swap the player character image with the selection from the Dropdown, complete the following steps:

1. Create a new C# script in your `Assets/Scripts` folder named `PlayerCharacterSwap.cs`.

2. For us to access UI variable types, add the `UnityEngine.UI` namespace to the top of the script with the following line:

   ```
   using UnityEngine.UI;
   ```

3. We only need two variables, one to represent the `Image` that will be swapped with the selection from the Dropdown menu and one to represent the Dropdown menu. We'll attach this script to the `Dropdown` object, so we don't have to make the variable referencing it `public`. Add the following variable declarations after the namespace declarations:

   ```
   public Image characterImage;
   Dropdown dropDown;
   ```

4. Initialize the `dropDown` variable in an `Awake()` function with the `Dropdown` component attached to the object this script will be attached to:

   ```
   void Awake(){
       dropDown=GetComponent<Dropdown>();
   }
   ```

5. The default event on the Dropdown component is the `On Value Changed` event, and it accepts an integer argument. Create a public function that accepts an integer parameter with the following:

```
public void DropDownSelection(int selectionIndex){
}
```

6. The `DropDownSelection` function will get the integer value of the property **Value** from the Dropdown component. **Value** represents the index of the option currently selected within the **Options** list. If we pass the value of **Value** as an argument to the function, we can then reference it with the parameter `selectionIndex` within our script. Add the following two lines to your `DropDownSelection` function:

```
Debug.Log("player selected "
+dropDown.options[selectionIndex].text);
characterImage.sprite=dropDown.options[selectionIndex].image;
```

The first line will find the `text` on the option at the specified index in the `options` list and print it to the console.

The second line will find the `sprite` on the option at the specified index in the `options` list and change the `sprite` on the `characterImage` to that sprite.

7. We're now done with the script and can hook it up in the Unity Editor. Drag the `PlayerCharacterSwap.cs` script onto `Dropdown` to attach it. Remember, the `dropDown` variable is not `public`, because we expected to attach this script as a component to the `Dropdown`.

8. The `public` variable `characterImage` needs to be assigned. Drag the `Character` Image form the **Hierarchy** (`HUD Canvas | Top Left Panel | Character Holder | Character`) to the **Character Image** slot on the Player Character Swap component.

9. Now we need to call the **DropDownSelection** function on the **PlayerCharacterSwap.cs** script from the **On Value Changed** event on the Dropdown component. Select the plus sign (+) in the **On Value Changed (Int32)** event list to add a new **On Value Changed** event. Drag **Dropdown** from the **Heirarchy** into the object slot and select the **DropDownSelection** function from the **Dynamic int** list of the **PlayerCharacterSwap** script. The **On Value Changed (Int32)** event list should appear as follows:

That's it! Now play the game and watch the player character's image swap with the image selected from the Dropdown:

Summary

Who knew there were so many different types of interactable UI objects! Having templates for these different UI objects is incredibly helpful. Technically, they can all be built "by hand" with Buttons, Images, and Text, but that is a lot of effort you don't have to do, because Unity has done it for you.

In this chapter, we discussed the following topics:

- Applying masks to UI objects
- Implementing the UI Toggle, UI Slider, UI Scrollbar, UI Scroll View, UI Dropdown, and UI Input Field templates
- How to use the TextMeshPro-Dropdown and TextMeshPro-Input Field objects
- Hooking up the default events attached to each interactive UI item
- How to add a Scroll Rect component to a preexisting menu to make a scrollable menu

Next, we will cover using animations and particles in the UI.

8

Animations and Particles in the UI

Since we have already discussed how to create animation transitions for buttons (Chapter 5, *Buttons*), in this chapter, we'll take a look at animation transitions more thoroughly and discuss how to create animations for UI elements in a more general sense.

This chapter will demonstrate how to create animations within the UI and use Particle systems within the UI.

In this chapter, we will discuss the following topics:

- Applying animations to the various UI elements
- Displaying particle systems in front of UI elements
- Creating a pop-up window that fades in and out
- Creating a complex animation system with a State Machine and Animation Events

 As with previous chapters, all of the examples shown in this section can be found within the Unity project provided in the code bundle. They can be found within the scene labeled Chapter8Text in the Assets/Scene/ExamplesInText/Chapter8Text folder.

This chapter assumes that you have a basic understanding of Unity's Animation System and will not go into detail describing the names of the various menus and layout of the Animation Window and Animator Window. Animation Clips and Animators will be described briefly, with a focus on how they relate to UI and the implementation that will be discussed in the examples at the end of the chapter.

Even though I am assuming that you have a basic understanding of Unity's Animation System, I do want to emphasize the difference between an Animation Clip and the Animator.

When creating animations for items in Unity, you start with **Animation Clips**. An Animation Clip should represent a single distinct action or motion. So, for example, if you had a menu that performed two separate actions, bouncing and zooming, you'd make each of those actions a separate Animation Clip. Although you can have multiple things happen in a single Animation Clip, it is very important not to put multiple actions in a single clip unless they are always going to happen at the same time.

Every GameObject can have multiple Animation Clips. The **Animator** determines how all of these Animations link together. So, a Game Object's Animator will have all of its Animation Clips within it.

I wanted to make this distinction, because, in the past, I have seen projects with epic Animation Clips containing multiple actions, which should have been broken down into more simple motions.

Animation clips

The great thing about the Unity Animation System is that you can animate nearly any property of the UI. To create an Animation Clip, simply open the Animation Window (**Window** | **Animation** or *Ctrl + 6*), and with the UI element you want to animate, select **Create**:

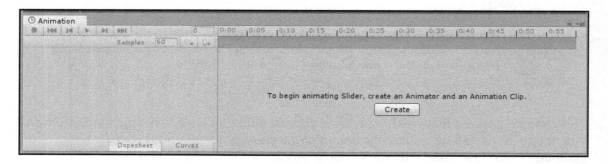

Once you do so, you'll be prompted to save the Animation Clip.

After creating the Animation Clip, you can then add any property to the clip's timeline by clicking on **Add Property**:

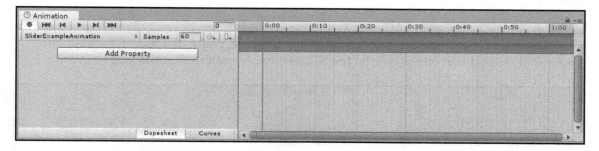

Doing so will bring up every component of the object, as well as a list of all of its children:

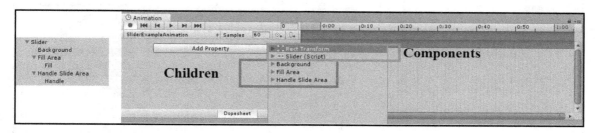

You can also view the components and children of each child:

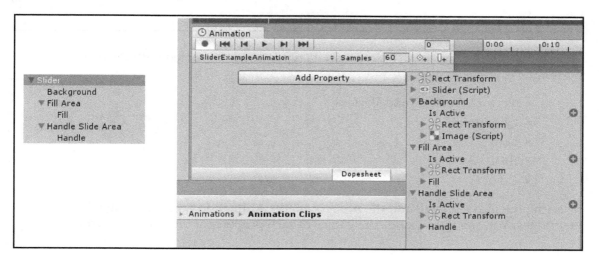

Then, you can view the components and children of those children. You can continue on in this manner until you have exhausted the list of GameObjects that are nested under the selected GameObject.

If you expand a component of GameObject or one of its children, you will then note a list of all properties of that component that can be animated. As you will notice in the following screenshot, almost every property on the **Slider** component can be animated in this way:

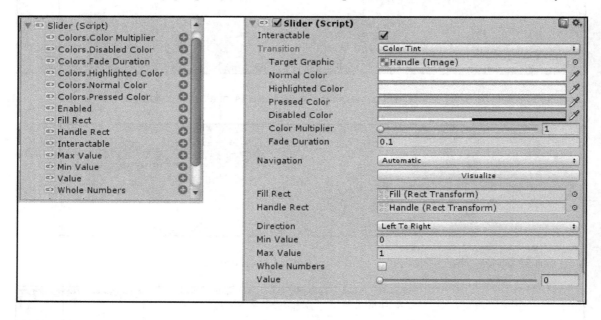

Only properties that have the following data types can be animated with the Animation System:

- Vector2, Vector3, and Vector4
- Quaternion
- bool
- float
- Color

Selecting the plus sign will add the property to the Animation timeline along with two keyframes. You can then change the values of each property at the various keyframes.

A **keyframe** is an important or "key" (hence the name) frame within an animation. It represents the start or end point of a transition within an animation.

In the preceding screenshot, the values encased in the red boxes represent the value of the property at the particular frame. Boolean values are represented by checkboxes, and float values are represented by numbers. Each type can be edited directly by selecting them.

Unity will fill in the values between the keyframes so that they change (or interpolate) on a curve. You can view the interpolation curve by selecting the **Curve Tab**.

You can watch the changes occur throughout all frames by playing the animation or scrubbing the playhead.

The **playhead** is the marker that indicates what frame is currently being displayed. "**Scrubbing** the playhead" means to drag the playhead across the timeline to view changes over individual frames.

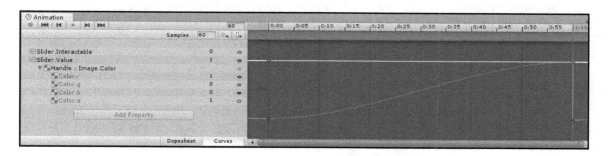

Boolean properties are interpolated on a linear curve. All other properties (since they are combination of floats) are interpolated along an ease-in-out curve. You can adjust these by adjusting the handles of the tangents at the keyframes by right-clicking on the keyframe.

Often times, these ease-in-out curves will cause your UI to appear *bouncy*, and adjusting the interpolation curve can remove that bounce. For example, animating an object between two points may make the object go past the destination point momentarily due to the ease-in-out nature of the default interpolation curve.

Animation Events

One of my favorite things about Animation Clips is the ability to add Animation Events to frames on the timeline. Animation Events allow you to call functions that exist on the GameObject at specified frames. They are represented by white *flags* above the timeline, and hovering over them will show the name of the function called by the Animation Event.

An Animation Event can only call a function that exists somewhere on the GameObject the Animation Clip is attached to. The function can be public or private and can also have a parameter. The parameter can be of the following types:

- `float`
- `int`
- `string`
- An object reference
- An `AnimationEvent` object

You can add an Animation Event to the Animation Clip's timeline by right-clicking on the area above the frame in which you wish to place the Animation Event and clicking on either the **Add Animation Event** or **Add Event** button. Selecting the Add Event button will add the Animation Event wherever the playhead currently rests.

You can delete the Animation Event by selecting the white flag and clicking on **Delete**, and you can move it by clicking on it and dragging it.

The appearance of the Animation Event's Inspector depends on whether the Animation Clip is attached to a GameObject and whether the GameObject is currently selected. The two appearances are shown in the following screenshot:

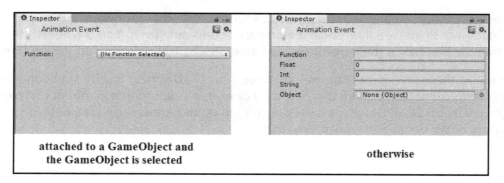

attached to a GameObject and the GameObject is selected | otherwise

If the Animation Clip is attached to a GameObject and the GameObject is selected, a drop-down menu will appear with a list of all available functions. If the selected function has a parameter, then options concerning the parameter will be made available (take a look at the preceding screenshot). Otherwise, the name of the function and the parameters to pass will have to be entered manually.

Animator Controller

Whenever an Animation Clip is created for an object, an **Animator** is automatically created for it (if one does not already exist). An Animator component is also automatically added to the object. When we created the `SliderExampleAnimation` Animation Clip on the `Slider` in the preceding section, an Animator named `Slider` was created and the Animator component was attached to the `Slider`:

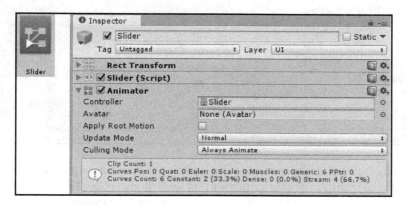

An Animator is needed to play Animation Clips because it determines when Animation Clips are played.

An Animator is a type of decision tree known as a **state machine**. It holds a collection of **states**. States are essentially "statuses at a moment in time." The **current state** of a state machine would be a representation of what is happening at this moment. So, for example, if there was a state machine describing my actions and behaviors, my *current state* would be *typing on the keyboard*. My state machine would have other states that I could eventually transition to, such as *sleeping* or *crying about approaching deadlines* if certain conditions are met.

States in the Animator are represented by rectangles called **nodes**. States are connected by transitions that are represented by arrow lines. These transitions occur after either a predetermined time or a set of conditions have been met. The current state will have a blue, animated status bar on it telling you the percentage of the state that has been completed. If the current state is waiting on a transition to occur, this status bar may loop or stop in the full position until the conditions of the transition are met:

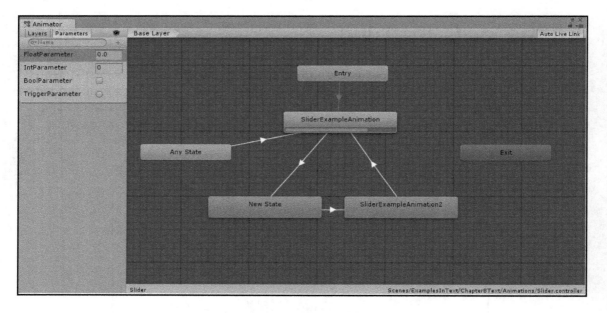

The bottom-right corner of the Animator Window displays the name of the current Animator controller as well as its folder location. This can be very helpful when you have many different Animators, as it tells you which Animator you are working with.

States can be empty or represent Animation Clips. If a state represents an Animation Clip, it will have an Animation Clip set to its **Motion** property in its **Inspector**, as with the following screenshot:

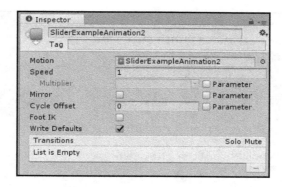

Most states will be colored gray, but those colored otherwise will represent special states. Every Animator will have an `Entry` node (green), an `Exit` node (red), and a `Any State` node (blue) within it. The first state you add to an Animator will be assigned the Default Layer State (orange). You can change the state of the Default Layer State at any time. Note that Animator Layers are discussed in a later section.

The `Entry` and `Exit` nodes essentially work as "gates" between state machines. You can have state machines within state machines, and these "gates" decide what happens after the state machine is entered and exited, respectively. So, the `Entry` node represents the instance the state machine starts, and the `Exit` node represents the instance it stops.

The `Entry` node always transitions to the Default Layer State, and you cannot define the conditions of the transition, so the transition will always happen automatically and instantly. Therefore, you can think of the Default Layer State as the *first* state that will occur when the state machine begins.

The `Any State` node is an *all encompassing* state. You use this state when you want a transition to happen, regardless of the current state. You can only transition away from the `Any State` node. Continuing with the example of a state machine that describes my behavior, I would have a transition from `Any State` to the state of *crying about approaching deadlines*, because no matter what I am currently doing, I could burst into tears if the condition "deadline is within 24 hours" is met.

As stated before, the Animator will stay on the current state until a specified amount of time has passed or a set of conditions have been met. Selecting a transition arrow will display the conditions of transition:

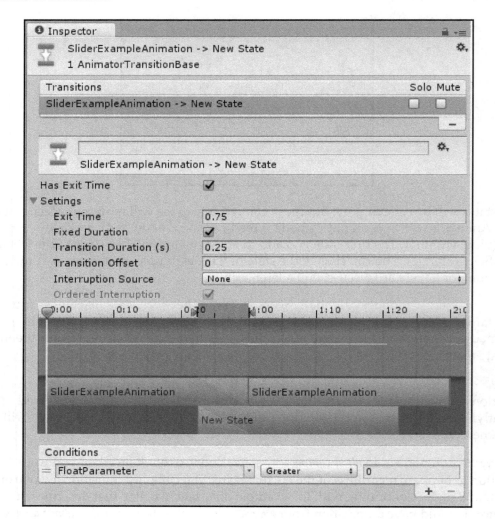

The transition from the preceding screenshot requires both a specified amount of time and a condition. The transition also isn't instantaneous and takes 0.25 to complete.

The **Conditions** that must be met for a transition to occur are set by the Animator's **Parameters**, which can be found and created in the top-left corner of the Animator Window:

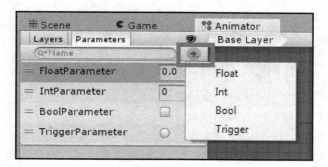

The values of these parameters can be set from scripts. There are four types of parameters: Float, Int, Bool, and Trigger. The first three are named for their value type, but a Trigger is a little less obvious. A Trigger is a Boolean parameter that instantly resets itself to False after it is used by a transition. Trigger Parameters are helpful for creating floodgate type actions where the animation has to stop and wait before it can proceed to the next state. These are preferred over Bool Parameters in instances where the states and transitions form a loop, because a Bool Parameter would have to be manually reset before the state looped back around.

When you look at the list of **Parameters**, you can tell which type they are by the value on the right. Float Parameters have decimal numbers, Int Parameters have integers, Bool Parameters have square checkboxes, and Trigger Parameters have circular radio buttons.

Since Animators are state machines, they can be used to accomplish much more than animations. Animators can be used to keep track of complex game logic. For example, I created the following state machine for a match three RPG to keep track of what was currently happening in the game. Using it to keep track of the current state of the game allowed me to restrict what the player could do based on what was happening in the game.

For example, if the enemy character was attacking, the player would not interact with the pieces on the board:

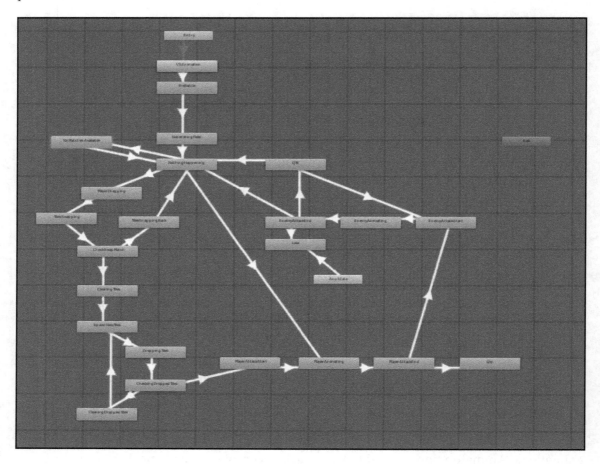

The Animator of Transition Animations

In Chapter 5, *Buttons*, we took a look at Button Animation Transitions and created a simple animation for a Button. We let the Button component automatically generate the Animator for us, but never looked at the Animator or did anything with it. Now that we've discussed Animators, let's look at the Animator of the Play Button saved in Assets/Animations:

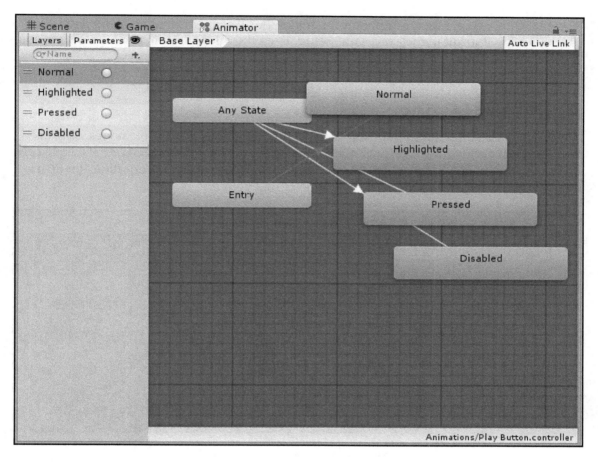

As you can see from the preceding screenshot, the Animator that was automatically generated for us isn't particularly complicated and its setup is pretty self-explanatory. It contains states to hold the following four Animation Clips: `Normal`, `Highlighted`, `Pressed`, and `Disabled`. All of the Animation Clips transition from `Any State`. Also, there are four `Trigger` Parameters: `Normal`, `Highlighted`, `Pressed`, and `Disabled`.

Automatically generating an Animator for any of the UI elements that allow for Transition Animations will result in the exact same setup. Even though this Animator is preset for you, you are free to adjust it however you see fit.

Animator layers

When using the Animator, if you have a state with transitions to multiple nodes, only one transition can occur. For example, in the following screenshot, the `ChooseAState` state can only transition to one of the other states at once, even if the transition conditions for all are met; this is true regardless the type of Parameter that you use:

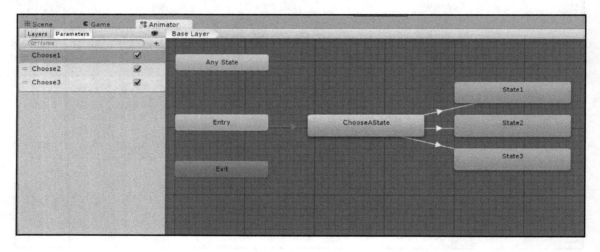

A Forking Animation example in the Chapter8Text Scene

If you want multiple animations to trigger at once, you can use Animation Layers. The following layer set up will have all three states running simultaneously:

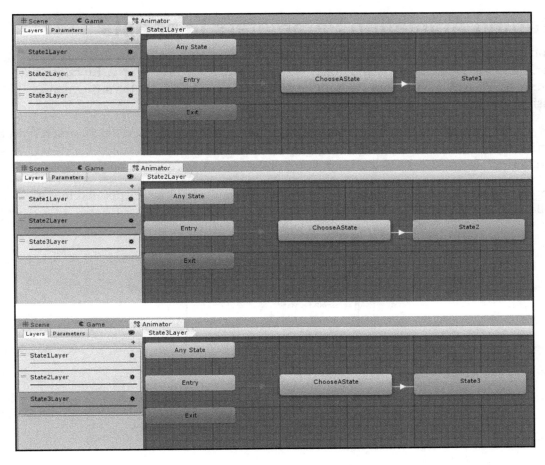

An Animation Layers example in the Chapter8Text Scene

I've found that the most common need for something like this is when you have an object made of multiple sprite sheets and you want multiple sprite sheet animations to trigger at the same time, and putting them all on the same Animation Clip doesn't make sense. For example, I've worked on a game where a 2D character had multiple interchangeable parts, and each part had its own sprite sheet animation. It was necessary to have the "idle" animation for each part start all at the same time. Since the parts could be swapped out, there were multiple combinations of parts that could be achieved, and it would not have made sense to make all the different possible idle animation combinations. It also wouldn't have made sense to give each possible part its own Animator. So, I made a layer for each body part and was able to have the individual sprite animations all play at the same time.

Setting Animation Parameters in scripts

You can set the values of the Animator Parameters via scripts using the `SetFloat()`, `SetInteger()`, `SetBool()`, and `SetTrigger()`, and `ResetTrigger()` functions of the Animator class. You reference the Animator Parameter variables by the string names assigned to them within the Animator.

To set the Animation Parameters, you first get the Animator on which the Parameters were defined; you can do this with either a public `Animator` variable or using `GetComponent<Animator>()`. Then, you call the necessary function on the `Animator`.

For example, the following script would set the Animator Parameters defined in the following screenshot:

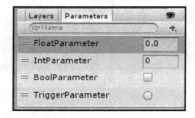

```
using System.Collections;
using System.Collections.Generic;
using UnityEngine;

public class Chapter8Examples : MonoBehaviour {
    Animator theAnimator;

    void Awake(){
        theAnimator=GetComponent<Animator>();
    }

    public void SetAnimatorParameters(){
        theAnimator.SetFloat("FloatParameter", 1.0f);
        theAnimator.SetInteger("IntParameter", 1);
        theAnimator.SetBool("BoolParameter", true);
        theAnimator.SetTrigger("TriggerParameter"); //sets to true
        theAnimator.ResetTrigger("TriggerParameter"); //sets to false
    }
}
```

The benefit of using a Trigger is that you usually don't have to reset it, as it instantly resets the moment a transition uses it. However, if you will set a Trigger and the transition is never reached, you will need to reset it using `ResetTrigger()`.

Animator behaviours

If you want to write code that fires at specific points within a state, you can use a unique class of scripts known as State Machine Behaviours. State Machine Behaviours can be added to any state node you create within the Animator. I specify "you create" because you cannot add them to the `Entry` node, `Exit` node, or `Any State` node.

You can create a new State Machine Behaviour by selecting a state and clicking on **Add Behaviour**:

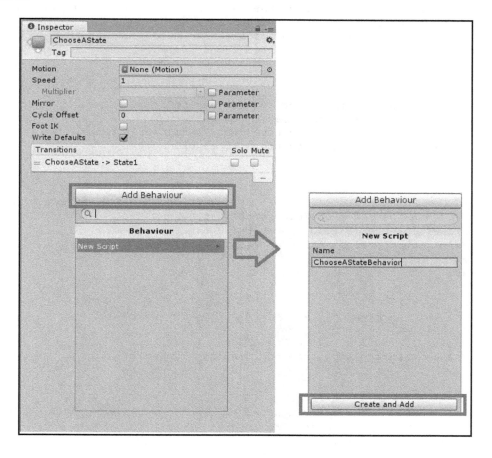

All new State Machine Behaviours created in this way are saved in the `Assets` folder.

When you open the script, it will be automatically populated with the following code:

```
using System.Collections;
using System.Collections.Generic;
using UnityEngine;

public class ChooseAStateBehavior : StateMachineBehaviour {

    // OnStateEnter is called when a transition starts and the state
    //machine starts to evaluate this state
    //override public void OnStateEnter(Animator animator,
    //AnimatorStateInfo stateInfo, int layerIndex) {
    //
    //}

    // OnStateUpdate is called on each Update frame between
    //OnStateEnter and OnStateExit callbacks
    //override public void OnStateUpdate(Animator animator,
    //AnimatorStateInfo stateInfo, int layerIndex) {
    //
    //}

    // OnStateExit is called when a transition ends and the state
    //machine finishes evaluating this state
    //override public void OnStateExit(Animator animator,
    //AnimatorStateInfo stateInfo, int layerIndex) {
    //
    //}

    // OnStateMove is called right after Animator.OnAnimatorMove().
    //Code that processes and affects root motion should be
    //implemented here
    //override public void OnStateMove(Animator animator,
    //AnimatorStateInfo stateInfo, int layerIndex) {
    //
    //}

    // OnStateIK is called right after Animator.OnAnimatorIK(). Code
    //that sets up animation IK (inverse kinematics) should be
    //implemented here.
    //override public void OnStateIK(Animator animator,
    //AnimatorStateInfo stateInfo, int layerIndex) {
    //
    //}
}
```

Note that this class is derived from StateMachineBehaviour rather than MonoBehaviour, like the scripts we attach to GameObjects.

There are a few functions prewritten in the script for you, along with descriptions on how to use them. Just as Awake(), Start(), and Update() are predefined functions for MonoBehaviour, OnStateEnter(), OnStateUpdate(), OnStateExit(), OnStateIK(), and OnStateMove() are predefined functions that call as specific times. You can delete whichever functions you don't want to use. You can also write other functions within this script, and they are not restricted to these predefined ones.

These functions can do whatever you want them to do, even set the Animator Parameters of your Animator.

I find State Machine Behaviours to be incredibly helpful, because I use state machines extensively to control the logic of my games. Earlier, in this section, I showed you a state machine I created for a match three RPG. I used multiple State Machine Behaviours to let my other scripts know when the states had changed, call functions from other scripts at specified times, and so on.

Particles in the UI

Using particles in UI is a hot topic. It seems like nearly every mobile game with loot boxes uses particles, but there is no standardized way to implement them. The problem with trying to use particples in the UI is that particles render behind UI on canvases that have their **Render Mode** set to **Screen Space - Overlay**:

The preceding screenshot shows two UI canvases from our working examples and a particle system (the white dots). The pink background is on the Background Canvas, which renders with **Screen Space - Camera**. The circular meter and the panel with the cat are on the HUD Canvas, which renders with **Screen Space - Overlay**. The particles are rendering in front of the Background Canvas and behind the HUD Canvas. However, I want the particles to be displayed also in front of the HUD Canvas.

There are a few solutions to this problem. My two preferred solutions are as follows:

- Change the **Render Mode** on HUD Canvas to **Screen Space - Camera** and adjust the sorting order of it and the particles to make the particles appear in front
- Use a second Camera and a Render Texture to display the particles on a raw image in the Canvas

There are benefits and downfalls to both methods. The first method is by far the easiest. It allows you to view particles in front of your UI with only one or two modifications to your scene. However, using **Screen Space - Camera** for your UI's **Rendering Mode** may not be practical for your project. If you edit the properties of the Camera in your game, the properties of the UI will be changed. Additionally, changing the Rendering Mode of your Canvas after you have already set everything up can cause your UI to stop displaying the way you initially intended.

The second method isn't terribly complicated to implement, but does require more work than the first. It's main benefit is that you can render particles in front of UI on Canvases that render with **Screen Space - Overlay**. Its main downfall, other than needing more work to set up, is that you may have to make some complicated decisions about what your two cameras are going to render and may slightly affect performance. An example covering this method is discussed in the *Examples* section.

There are other solutions to this problem, each more complicated (or costly) than the next, and what you choose to do depends on your project. Some projects forego particles entirely and pre-render their particles as sprite sheets using software, such as After Effects. Some projects use assets available in the Asset Store, and others handle everything entirely with scripts and shaders. Although I can't foresee any reason why the second solution I proposed will not work for your project, it's certainly possible that your project has a fringe case I am not considering. Hopefully, if that is the case, you will be able to modify my solution with minimal effort to work in your project.

My best advice to you would be to decide early whether you will use particles in your UI. If you know you are going to use them, plan ahead with your UI layouts and camera setups. Also, if you and use the first method, do it.

It's really too bad that there is no standard method for this implemented by Unity. I assume that one day there will be a pre-built UI Particle object that will make the process both simple and performant.

Examples

The main point in this chapter is providing examples of how to create common UI animations and effects, so let's get to it.

Animating pop up windows to fade in and out

With our first example, we will continue to work on our main scene. Duplicate the `Chapter7` scene to create a new scene named `Chapter8`. Open the `Chapter8` scene and complete this example within it.

Currently, we have a `Pause Panel` and `Inventory Panel` that instantly appear when the *P* or *I* key is pressed. That's not terribly interesting, so let's add some animations to have the panels *pop* in and out with fade and scale animations.

It can get rather tedious having to expand all of the parents to see their children every time you go to a new scene. A shortcut to open all parents is to select everything in the Hierarchy and then press the right arrow key on the keyboard. You can do this multiple times if you have multiple nestings. The left arrow key will collapse the parents.

Our workflow to set up these animations and their functionality will be to create Animation Clips, set up our Animator, and then write code that sets the Animator's parameters at the appropriate times. To make the steps easier to digest, I've broken them into sections. The first section covers all of the steps involved with setting up the Animation Clips and Animator and the second section covers the sets involved with writing code.

Setting up the animations

To create a "pop" in and out animation on the `Pause Panel` and `Inventory Panel`, perform the following steps:

1. We'll start by adding an Animation Clip to the `Pause Panel` that will cause it to scale and fade in. Open the Animation Window and select `Pause Panel` from the **Hierarchy**. Select **Create** to add a new Animation Clip. Save the new Animation Clip in the `Assets/Animation` folder and name it `FadeAndScale`.

2. We want to control four properties of this panel: its scale, its alpha value, its ability to be interacted with, and its raycast blocking. Let's start with scale. We can adjust this property from the Rect Transform component. Select **Add Property** and click on the plus sign next to **Scale** under **Rect Transform**, as follows:

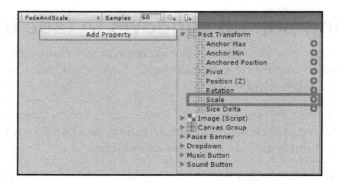

3. Two keyframes are initialized for the **Scale** property at **0:00** and **1:00**. This means that the animation will last 1 second, which is a bit long for a pop-in animation. Select the keyframe at **1:00** and drag it to **0:30** to make the animation half a second long:

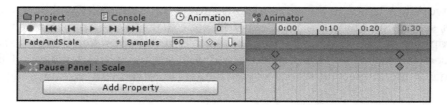

4. We want the panel to start out small and then get big. To achieve this, we will need to adjust the x and y scale. Expand the **Scale** property (select the arrow next to **Pause Panel : Scale**) to view the x, y, and z properties of **Scale**. Currently, the scale for all three coordinates are set to 1 at both keyframes. Since we want the scale to start small and then enlarge to its normal size, we want it to scale from 0 to 1. We only need to adjust the x and y scale since z scale doesn't really affect a 2D object. So, at the keyframe **0:00**, change the **Scale.x** and **Scale.y** properties to 0 by typing 0 in their property boxes, as follows:

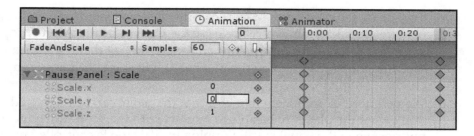

If you play the animation, you'll note that the `Pause Panel` quickly scaling in. Since parent/child relationships scale children with their parents, we don't have to animate the scale of all the `Pause Panel` children separately.

5. Now, let's control the alpha of the panel to fade it in. We don't want to animate the alpha on the **Color** property of the Image component of `Pause Panel`. Doing so would only affect the alpha of the panel's background image and would not affect the children. Instead, we want to animate the alpha value on the Canvas Group component. This will make the alpha of the Pause Panel and all its children work in unison. Remember that this was the whole reason we used a Canvas Group component to begin with.

   Let's select **Add Property | Canvas Group | Alpha**:

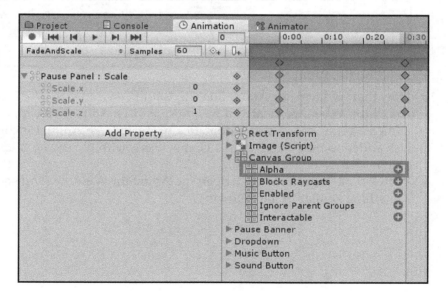

6. To fade in, the panel should start completely transparent and end completely opaque. Both keyframes already have the **CanvasGroup.Alpha** property set to 1, so change the **CanvasGroup.Alpha** property to 0 at the first keyframe. Playing the animation (or scrubbing the playhead) will show the panel and all of its children fading in.

7. We will need to animate whether or not the panel can be interacted with. We don't want the player to be able to interact with the drop-down menu or mute buttons when the panel is still popping in. This too is controlled by the Canvas Group component—select **Add Property | Canvas Group | Interactable**.

8. The Pause Panel and its children should be interactable only after it has fully popped in to the scene. So, deselect the checkbox next to **CanvasGroup.Interactable** at the first keyframe to make the Canvas Group animate from interactable to not interactable. When you scrub the playhead, you'll see that the property does not turn back on until the very last frame.

9. The last item we will need to animate is its raycast blocking. Select **Add Property | Canvas Group | Blocks Raycast**. Animate it from false to true as you did with the **Interactable** property.

   Your FadeAndScale Animation Clip's timeline should now appear, as follows:

10. Now that we have our Animation Clip set up, we can start working inside the Animator. When we created the FadeAndScale Animation clip, an Animator named Pause Panel was automatically created. An Animator component was also added to the Pause Panel GameObject, with the Pause Panel Animator assigned to it.

   With Pause Panel selected, open the Animator Window. You should see something similar to the following:

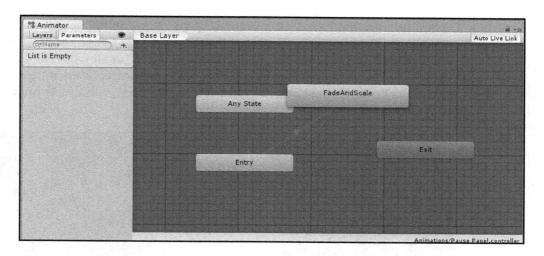

You will see a state named FadeAndScale. This state uses the FadeAndScale Animation Clip as its **Motion**. Selecting the FadeAndScale State will show the following properties in the **Inspector**:

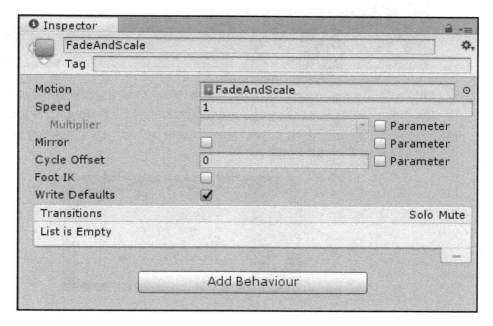

11. Currently, since the `FadeAndScale` state is connected to the `Entry` node and set as the Layer Default State, when we play the game, the `FadeAndScale` animation will play instantly. It will also play on loop. That's not at all what we want, obviously. Let's stop it from playing when the game starts by creating an empty state as the Layer Default State. Right-click anywhere within the Animator and select **Create State | Empty**:

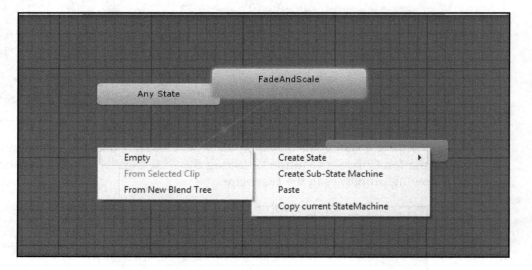

This will add a gray colored state named `New State` to the Animator.

12. Rename `New State` to `Empty State` by changing its name in its **Inspector**.

13. Set `Empty State` to the Layer Default State by right-clicking on it and selecting **Set as Layer Default State**:

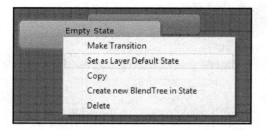

It will now be connected to Entry via a transition. FadeAndScale will also now no longer be the Layer Default State and will not have any transitions connected to it:

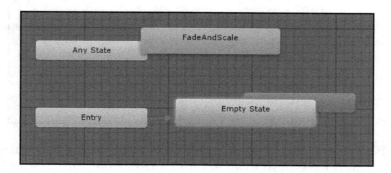

We used an empty state as our Layer Default State, because we want the panel to do nothing, while it waits for us to tell it to start animating.

14. Rearrange the items to a more viewable layout. I personally like the following layout for this Animator:

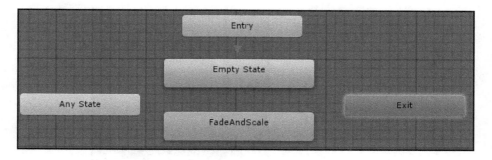

15. The FadeAndScale Animation Clip now no longer instantly plays when the game starts. It is still set to have its animation loop, however. To fix this, select the FadeAndScale Animation Clip from your **Project** folder view. This will bring up its **Inspector**.

Deselect the **Loop Time** property to disable looping on the animation:

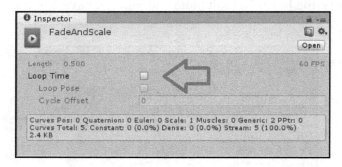

16. We want the `Pause Panel` to be able to fade in and fade out on command, but we don't have an Animation Clip for fading out, only one for fading in. We actually don't need to create a whole Animation Clip to achieve this motion. We can simply play the `FadeAndScale` Animation Clip backward.

    Duplicate the `FadeAndScale` state by selecting it and pressing *Ctrl + D*. This will give you a new state named `FadeAndScale 0` that has the `FadeAndScale` Animation Clip set as its **Motion**:

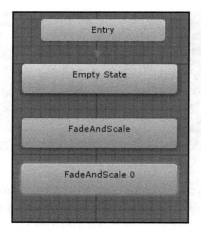

17. Rename the `FadeAndScale` state to `FadeAndScaleIn` and the `FadeAndScale 0` state to `FadeAndScaleOut`.

18. To set the `FadeAndScaleOut` state to play the `FadeAndScale` Animation Clip backward, we simply have to change its **Speed** to −1 in its **Inspector**:

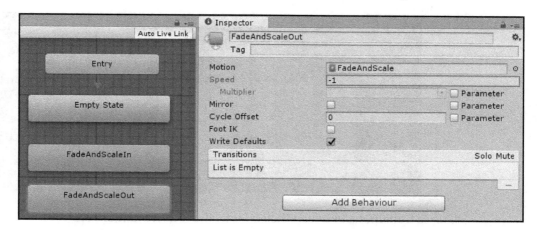

19. Now that we have all of our states set up properly, we can create the transitions between them. Start by creating two Trigger Parameters named `FadeIn` and `FadeOut`:

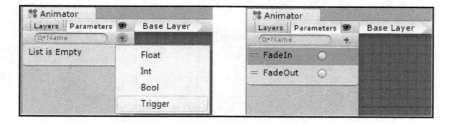

We are using Trigger Parameters here because we want these values to instantly reset after we've used them. That way, we can create an animation "cycle" without having to write code that resets the parameter values.

20. You create transitions between states by right-clicking on the first state, selecting **Make Transition**, and then clicking on the second state:

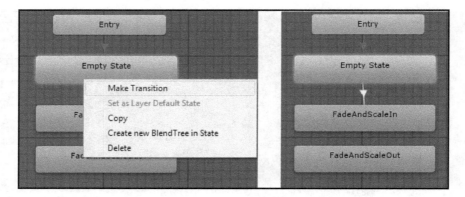

Create transitions between the states in the following manner:

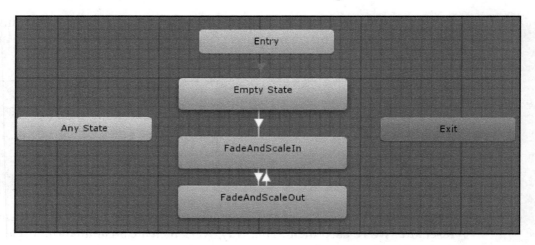

This transition flow will allow the panel to transition from no animation to the FadeAndScale Animation, then to the reversed FadeAndScale Animation, and back and forth between the two.

21. If you play the game, `Pause Panel` will instantly go from the `Empty State` to the `FadeAndScaleIn` state and then to the `FadeAndScaleOut` state, and back and forth between the two indefinitely. This is because transitions are automatically set to occur after an animation is complete. To stop this, you have to tell the transitions to only occur after a parameter has been set.

    Select the transition between the `Empty State` and the `FadeAndScaleIn` state. Select the plus sign in the **Conditions** list to add a new condition. Ensure that the condition is set to the `FadeIn` trigger. Since we don't want timing to be a factor of our transition, deselect **Has Exit Time**:

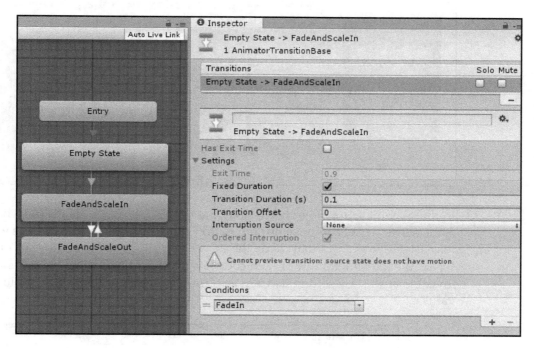

22. Complete the same steps for the transitions between the `FadeAndScaleIn` and `FadeAndScaleOut` states. Set the condition from the `FadeAndScaleIn` and `FadeAndScaleOut` state to the `FadeOut` trigger, and set the condition from the `FadeAndScaleOut` and `FadeAndScaleIn` state to the `FadeIn` trigger. Additionally, deselect **Fixed Duration** and set all values to 0 to ensure an instant transition:

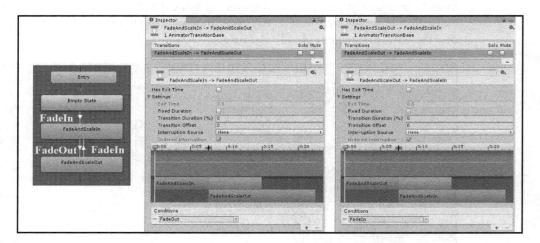

23. If you play the game now, you'll note that the `Pause Panel` is visible when the game starts. This is because our animation states supersede the code we wrote in `ShowHidePanels.cs` that made the `Pause Panel` invisible at the start of the scene. We'll deal with our broken code later, but for now, make the `Pause Panel` invisible at start by setting its **Canvas Group** component to have the following values:

Now when you play the game, the `Pause Panel` will not appear at the start.

24. We've completed setting up the animations for the Pause Panel, but before you proceed to the Inventory Panel, check whether the animations are working correctly. To do so, arrange your windows so that your Game View and Animator window are both visible:

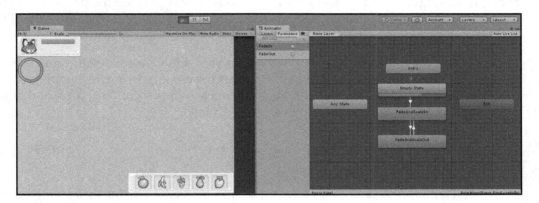

You'll see the progress bar on the current state of Pause Panel running. To force the transitions, click on the circles next to the appropriate Trigger parameters.

25. If your animations are working the way they should, you can now set up the animations on the Inventory Panel. You may be thinking, "Ugh, now I have to do all of this again for the Inventory Panel?!" However, worry not, you don't have to do it again, because you can reuse the Animator for the Pause Panel on the Inventory Panel. All of the properties we changed on the Pause Panel in the FadeAndScale Animation Clip also exist on the Inventory Panel. So, to give the same set of animations and controls to the Inventory Panel, we can simply attach the Animator we created to Inventory Panel.
Since we will be using the Animator we created on two different objects, it's a good idea to rename it. Change the name from Pause Panel to PopUpPanels. Now, drag it on to the Inventory Panel.

26. Just as we had to change the properties of the Canvas Group on Pause Panel to stop it from appearing when the scene starts, we also have to change the properties on the Canvas Group of the Inventory Panel. Set the properties as they appear in step 23.

Now that we are done setting up our animations for our two panels, we can begin writing code that will trigger the animations when the P and I keys are hit to bring up the panels.

Setting the Animator's Parameters with code

We have a script named `ShowHidePanels.cs` attached to the `Main Camera` that would bring the `Pause Panel` and `Inventory Panel` up when the P and I keys are pressed. Sadly, it no longer functions, since the animations now supersede the properties of the Canvas Groups we set within it. We can reuse the logic, but will have to do a bit of work to get out panels popping again.

 The changes that we will make to ShowHidePanels.cs will cause the panels in preceding chapter scenes to stop appearing. If you plan on accessing the previous chapter scenes, save a secondary copy of this script as it is now so that you can access it later.

To trigger the animations on the `Pause Panel` and `Inventory Panel` with code, complete the following steps:

1. Open the `ShowHidePanels.cs` script. We have to delete everything related to Canvas Groups and their properties. After you delete all the code related to Canvas Groups, you'll have a barebones script that appears, as follows:

```
using System.Collections;
using System.Collections.Generic;
using UnityEngine;

public class ShowHidePanels : MonoBehaviour {
    public bool inventoryUp=false;
    public bool pauseUp=false;

    // Use this for initialization
    void Start () {
    }

    // Update is called once per frame
    void Update () {
        //inventory panel
        if(Input.GetKeyDown(KeyCode.I) && pauseUp==false){
            //not visible
            if(inventoryUp==false){
                inventoryUp=true;

            //already visible
            }else{
                inventoryUp=false;
            }
        }
```

```
//pause panel
if(Input.GetButtonDown("Pause")){
    //not visible
    if(pauseUp==false){
        pauseUp=true;
        Time.timeScale=0;
    //already visible
    }else{
        pauseUp=false;
        Time.timeScale=1;
    }
}
```

2. Instead of referencing the `Pause Panel` and `Inventory Panel` with their Canvas Group components, we'll now reference them with their Animator components. Create the following two variable declarations at the top of the class:

```
public Animator inventoryPanelAnim;
public Animator pausePanelAnim;
```

3. Now, all we have to do is set the appropriate animation trigger parameters when we want the panels to appear and disappear. We will do that using the `SetTrigger()` function. To call and dismiss the inventory panel, add the following two lines to your if statement that checks for the I key to appear as follows:

```
if(Input.GetKeyDown(KeyCode.I) && pauseUp==false){
    //not visible
    if(inventoryUp==false){
        inventoryUp=true;
        inventoryPanelAnim.SetTrigger("FadeIn");

    //already visible
    }else{
        inventoryUp=false;
        inventoryPanelAnim.SetTrigger("FadeOut");
    }
}
```

4. Now, update the if statement for the pause key with the following two lines:

```
if(Input.GetButtonDown("Pause")){
    //not visible
    if(pauseUp==false){
        pauseUp=true;
        Time.timeScale=0;
        pausePanelAnim.SetTrigger("FadeIn");

    //already visible
    }else{
        pauseUp=false;
        Time.timeScale=1;

  pausePanelAnim.SetTrigger("FadeOut");
  }
}
```

That's all we have to do to the code.

5. Drag the `Inventory Panel` and the `Pause Panel` into their appropriate slots on the Show Hide Panels component:

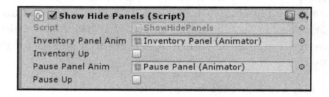

6. Play the game and watch it kind of work. `Inventory Panel` should appear and disappear as necessary, but the `Pause Panel` won't work the way it is supposed to. This is because the following line of code stops all animations from happening that depend on time scale:

```
Time.timeScale=0;
```

That line of code was used to effectively pause the game. However, that means its pausing our `Pause Panel` pop-up animation. Don't worry, you can still use this simple pause code and run animations when the game is paused. All you have to do is tell the Animator on the `Pause Panel` that it can still function when the time scale is set to 0. You do this by changing the **Update Mode** on the Animator component from **Normal** to **Unscaled Time**:

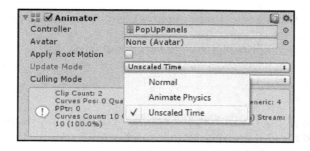

You only need to do this on the Animator component of `Pause Panel`. `Inventory Panel` will not be animating when the game is paused, so its **Update Mode** can remain as **Normal**.

Play the game, and you should have smoothly animating Pause and Inventory Panels.

Animating a complex loot box with Particle System

For this example, we'll work with a new scene. The animation we will create is a bit complicated—a chest will fly in to the scene and then wait for the player to open it. Once the player opens it, the chest will animate open with a particle system that pops in front of it. Then, three collectibles will fly out in sequence. Each collectible will have its own "shiny" animation that begins to play. The following figure is a storyboard of sorts that shows a few key frames of the animation playing out:

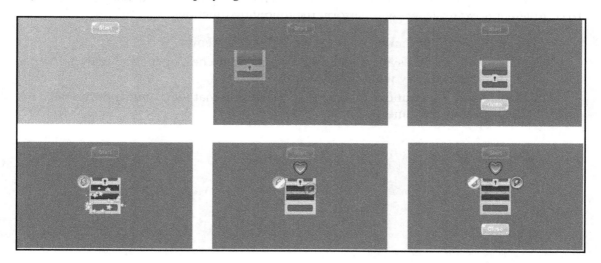

The chest sprite sheet was obtained from `https://bayat.itch.io/`
`platform-game-assets`
and the item sprite sheets were obtained from `https://opengameart.org/`
`content/shining-coin-shining-health-shining-power-up-sprite-`
`sheets`.

This example has a lot going on with it. It's not particularly complicated to build out, but
providing the steps to build it entirely from scratch would require too many steps. I don't
have the page count to do all of that; at this point in the text, you can hopefully look at a
scene already built out and understand how it was achieved. Therefore, we will start this
example with a package file that has all the items placed in the scene, some of the
animations already created, and all of the new sprite sheets included.

Before you begin, import the `Chapter 8 Example 2-Starting.unitypackage` asset
package.

If you'd like to view the completed example, view the package labeled `Chapter 8`
`Example 2-Completed.unitypackage`—a video demonstrating the completed example
is provided as well.

Note that Unity Layers do not save in Unity asset packages. The example
will describe creating a Layer named UI Particles and having the cameras
ignore or include the layer, but this does not get displayed in the provided
package.

To make the example easier to absorb, I have broken the steps into three distinct sections.
To complete this example, we will perform the following functions:

1. Set up the various animations for the individual items
2. Create the particle system that displays when the chest opens and make sure that
   it displays properly within the UI
3. Tie all of the animations together and make sure that their time appropriately
   using a state machine

Setting up the animations

Let's start this section by creating the animations for each of the objects within the scene. To create all the animations for this scene, complete the following steps:

1. If you have not done so already, import the Chapter 8 Example 2-Starting.unitypackage package. You should see a scene that has two Canvases--one with a button and a background image and another with a chest, items, and a button, as shown in the following screenshot:

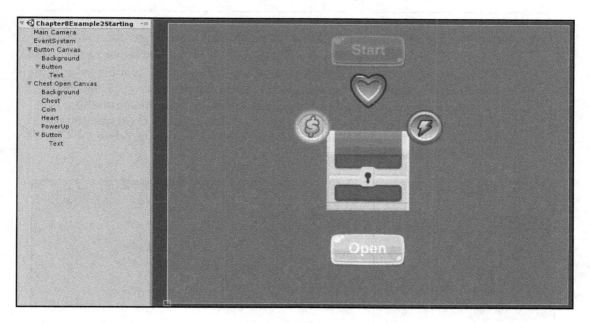

In the preceding screenshot, you will also note that there are a few animation clips and controllers provided in the asset folder.

2. The Chest object needs two animations, flying in from the side of the screen and one of its sprite sheet opening. Let's make the flying in animation first. Select the Chest object in the Hierarchy and then select **Create** in the Animation window to create a new Animation Clip. Name the new Animation Clip ChestFlyingIn.anim and save it in the Assets/Animations/Clips folder.

3. A new Animation Controller named Chest.controller was automatically created. Move it to the Assets/Animations/Controllers folder.

4. Select **Add Property** and expand **Rect Transform**. Click on the plus sign next to **Anchored Position**. This will allow us to animation the position of the Chest position within the Canvas:

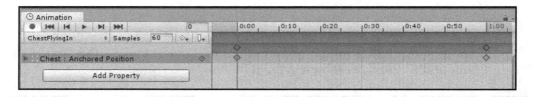

5. Currently, the animation is 1 second long, which is a bit longer than we want. Move the second keyframe to the 0:30 mark so that it will be half a second long.

6. The position of the chest in the scene right now is where we want it to be at the end of the fly-in animation, so we will not affect the position at the second keyframe. However, we want it to start off screen, so with the animation playhead on the first frame, use the **Move** tool to move the chest outside of the Canvas area. Since record is automatically selected, this will update the Chest's position at the first frame:

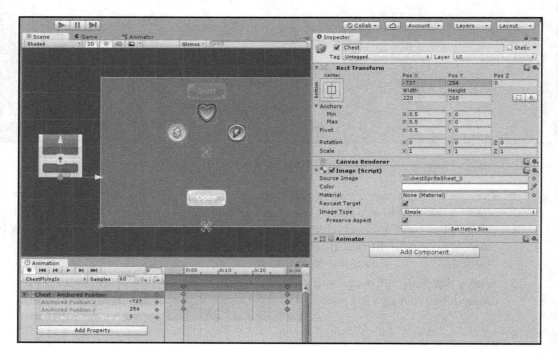

If you scrub the playhead, you will see the chest move from left to right.

7. Now, let's make the chest fly in at an arc instead of the straight line. We'll do this with Animation Curves. Select the **Curves** tab, as follows:

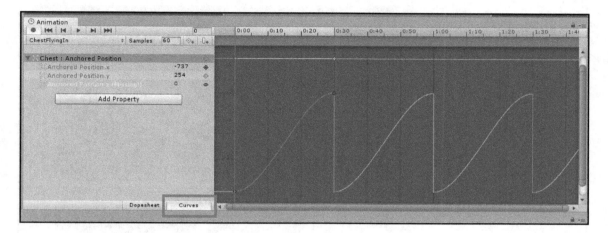

The green line represents the y property of the anchored position. Select the **Anchored Postion.y** property to focus on it.

8. Select the first and second key frame anchors to affect their handles. Move their handles until the green curve looks more like an arc:

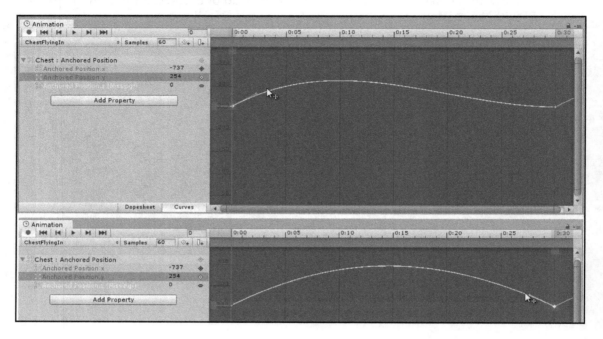

Now, when you play the animation, you will see the chest move in an arcing path.

9. Let's have the chest fade in as it flies by adding a color property to the animation. Select **Add Property**, then expand **Image**. Click on the plus sign next to **Color**. On the first frame, change the **Color.a** property to 0 to make the chest invisible on the first frame:

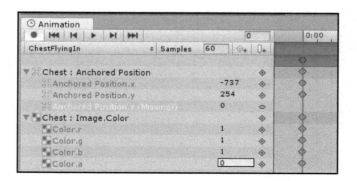

10. Whenever a new animation is created, it is automatically set to loop. We don't want this animation to play on a loop, so select the `ChestFlyingIn` Animation Clip from the Project view to see its Inspector properties. Deselect the **Loop Time** checkbox.

11. We don't want the `ChestFlyingIn` Animation Clip to automatically play when the scene starts. Since this was the first Animation Clip created for the `Chest`, it will be set to the Animator default state. With the `Chest` selected, open the **Animator Window**.

    Create a new default state by right-clicking within the Animator Window and selecting **Create State | Empty**. Rename the new state `Empty State` and set it as the default state by right-clicking on it and selecting **Set as Layer Default State**. We will do more with the Chest's Animator later, but for now, this is all we are going to do.

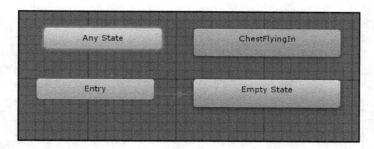

12. Now, let's set up the chest opening animation. With Chest still selected, in the Animation window, select **Create New Clip...** from the Animation Clip dropdown list:

    Name the new Animation Clip `ChestOpening.anim` and save it in the `Assets/Animations/Clips` folder.

13. This Animation Clip will contain all of the sprites from the sprite sheet. From the Project view, drag and drop all of the sub-sprites into the Animation timeline. A new property for **Image.Sprite** will automatically be added, and all of the sub-sprites will be added to the timeline in a sequence:

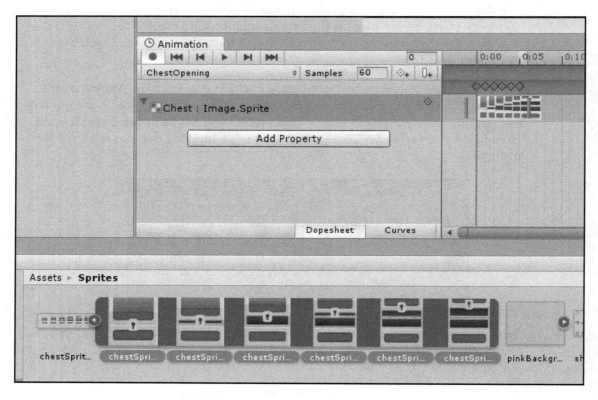

14. Right now, the animation is way too fast. The animation is running at 60 frames per second, and there are only 6 frames. Change the animation's **Samples** value to 12; this will change the animation's frame rate to 12 fps:

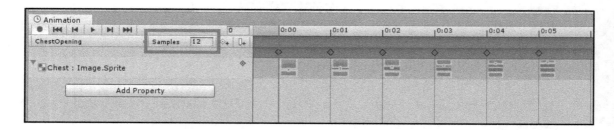

15. Since the `Chest` has an animation that will affect its alpha value, let's ensure that this animation has full alpha whenever it plays. Select **Add Property**, then expand **Image**. Click on the plus sign next to **Color**. The first frame already has its alpha set to 1. On the sixth frame, change the **Color.a** property to 1 by simply adding a keyframe to the last frame:

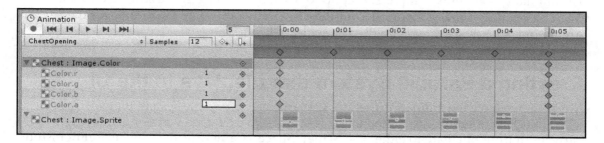

Technically, we only need the alpha set to 1 on the first frame, but I like to add a start and end frame here so that I am very sure about what the animation is doing with that value.

16. We don't want this animation to play on a loop, so select the `ChestOpening` Animation Clip from the Project view to take a look at its Inspector properties. Deselect the **Loop Time** checkbox.

17. All of the other animations needed for this example have been already set up. They are very similar to this one in set up or similar to the ones created in the preceding example. However, they are not hooked up to the correct GameObjects.
Let's give the other objects in the `Chest Open Canvas` their animations. Drag the `Coin` animator to the Inspector of the `Coin` Animator, the Heart Animator to the Inspector of the `Hearts`, and the `PowerUp` Animator to the PowerUp's Inspector. You can now preview the animations of all the items popping out of the chests and shining.

18. Let's initialize the chest and all of the objects as invisible. Select the `Chest`, `Coin`, `Heart`, and `PowerUp` GameObjects from the Hierarchy. In their Image component, change their alpha values to 0.

19. The `Chest Open Canvas` and the `Button` on that Canvas both have animations, as well. These animations will affect a Canvas Group component on the objects. Right now, they don't have Canvas Group components, though. So, add a Canvas Group component to `Chest Open Canvas` and its child `Button`.

20. Initialize the new Canvas Group components to have **Alpha** values of 0 and their **Interactable** and **Blocks Raycasts** properties set to `false`.

21. Now, add the `CanvasGroupFadeInOut` Animator to `Chest Open Canvas` and its child `Button`.

The animations are now completely set up for each of the objects. We still need to finish working on the Animator Controller for the `Chest` and add some more logic for the various Animators, but we are done with the Animation Clips for now.

Creating a Particle System that displays in the UI

Now that we have the animations set up, we can create a particle system that will "pop" when the chest opens up. As stated in the text, my two preferred ways of displaying particles in front of UI are to either use **Screen Space - Camera** as the Canvas **Render Mode** or to use a Render Texture. Since the second option is more complicated, it merits an example. You'll notice that our Canvases all have their Render Modes set to **Screen Space - Overlay,** so using a Render Texture is the best method for the way the project is currently set up.

We will create a particle system that is rendered to a texture via a second camera and then have that texture displayed on a Raw Image within the UI.

To create a particle system that displays in the UI, complete the following steps:

1. The first thing we will need to do is create a material that will be used for the particle. Create a new folder in the `Assets` folder named `Textures and Materials`. Now, right-click within the new folder and select **Create | Material**. Name the new material `StarsMaterial`.

2. Set the `StarsMaterial` **Shader** to **Unlit/Transparent** and drag the star icon sprite into its texture slot.

3. To display the particles in front of the UI objects, we will need a second Camera. Duplicate the `Main Camera` using *Ctrl + D* and rename the duplicate `UI Particles Camera`.

4. You can only have one Audio Listener in the scene, so delete the Audio Listener component on the new camera.

5. You also won't want any code later to think this might possibly be the `Main Camera`, so change the tag from `MainCamera` to **Untagged**.

6. This camera will be used only to display the particle pop we're going to make, so we might as well make the particle system a child of this camera by right-clicking on the `UI Particles Camera` and selecting **Particle System**.

Since this book isn't about Particle Systems, but about UI, we will not spend time going over every property of Particle Systems. Luckily, most are somewhat self-explanatory and fiddling with the various properties let you see what they can do. Therefore, rather than going through each property of the `Particle System`, I will simply provide screenshots of the necessary properties. When you apply the properties, I suggest adding the material in the **Renderer** properties first, so you get a better idea of what the `Particle System` will look like:

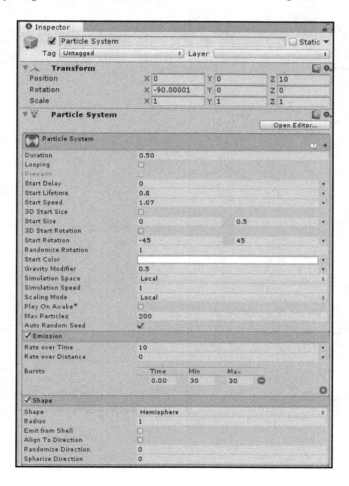

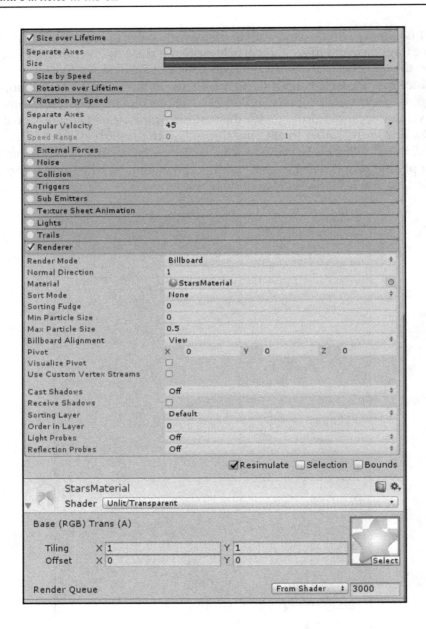

7. It will be a lot easier to take a look at whether what we are about to do is working if we have the particle system constantly playing. Therefore, for now, re-select **Looping** and **Play on Awake** so that we can see the particle system constantly playing when the game is playing.

8. We want to make sure that the `UI Particles Camera` displays only the `Particle System` and the `Main Camera` displays everything but the `Particle System`. That way, we will accomplish this with **Layers**. Select the **Layers** drop-down menu and select **Add Layer...** Add a new **User Layer** named `UI Particles`. Now, assign `UI Particles` to the **Layer** property of `Particle System`.

9. Now, tell each of the cameras what they will be displaying using their **Culling Mask** property. Set the **Culling Mask** property of the `UI Particles Camera` to only display **UI Particles** and the **Culling Mask** property of the `Main Camera` to exclude **UI Particles**.

10. Now, let's have the `UI Particles Camera` render to a texture. Within the `Textures and Materials` folder, right-click and select **Create | Render Texture**, and name it `StarPopRenderTexture`. Change its **Size** to 512 x 512.

11. Assign the `StarPopRenderTexture` to the **Target Texture** property of the `UI Particles Camera`'s Camera component.

12. The only thing left to do is have the render texture display in the UI. Create a new UI Canvas with **Create | UI | Canvas**. Rename the Canvas to `Particle Canvas`.

13. With the `Particle Canvas` selected, select **Create | UI | Raw Image**. Rename it `Particle Renderer`.

14. Change the **Width** and **Height** of the `Particle Renderer` to 512 and 512, respectively, to match the properties of `StarPopRenderTexture`.

15. Assign `StarPopRenderTexture` to the **Texture** property of the Raw Image component of the **Particle Renderer**.

16. We don't want this image to block our mouse clicks, so deselect **Raycast Target** from the Raw Image component.

17. Now, we just need to make sure that the `Particle Canvas` displays in front of the other two Canvases. Set the **Canvas Sort Order** to 2 on the `Particle Canvas`' Canvas component.

18. Play the game now, and you should now see the particles displaying the the scene.

19. We set the Particle System to be constantly playing, so deselect **Looping** and **Play on Awake** to reset the values to what they should be.

Now that the particle system is set to display in front of the UI, we can set up the logic to have the animation trigger in the correct order.

Building a State Machine and timing the animations

The last thing to do is set up the state machine and write the code that will make the various animations play.

To hook up the various animations and have them play at the correct time, complete the following steps:

1. We'll start by creating the state machine that will work as the logic for our animation sequences. Create a new Animator Controller named `ChestOpeningStateMachine.controller` in `Assets/Animations/Controllers`.

2. Open the `ChestOpeningStateMachine` Animator Controller and create 12 new empty states. Arrange, name, and transition the states, as shown in the following screenshot:

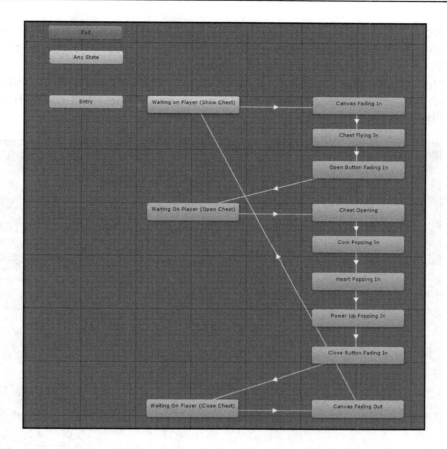

The state machine shown in the preceding screenshot demonstrates the sequence of events for the animations and interactions of the chest opening. The states labeled with **Waiting On Player** will "play" when the game is waiting for the player to press a button to proceed the animation. The other animations will automatically play based on timed events.

3. The state machine created in the previous steps will not actually contain any animations. It is simply a flow chart describing what is currently happening in the game. We will also use it to send information to the various objects in the scene to let them know what they should or should not be doing. Since we just want this to control the logic of this sequence, and not actually animate anything in the scene, we can add it on an Animator component to any object in the scene. Therefore, let's add it to the "ubiquitous" `Main Camera`. Drag the `ChestOpeningStateMachine` Animator from the project view to the Inspector of the `Main Camera`.

4. Now, we will need to set the conditions of transition for the various states within the state machine. Create four animation Trigger Parameters named ShowChest, OpenChest, CloseChest, and AnimationComplete.

5. Now, set Trigger Conditions for each transition, as shown with the following screenshot; with each transition, make sure that you deselect **Has Exit Time** and **Fixed Duration**:

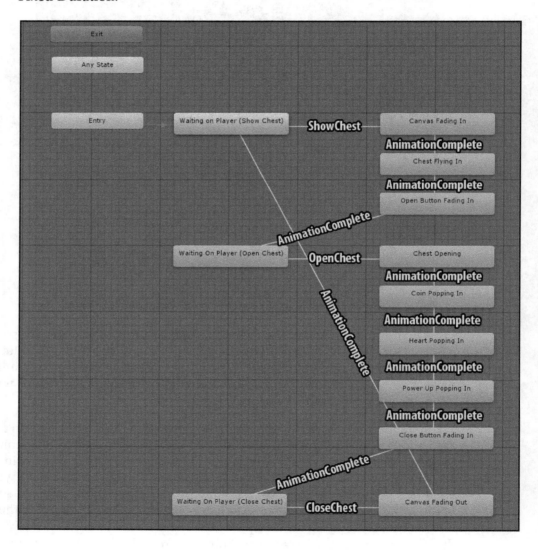

I highly recommend that you bookmark this image or print out a screenshot of your `ChestOpeningStateMachine` Animator while working through this example. Having this as a flow chart that you can easily reference while working this example will make the steps being completed a lot easier to follow.

6. Before we proceed to write code, let's set up the Animator for the `Chest`. Currently, the Animator of the `Chest` should look something as follows:

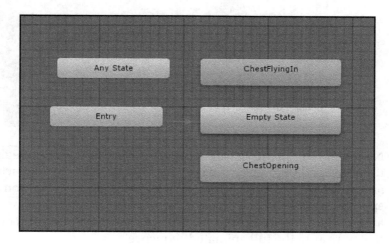

The Animator only contains the animation states, but does not yet indicate how they are all connected. We will need to create transitions and set up the Animation Parameters. Rearrange the states and add transitions to the Animator so it appears as follows:

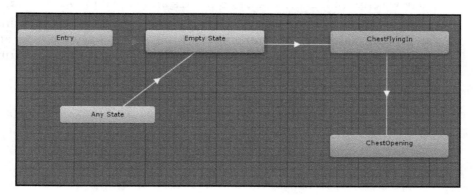

7. Create three animation Trigger Parameters named `ShowChest`, `OpenChest`, and `Reset`.

8. Now, set Trigger Conditions for each transition, as shown with the following screenshot; with each transition, make sure that you deselect **Has Exit Time** and **Fixed Duration**:

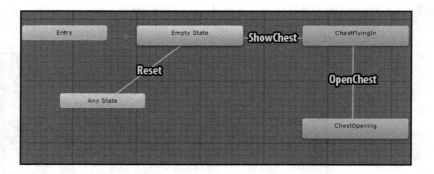

9. Now that our Animators are all appropriately set, we can begin coding. We will use the `ChestOpeningStateMachine` Animator to make each appropriate animation play when the player clicks on the specified button during the specified state. The `ChestOpeningStateMachine` Animator will then automatically set the appropriate triggers on the Animators on the various objects that appear in the full animated sequence.

   We need a way to keep track of which items in the scene have Animators that will be controlled by the `ChestOpeningStateMachine` Animator, what their various parameters are, and what conditions need to be met to have those parameters set. We'll keep track of all of this information on a single script. Create a new script called `ChestAnimControls` and save it in `Assets/Scripts`.

10. To give us a nice clean way of keeping track of all of the necessary information, we'll use classes and an enumerated list (I'll explain what these are and why we are using them momentarily). Delete the `Start()` and `Update()` functions from the `ChestAnimControls` class, and write the following code:

```
//the different types of parameters
public enum TypesOfParameters{floatParam, intParam, boolParam,
triggerParam};

//properties of animation parameters
[System.Serializable]
public class ParameterProperties{
    public string parameterString; //what string sets it?
    public string whichState; //name of the state its called from,
```

```
null=not called by the state machine
    public TypesOfParameters parameterType; //what type of Animator
Parameter is it?
    public float floatValue; //float value required, if float
    public int intValue; //int value required, if int
    public bool boolValue; //bool value required, if bool
}
//make a list of all animatable objects and their parameters
[System.Serializable]
public class AnimatorProperties{
    public string name; //so the name will appear in the inspector
rather than "Element 0, Element 1, etc"
    public Animator theAnimator; //the animator
    public List<ParameterProperties> animatorParameters; //its
parameter properties
}
```

You'll note that the preceding code is in the following three parts: the enumerated list `TypesOfParameters`, the class `ParameterProperties`, and the class `AnimatorProperties`.

First, let's look at the enumerated list `TypesOfParameters`. This is a list of the types of Animator Parameters that can be used within an Animator. An enumerated list is a custom type that contains a set of constants that are represented with names. A benefit of using an enumerated list is that the list appears as a drop-down menu within the Inspector.

Now, let's look at the `ParameterProperties` class. Each object that is animated within the scene has a set of properties related to its Animator Parameters that we need to keep track of. A class can be an effective tool for grouping sets of data together. Therefore, I used a class to group together the name of the parameter, which state the parameter will be set in, what type of parameter it is, its value if it is a float, integer, or Boolean parameter. Note that the type of parameter is defined using the enumerated list, `TypesOfParameters`. This was done because there are a finite and specific set of parameters available for each animator parameter.

Now, let's look at the `AnimatorProperties` class. For each object in the scene, we will need to keep track of its name, its animator, and all of its parameters along with the conditions in which they are set. Note that the list of parameters and their properties is defined by the `ParameterProperties` class.

A big benefit of working with Unity is the ability to assign and view public variables in the inspector. However, when you create a class within a class, the public variables are not visible within the inspector unless you place `[System.Serializable]` above the class. This gives the subclass the serializable attribute and allows its public variables to be visible in the Inspector.

I would like to point out that this code allows for the Animators to have Float, Int, and Bool parameters, even though the only parameters we use in any of our Animators are Triggers. I wrote it in this way to make it work more universally so that you can reuse this code for other animations in the future.

11. If the code we wrote in the preceding step is overwhelming you, don't worry—seeing it all listed out in the Inspector will clear it up a bit. All we've done so far is set up a few different groups of data. Now, we will need to actually create a variable that will use the information. We need a list of all animated items, so add the following code to your script:

```
public List<AnimatorProperties> animatedItems; //all the animated
items controlled by this state machine
```

12. Attach the `ChestAnimControls` script to the `Main Camera` by dragging it into its Inspector.

13. In Inspector of the `Main Camera`, click on the arrow next to **Animated Items** to expand the list:

We have a total of six items that need to have their Animators controlled by this script and the State Machine we created. So, change **Size** to 6. Expand **Animator Parameters** of **Element 0** and **Element 0**:

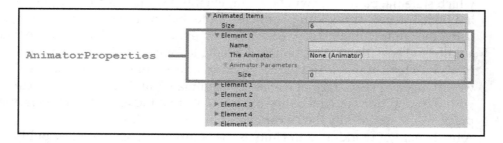

Remember that the `animatedItems` variable was a list of `AnimatorProperties`. So, **Element 0** (and all the other **Elements** for that matter) contains all of the items that were grouped in the `AnimatorProperties` class.

14. The first item we will need to list data for is the `Chest Open Canvas` GameObject. Type **Chest Open Canvas** in the **Name** slot and drag the `Chest Open Canvas` from the Hierarchy in to the **The Animator** slot.

    Once you type **Chest Open Canvas** in the **Name** slot, you'll see that the label **Element 0** is replaced with **Chest Open Canvas**. Whenever you have a list of objects in Unity's inspector, if the first item in the object is a string, the string will replace the **Element x** label:

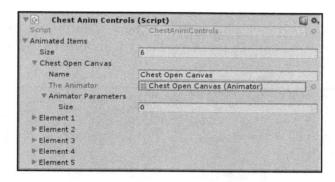

15. Now, we will need to list out all of the parameters that are used with in the `Chest Open Canvas`'s Animator and the conditions in which it is set. It has two parameters that we need to list data for, so change the **Size** of **Animator Parameters** to 2. Expand the two resulting **Elements**, as follows:

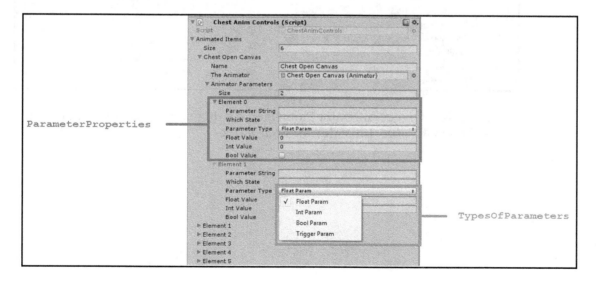

Remember that the `animatorParameters` variable was a list of `ParameterProperties`. So, the two **Elements** contain all of the items that were grouped in the `ParameterProperties` class. Additionally, within the `ParameterProperties` class, the `parameterType` was a `TypesOfParameters` variable. `TypesOfParameters` was an enumerated list, so any variable of that type will appear as a drop-down menu with the options that appeared within the defined list.

16. We now need to list out each parameter of the `Chest Open Canvas`, which state in the `ChestOpeningStateMachine` will cause the parameter to be set, and specify its parameter type:

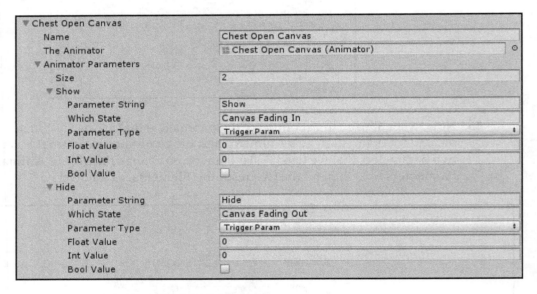

Since each is a Trigger Animator Parameter, we do not have to worry about the values for **Float Value**, **Int Value**, or **Bool Value**.

17. Now, we can fill in the Animator information for the other five animated objects in the same way we filled out the information for the Chest Open Canvas. Fill in the information for the animator of Chest, as follows:

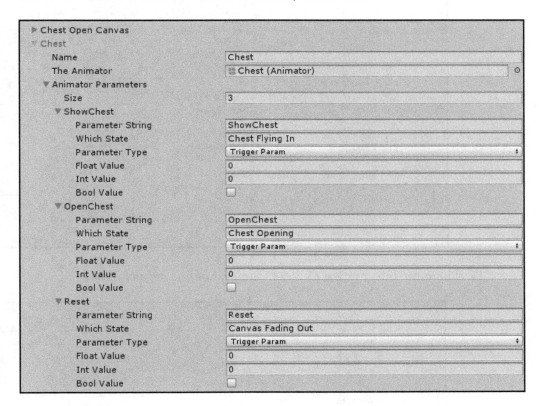

18. Fill in the information for the Animator of `Coin`, as follows:

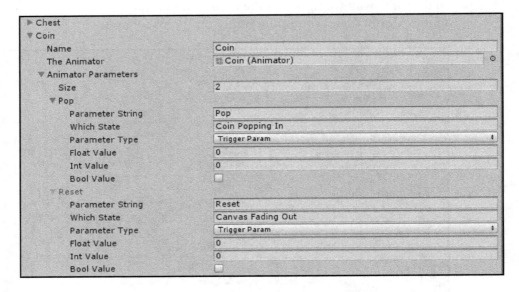

19. Fill in the information for the Animator of `Heart`, as follows:

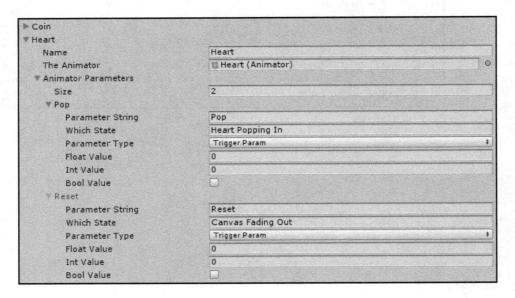

20. Fill in the information for the Animator of `PowerUp`, as follows:

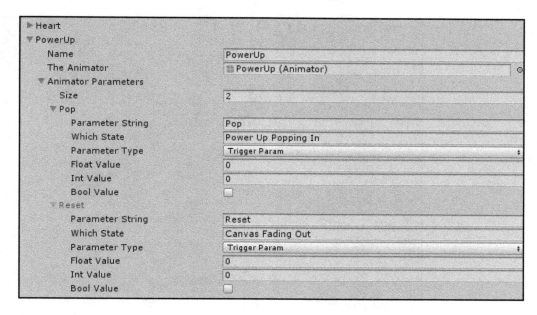

21. Fill in the information for the Animator of `Button`, as follows:

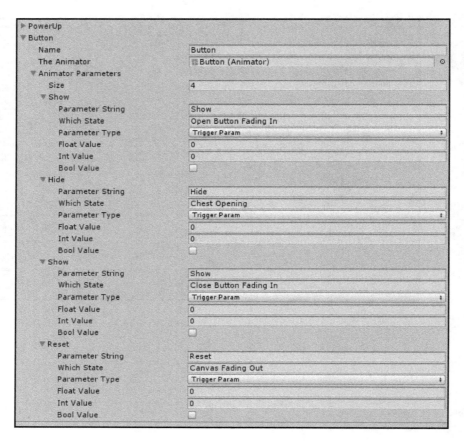

22. Now that we have all the appropriate data values for the State Machine initialized and defined, let's actually have the State Machine perform its appropriate logic. First, we will need to create a variable for the Animator. Add the following variable initialization to your script:

```
Animator theStateMachine; //the state machine animator component
```

23. Now, initialize the State Machine's Animator in an `Awake()` function:

```
void Awake(){
    theStateMachine=GetComponent<Animator>(); //get the state
machine
    }
```

24. To have the State Machine automatically set the various parameters of the individual Animators at the appropriate state, we will need to loop through all of the animated items we have listed and each of their listed parameters. If the animated item has a parameter, which is to be set at the current state of the State Machine, we will set it based on the conditions listed. Create the following function to perform that functionality:

```
//check if any of the animations need their parameters set
//called from enter state
public void CheckForParameterSet(){
    //loop through all of the objects
    foreach (AnimatorProperties animatorProp in animatedItems){
        //loop through its set of parameters
        foreach(ParameterProperties parameter in
        animatorProp.animatorParameters){
            //find the ones called on the current state
            if(theStateMachine.GetCurrentAnimatorStateInfo(0)
            .IsName(parameter.whichState)){
                //determine parameter type
                //float types
                if(parameter.parameterType==
                TypesOfParameters.floatParam){
                    animatorProp.theAnimator.
                    SetFloat(parameter.parameterString,
                    parameter.floatValue);
                //int types
                }else if(parameter.parameterType==
                TypesOfParameters.intParam){
                    animatorProp.theAnimator.
                    SetInteger(parameter.parameterString,
                    parameter.intValue);
                //bool type
                }else if(parameter.parameterType==
                TypesOfParameters.boolParam){
                    animatorProp.theAnimator.
                    SetBool(parameter.parameterString,
                    parameter.boolValue);
                //trigger type
                }else{
                    animatorProp.theAnimator.
                    SetTrigger(parameter.parameterString);
                }
            }
        }
    }
}
```

25. The `CheckForParameterSet` function will determine whether a specified Animator needs a parameter set at the current state of the State Machine. However, this function is not currently called anywhere. We want this function to be called whenever a state in the State machine starts. We can accomplish this with a State Machine Behaviour. Open the `ChestOpeningStateMachine` Animator and select the **Canvas Fading In** state. In the state's **Inspector**, click on the **Add Behaviour** button. Select **New Script**, enter `ChestStateMachineBehaviour`, and click on the **Create and Add** button. A new script named `ChestStateMachineBehaviour` will be added to the `Assets` folder. Move it to the `Assets/Scripts` folder and open it.

26. A lot of stuff is included within this State Machine Behaviour. We only need the `OnStateEnter` function. Adjust the code within the `ChestStateMachineBehaviour` class to include the following to call the `CheckForParameterSet` function on the `ChestAnimControls` script when it starts:

```
ChestAnimControls theControllerScript;

public void Awake(){
    //get the script that holds the state machine logic
    theControllerScript=FindObjectOfType<ChestAnimControls>();
}

// OnStateEnter is called when a transition starts and the state
machine starts to evaluate this state
override public void OnStateEnter(Animator animator,
AnimatorStateInfo stateInfo, int layerIndex){
    theControllerScript.CheckForParameterSet();
}
```

27. We will need this script to on every state that does not say **Waiting On Player**. Add the `ChestStateMachineBehaviour` to each of the states in the right-hand column (the ones that do not say **Waiting On Player**) by clicking on the **Add Behaviour** button and selecting `ChestStateMachineBehaviour` in their Inspector.

    The State Machine will now appropriately call each of the individual item's animations when the appropriate states are entered, but we don't have anything that actually controls the flow of the state machine. Right now, it's going to just stay in the **Waiting on Player (Show Chest)** state. We will need to write up some logic to control the flow within the State Machine. Remember that each of the states that say **Waiting on Player** are going to wait on the player to perform some interaction with the game before proceeding to the next state. So, let's start our State Machine logic by making a script that can be used by the buttons when the player clicks on them. Let's start with the button that is on the `Button Canvas` that says **Start**.

    Add the following function to your script:.

    ```
    public void PlayerInputTrigger(string triggerString){
        theStateMachine.SetTrigger(triggerString);
    }
    ```

    This function will trigger State Machine's trigger parameter specified by the string sent as an argument.

28. We will need to call that function from the **Start** button, so add the following **On Click ()** Event to the `Button` on the `Button Canvas`:

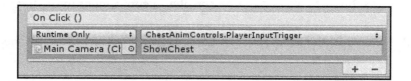

29. Now, we will need to create some logic that will have the `Button` on the `Chest Open Canvas` transition from the other two **Waiting On Player** states. Create a new script called `OpenCloseButton` in the `Assets/Scripts` folder.

30. Add the `UnityEngine.UI` namespace to the `OpenCloseButton` script with:

    ```
    using UnityEngine.UI;
    ```

31. Now, add the following code to the OpenCloseButton script:

```
Text buttonText;
Animator chestAnimController;

void Awake(){
    buttonText=transform.GetComponentInChildren<Text>();
    chestAnimController=Camera.main.GetComponent<Animator>();
}

public void OpenOrClose(){
    Debug.Log("click");
    if(buttonText.text=="Open"){
        chestAnimController.SetTrigger("OpenChest");
        SetText("Close");
    }else{
        chestAnimController.SetTrigger("CloseChest");
        SetText("Open");
    }
}
public void SetText(string setTextTo){
    buttonText.text=setTextTo;
}
```

The OpenOrClose() function will be called by the button's **On Click ()** Event. The Button on the Chest Open Canvas will be used to open and close the chest. It will set the appropriate trigger based on the current text written on the button and will change its text to "Open" or "Close" with the SetText() function.

32. Add the OpenCloseButton script as a component to the Button on the Chest Open Canvas.

33. Now, add the following **On Click ()** Event to the Button on the Chest Open Canvas:

34. If you play the game now and click on the **Start** button, all that happens is that the Canvas fades in. This is because we still haven't done anything to set the `AnimationComplete` trigger in the `ChestOpeningStateMachine` Animator. We will need another script to set this trigger. Create a new script called `AnimationControls` in the `Assets/Scripts` folder.

35. Adjust the code within the `AnimationControls` class, as follows:

```
Animator chestAnimController;

void Awake(){
  chestAnimController=Camera.main.GetComponent<Animator>();
}

//call as an animation event on last frame of animations
public void ProceedStateMachine(){
  chestAnimController.SetTrigger("AnimationComplete");
}
```

36. The preceding code simply sets the `AnimationComplete` trigger with the `ProceedStateMachine()` function.

37. This trigger is used to allow each of the individual animations to play fully before the next state is started. To make sure that the animation trigger isn't set until the entire animation has played, we'll use Animation Events to call the `ProceedStateMachine()` function at the appropriate time within the necessary animations.
When you use an Animation Event, the function you want to call must be on a script attached to the same object as the animation. We want the function to be called at the end of animations on the `Chest Open Canvas`, the `Chest`, the `Coin`, the `Heart`, the `PowerUp`, and the `Button` on the `Chest Open Canvas`. Therefore, add the `AnimationControls` script as a component to each of them.

38. Now, we will need to add the `ProceedStateMachine()` function as an Animation Event to the various animations. Select the `Chest Open Canvas` and view its `CanvasGroupFadeIn` animation. On its last animation frame, right-click on the top dark gray area of the timeline and select `Add Animation Event`. In the Inspector, select **ProceedStateMachine()** from the drop-down menu. It will be the very last function in the list. You should now have a white flag above the last keyframe that says **ProceedStateMachine** when you hover over it:

39. If you play the game now and click on the **Start** button, the Canvas will fade in
    and the chest will fly in. The State Machine will stay on the "Chest Flying In
    Animation". To have the animation sequence finish out, add the
    `ProceedStateMachine()` function as an Animation Event to each of the
    following animations at the following locations:

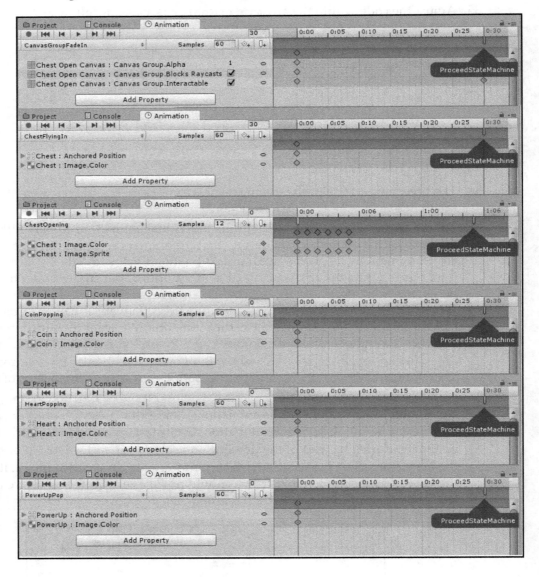

40. Playing the game now almost works the way it should. There's a bit of an issue with the timing on the items popping out of the chest when you replay the animation sequence. Currently, there is a bit of a problem with the `AnimationComplete` trigger. We need that trigger to definitely be unset whenever any of the **Waiting On Player** states start. Otherwise, it will be set to true when the State Machine restarts, causing some timing issues. To fix this, we need one more State Machine Behaviour. Select the **Waiting on Player (Show Chest)** state and **Create and Add** a new State Machine Behaviour called `ResetTriggers` in its Inspector. Remember that whenever you create a new State Machine Behaviour, it is added to the `Asset` folder, so move it to the `Asset/Scripts` folder.

41. We want the Trigger Parameter `AnimationComplete` to reset whenever a **Waiting On Player** states start, so change the code in the `ResetTriggers` class, as follows:

```
// OnStateEnter is called when a transition starts and the state
machine starts to evaluate this state
override public void OnStateEnter(Animator animator,
AnimatorStateInfo stateInfo, int layerIndex){
    animator.ResetTrigger("AnimationComplete");
}
```

42. Now, add the `ResetTriggers` State Machine Behaviour to all three of the **Waiting on Player** states. Playing the game now should have the animation sequence firing correctly, with everything but the particle system. We want the particle system to play when the chest opens. Create a new script called `PlayParticles` in the `Assets/Scripts` folder.

43. Edit the `PlayParticles` class to have the following code:

```
public ParticleSystem stars;

void PlayTheParticles(){
    if(!stars.isPlaying){
        stars.Play();
    }
}
```

44. All this code does is check whether the particle system is currently playing with the function `PlayTheParticles()`. If it is not playing, it plays when the function runs.

45. We'll have this function triggered via an Animation Event on the `Chest`. So, add the script to the `Chest` as a component and assign the `Particle System` from the Hierarchy to the **Stars** slot.

46. Add the `PlayTheParticles` function as an Animation Event on the very first frame of the `ChestOpening` Animation:

Playing the game now should result in all animations playing at the appropriate times and the particle system displaying when the chest opens. Wow! That was a doozy of an example to write up.

Summary

Animating UI elements is not significantly different from animating any other 2D object in Unity. Therefore, this chapter offered a brief overview of animation. Making particle systems appear in front of UI elements is a hot topic in the Unity-UI world, but it's not terribly difficult to achieve once you know the tips discussed in this chapter. This chapter also offered an example of the workflow for creating complex animations utilizing a State Machine and Animation Events.

In this chapter, we discussed the following topics:

- Applying animations to the various UI elements
- Displaying particle systems in front of UI elements
- How to create a pop up window that fades in and out
- How to create a complex animation system with a State Machine and Animation Events

In the next chapter, we will discuss how to use the World Space Canvas Rendering Mode to have UI elements appear directly in your Unity scene rather than "on the screen."

9
World Space UI

In Chapter 2, *Canvases, Panels, and Basic Layouts*, we discussed the three different Rendering Modes you can assign to a Canvas. We've used Screen Space-Overlay and Screen Space-Camera, but haven't used World Space yet. As described in Chapter 2, *Canvases, Panels, and Basic Layouts*, UI rendered in World Space is placed directly in the scene. We've already discussed the properties of the World Space Canvas rendering, so this chapter will just look at when to use it and examples of implementation.

In this chapter, we will discuss the following topics:

- When to use World Space UI
- General techniques to consider when working with World Space UI
- Using World Space Canvases in a 2D game to create status indicators positioned relative to characters
- Using World Space Canvases to create health bars that hover over enemies' heads in a 3D game

When to use World Space

There are many reasons you may want to use a World Space Canvas. The most common reasons for using this rendering mode are the following:

- To have better control of individual UI objects' positions in relation to objects in the scene
- To rotate or curve the UI elements

For example, the game *Mojikara: Japanese Trainer* uses World Space Canvases to have rotated panels and keep UI objects, such as Text, attached to 3D objects. As you can see from the following screenshot, the panel on the left is rotated just slightly in 3D space, because it is on a World Space Canvas:

Image provided by Lisa Walkosz-Migiacio, Intropy Games

Another example of rotated UI can be found in the game *Cloudbase Prime,* as shown in the following screenshot. It also used World Space rendering to provide create indicators that hover over objects and characters.

Image provided by Tyrus Peace, Floating Island Games

All the UI in *Cloudbase Prime* was done on World Space Canvases. This allowed the developer to create cool curving UI, as follows:

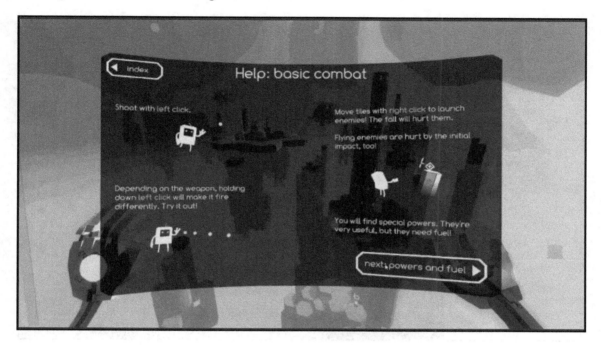

Image provided by Tyrus Peace, Floating Island Games

Here, you can see how the UI looks in the **Editor** versus how it looks to the player. This gives a nice peek at how the UI was built:

Images provided by Tyrus Peace, Floating Island Games

I recommend checking out the following site to see more ways in which *Cloudbase Prime* implemented World Space UI, as they are truly beautiful: `https://imgur.com/a/hxNgL`.

Another common usage of World Space UI is simulating computer screens and monitors within a scene. For example, I built out the following UI for a friend's VR game named *Cloud Rise*. The monitor was simulated by placing a World Space Canvas right on top of the in-game screen. I was then able to easily anchor and animate the UI; in the same way, I rendered the UI in Screen Space.

Image provided by Meredith Wilson, Bedhouse Games

In general, the interactive UIs of VR games are on World Space Canvases, since the player cannot interact with *the screen*. Common usages of VR UI are flat floating panels or wrapping panels.

Currently, if you subscribe to Unity Plus or Pro, you can choose to receive a free VR Essentials Pack, which provides functionality for Curved UI. You can find more information about Unity's VR Essential Pack at `https:/ /unity3d.com/learn/tutorials/topics/vr/worldspace-ui-curved-ui.` If you want to create Curved World Space UI but don't want to pay for a Unity subscription, you can create your own code to do so, or you can use one of the many resources available on the Asset Store.

Hovering indicators are by far the most common use of World Space UI; they are specifically used for health bars over the heads of in-game characters, as shown in the following screenshot of *Iris Burning*:

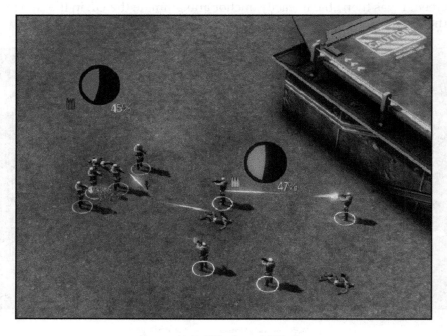

Image provided by William Preston, DCM Studios

Most people think of 3D games when they think of World Space UI because they think of UI that appears *far away*, but it's commonly used in 2D games as well! Management and RTS games use UI quite frequently to create buttons and progress bars, and other UI elements maintain their position with the object they interact with. The World Space UI can be on one Canvas that encompasses all items on the screen, with individual UI items matching the 2D World Space coordinates of the items they represent, or they can be on individual Canvases of their respective items. We will cover how to create a 2D game using World Space UI in an example at the end of the chapter.

I am lucky enough to have a lot of friends who work in game development and who were willing to provide screenshots of World Space Canvases for this section. For more information about the games described in this section, refer to the following:

Mojikara: Japanese Trainer images provided by Lisa Walkosz-Migiacio, Intropy Games
`http://www.intropygames.com`
`https://itunes.apple.com/us/app/mojikara-japanese-trainer/`
`id1292134443?mt=8`

Cloudbase Prime images provided by Tyrus Peace, Floating Island Games
`http://cloudbaseprime.com/`
`http://store.steampowered.com/app/511250/Cloudbase_Prime/`

Cloud Rise images provided by Meredith Wilson, Bedhouse Games
`http://www.bedhousegames.com/`

Iris Burning images provided by Will Preston, DCM Studios
`irisburning.com`

Appropriately scaling text in the Canvas

Whenever a Canvas is created, it is initialized with **Screen Space - Overlay** as its **Render Mode**. Therefore, when you change the **Render Mode** to **World Space**, the Canvas will be huge in your scene.

When you scale down the Canvas to the appropriate size in the scene, the text will likely be super blurry or not visible at all. Let's say we created the following Canvas in **Screen Space - Overlay** but decided to put it in **World Space**.

Converting it to **World Space** doesn't initially cause any problems, but once we scale it down to something like a **Width** of 4 and **Height** of 3 (since it was initially created with a 4:3 aspect ratio screen), the text will disappear!

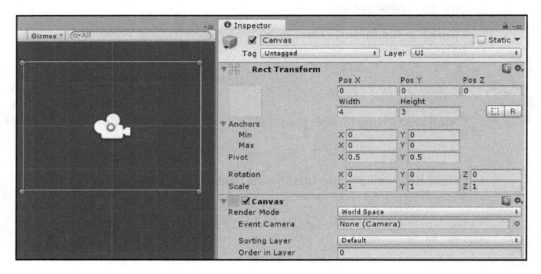

If I set the **Text** to allow **Horizontal** and **Vertical Overflow**, you'll see that it is super huge when compared to the Canvas! In the following screenshot, the tiny rectangle in the middle is the Canvas:

To fix this, and to get it looking the way we want, we need to adjust the **Dynamic Pixels Per Unit** property on the **Canvas Scaler** component (initially discussed in Chapter 2, *Canvases, Panels, and Basic Layouts*). This property is initially set to 1.

Usually, to determine the new **Dynamic Pixel Size**, I take the starting **Width** of the Canvas before I scaled it down, which is 905, divide it by the new **Width**, 4, and enter that division in my **Dynamic Pixels Per Unit** property. (Typing the actual division 905/4 in the box will perform the calculation.)

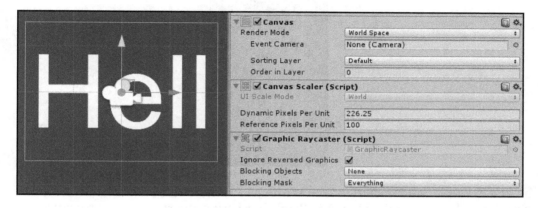

However, that calculation didn't get the exact look I was looking for, so I increased the size until it looks right:

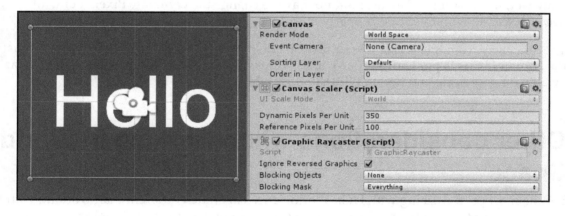

Dynamic Pixels Per Unit Property in the Chapter9Text Scene

Every time you change the **Width** and **Height** of the Canvas, you will have to adjust the **Dynamic Pixels Per Unit** property. Decreasing the size of the Canvas will mean increasing the **Dynamic Pixels Per Unit** property, and increasing the size of the Canvas will mean decreasing the size of the **Dynamic Pixels Per Unit** property.

Here are two Canvases, both one-fourth the size of the one from the previous image. In the top Canvas, I changed the **Width** and **Height** to 1 and .75. In the bottom Canvas, I changed the **Scale X** and **Y** to 0.25:

In the first example, since I changed the **Width** and **Height** of the canvas to one-fourth of the size, I typed 350*4 in the **Dynamic Pixels Per Unit** property, and it automatically calculated 1400 for me (I love that Unity performs calculations in the boxes).

However, in the second Canvas, I did not have to change the **Dynamic Pixels Per Unit** size, because scaling with the **Scale** property in this way does not require me to change it.

The takeaway from this is that if your text isn't displaying or looks incredibly blurry, adjust the **Dynamic Pixels per Unit** property until it looks the way it should or scale your Canvas by adjusting its **Scale** and not its **Width** and **Height**.

Other considerations when working in World Space

For the most part, working with UI in World Space isn't much different than working with UI in Screen or Camera Space. There are a few things you have to keep in mind, though.

When working with 3D scenes, you may want your UI to always face the player, regardless of how the player turns the camera—this is known as a **billboard effect**. You can achieve this with a simple `LookAt()` function on the transform of the object in the `Update()` function:

```
transform.LookAt(2*transform.position-theCamera.transform.position );
```

You can use a variation of the preceding code, depending on how you want the rotation to behave.

Another consideration with 3D World Space UI is the distance it is away from the camera. You may want to have UI only render when it is a specific distance from the camera, as it may be difficult to see when it is too far away.

Depending on your project, using World Space Canvases may cause difficulties with Raycasting, making interacting with UI a problem. Tyrus Peace of Floating Island Games recommends creating your own physics layer if you end up having to create your own Raycasting system, as he did with *Cloudbase Prime*, shown earlier in the chapter.

Examples

Working with World Space Canvases isn't significantly different than working with Canvases in Screen and Camera Space. World Space Canvases offer many benefits. If you have an object that exists within your scene that has UI specifically tied to its location, it is helpful to use a World Space Canvas so that the UI "follows" it wherever it is. This removes the necessity of trying to convert the object's World Space Coordinates to Screen Coordinates to ensure that the UI always lines up with the object. It also guarantees that the UI object will always display correctly with respect to the object's location, even when the screen's resolution changes. In this chapter, I will cover two common uses of World Space Canvases: one in 2D space and another in 3D space.

2D World Space status indicators

For this example, we will start a new scene. For you to not have to build out the scene, we will start with an **Asset** package that includes all the required items.

We'll create UI that allows a character to have a status indicator pop up above his head. After the scene has played for 3 seconds, a status-indicating button will appear over his head. Once the player clicks on the status indicator, a dialog will appear. After 5 seconds, the dialog will disappear. The status indicator will re-appear 10 seconds later.

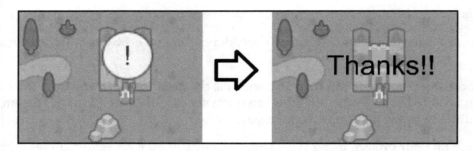

The art used in this example was accessed from `https://opengameart.org/content/medieval-rts-120`.

To create the status-indicating UI demonstrated by the previous example, complete the following steps:

1. Import the `Chapter 9 Example 1-Starting.unitypackage` package. This package contains a scene with a background image and a 2D sprite named `Mage`. The `Assets/Scripts/MageInteractions.cs` script included with the package controls the timers on the appearance of the status indicator and is included in the package. This script requires two Canvas Group items—`theExclaimationPoint` and `theDialogBox`—and contains a function, `ShowTheDialogBox()`, that can be called via a button's `On Click ()` event.

2. We want the status indicator and the dialog to be tied to the position of the `Mage` within the scene. Therefore, we will create a Canvas that is a child of the `Mage` in **World Space**.
   Right-click on the `Mage` in the Hierarchy and add a UI Canvas as a child of the `Mage`.

3. Select the newly created `Canvas`. Change the **Render Mode** on the Canvas Component to **World Space**.

4. Assign the `Main Camera` to the **Event Camera** slot.

5. Since this Canvas is a child of `Mage`, its coordinate system is relative to the `Mage`. To have it perfectly positioned over the `Mage`, change both the Rect Transform **Pos X** and **Pos Y** to 0.

6. The `Canvas` is significantly bigger than the `Mage`. Make the size more reasonable by changing both the Rect Transform **Width** and **Height** to 1.

7. Now that we have the Canvas scaled and positioned in the scene around the `Mage`, we can add UI Elements to it. Right-click on `Canvas` in the Hierarchy and create a UI Button. Name the new button `Alert`.

8. Resize the Button to match the `Canvas` by setting its **Rect Transform** stretch and anchor to stretch fully across the `Canvas`.

9. Change the **Source Image** on the `Alert` Button's Image component to the UI `Knob` image. It looks better as a circle than as the default button sprite:

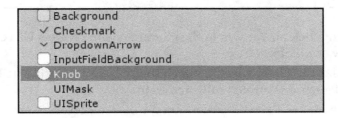

10. Change the `Text` child of `Alert` to display ! instead of `Button`.

11. The Button's text is not currently visible. To fix this, change the **Dynamic Pixels Per Unit** property on the **Canvas Scalar** component of `Canvas` to 1000.

12. Move the `Alert` Button so that it is positioned over the `Mage`'s head.

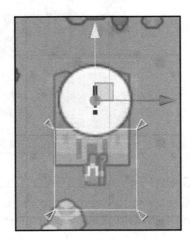

13. Add a **Canvas Group** component to the Alert Button.
14. Set the **Canvas Group** component's **Alpha** property to 0, and set both the **Interactable** and **Blocks Raycasts** properties to **False**.
15. Give the Alert Button an **On Click ()** Event that calls the ShowTheDialogBox() function on the MageInteractions script attached to the Mage:

16. Right-click on Canvas in the Hierarchy and create a UI Text object. Name the new Text object Dialog.
17. Resize the Text object to match the Canvas by setting its **Rect Transform** stretch and anchor to stretch fully across the Canvas.
18. Change the **Text** component on the Dialog object to say Thanks!!!. Also, center align the text and set the **Horizontal Overflow** to **Overflow**.
19. Move the Dialog object so that it is positioned above the head of the Mage:

20. Add a **Canvas Group** component to the Dialog Text object.
21. Set the **Canvas Group** component's **Alpha** property to 0, and set both the **Interactable** and the **Blocks Raycasts** properties to **False**.
22. Select the Mage and add Alert to **The Exclamation Point** property and add Dialog to **The Dialog Box** property.

If you play the game, you'll see the exclamation point Button appear after 3 seconds. Clicking on the Button will make the Text appear. Try moving around the Mage in the scene. You'll see that, no matter where he is, the exclamation point Button and Text appear over his head. This is a really helpful technique for creating UI elements that stay with moving characters.

I know that the example is a bit boring the way it is now, but I recommend using some of the techniques discussed in Chapter 8, *Animations and Particles in the UI*, to add a nice bouncy animation to the exclamation point and have the Text fade in and out.

3D hovering health bars

Making World Space UI in a 3D scene takes a little more work than making World Space UI in a 2D scene if the camera can be rotated and moved throughout the 3D space. If the camera can move and rotate, the UI likely needs to constantly *face* the camera. Otherwise, the player will not be able to see the UI Element.

For this example, we will once again create a new scene. For you to not have to build out the scene, we will start with an Asset package that includes all the required items.

We'll create a simple hovering health bar that constantly faces the camera. It will also receive clicks so that we can watch the health bar reduce:

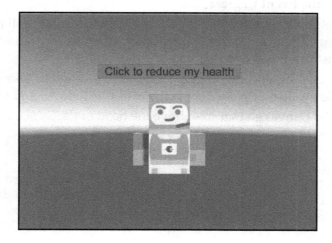

The art used in this example was accessed from `https://opengameart.org/content/space-kit`.

To create the health bar that always faces the camera and receives player-click input, complete the following steps:

1. Import the Chapter 9 `Example 2-Starting.unitypackage` package. This package contains a scene with a 3D character facing the camera. The camera uses the Standard Unity Asset `FreeLookCameraRig` provided by Unity. The package also contains a `ReduceHealth` script that is attached to the `astronaut` character. This script has a function, `ReduceHealthBar`, that we will call when the health bar above the character's head is clicked on.

2. We want the health bar to be tied to the position of the `astronaut` within the scene. Therefore, we will create a Canvas that is a child of the `astronaut` in World Space.
   Right-click on the `astronaut` in the Hierarchy and add a UI Canvas as a child of the `astronaut`.

3. Select the newly created `Canvas`, and change the **Render Mode** on the **Canvas Component** to **World Space**.

4. The `Main Camera` is a child of `FreeLookCameraRig/Pivot`. Assign the `Main Camera` to the **Event Camera** slot.

5. Since this Canvas is a child of `astronaut`, its coordinate system is relative to the `astronaut`. To have it perfectly positioned over the `astronaut`, change both the Rect Transform **Pos X** and **Pos Y** to 0.

6. The `Canvas` is significantly bigger than the `astronaut`. Make the size more reasonable by changing the Rect Transform **Width** to 10 and the **Height** to 1.

7. Position the Canvas so that it is above the head of the `astronaut`:

8. Now that we have the Canvas scaled and positioned in the scene around the astronaut, we can add UI Elements to it. Right-click on Canvas in the Hierarchy and create a UI Button. Name the new button Health Bar.

9. Resize the Button to match the Canvas by setting its **Rect Transform** stretch and anchor to stretch fully across the Canvas.

10. Change the **Source Image** on the **Image** component of the Health Bar to **None** to give it a white rectangle as an image:

11. Change the `Text` child of `Health Bar` to say `Click to reduce my health`.

12. Set both the **Horizontal Overflow** and **Vertical Overflow** properties of the Text component on the `Text` child to **Overflow**. This will allow you to see the size the text is currently rendering at in the scene:

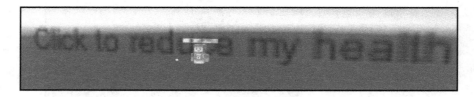

13. Set the Text's **Font Size** to `10`, and deselect the **Raycast Target** on the **Text** component.

14. Select the Canvas and hover over the **Dynamic Pixels Per Unit** property in the **Canvas Scaler** component until you see two arrows appear around your mouse cursor. Once you see those arrows, click and drag to the right. This makes the property work like a slider, allowing you to see how increasing the **Dynamic Pixels Per Unit** property continuously changes the way the text renders in the scene. Do this until the text fits within the Canvas:

When trying to get the text to look nice in 3D space, if only changing the **Dynamic Pixels Per Unit Size** results in *choppy* text, change the property until the text looks **Dynamic Pixels Per Unit Size** perfectly crisp in the scene. Then, use a combination of changing the Rect Transform **Scale** and **Font Size** of the `Text` object to find the *sweet spot*.

15. Right-click on the `Health Bar` Button and add a UI Image as a child. Name the new Image `Health Fill`.

16. Resize `Health Fill` to match the `Canv Health Bar` by setting its Rect Transform stretch and anchor to stretch fully across the `Health Bar`.

17. Now change the anchor and pivot to left stretch so that it will scale *leftward*.

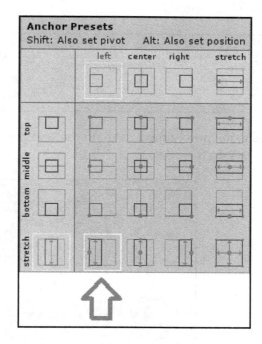

18. Reposition the `Health Bar` in the Hierarchy so that it is above `Text`. This will have the fill render behind the `Text` object.

19. On the **Image** component of the `Health Fill`, change the **Color** property to red and deselect the **Raycast Target** property.

20. Select the `astronaut` and assign the `Health Fill` object to the **Health Fill** property on the `ReduceHealth` component.

21. Add an **On Click()** Event to the `Health Bar` Button that calls the `ReduceHealthBar` function of the `ReduceHealth` script on the `astronaut`:

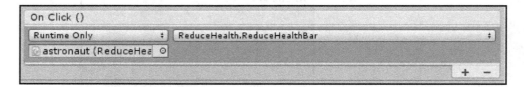

Playing the game now should result in the `Health Fill` reducing its fill value when you click on the `Health Bar` Button:

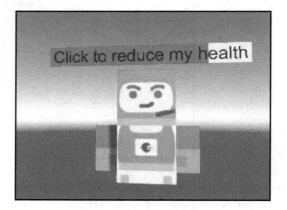

22. Now we just need to add a billboard effect to the `Canvas`. Create a new script called `BillboardPlane` in the `Assets/Scripts` folder.

23. Change the script of the `BillboardPlane` class to the following:

```
public Camera theCamera;

void Update(){
    transform.LookAt(2*transform.position-
theCamera.transform.position);
}
```

24. Attach the `BillboardPlane` script to the `Canvas`.

25. Assign the `Main Camera` to **The Camera** slot in the `BillboardPlane` component.

If you play the game now, you'll see that, as you move the camera around, the health bar always faces the `Main Camera`. Try changing the **Transform** position of the camera in the scene to see the `LookAt()` function work more drastically.

Summary

World Space UI is not significantly different in its implementation than the UI that renders in the Camera or Screen Space. Adding UI to your World Space gives you the ability to create cool effects and gives you more control over your UI's position relative to the objects in the scene.

In this chapter, we discussed the following topics:

- When to use World Space UI.
- General techniques to consider when working with World Space UI.
- How to use World Space Canvases in a 2D game to create status indicators positioned relative to characters.
- How to use World Space Canvases to create health bars that hover over enemy's heads in a 3D game.

In the next chapter, we will discuss mobile-specific UI elements and interactions.

10
Mobile-Specific UI

If you are creating a game for multiple platforms, you really have to consider making interfaces that either work on all platforms you plan on developing for, or make device-specific interfaces. One advantage of the Unity Event System is that it translates very well to mobile devices. An action such as clicking a button with a mouse translates perfectly to a touch or tap gesture. There are a few interactions that don't translate, however, such as keyboard key presses, right-clicking, and scrolling the mouse wheel. Let's discuss a few items of UI design that are specific to mobile/touchscreen devices.

In this chapter, we will discuss the following topics:

- The recommended button sizes for mobile games
- Laying out interactions based on the thumb zone
- How to access multi-touch
- When to use the accelerometer and gyroscope
- Creating on-screen D-pads

Recommended button sizes

When creating a mobile game, pretty much all of your interactions are controlled by button and screen taps. Buttons that are a reasonable size on a PC or console game may be too small for a mobile game.

Apple, Google, and Microsoft all have specific recommendations for the size of a button's touchable area when designing for their devices: Apple recommends that buttons be 44 points x 44 points; Google recommends 48 dp x 48 dp with 8 dp spacing between two more buttons; and Microsoft recommends 9 mm x 9 mm with 2 mm padding between two buttons. Annoyingly, all of these recommendations are in different units of measurement.

You can find information about designing touch/hit areas for each mobile platform at the following locations:

- **Apple:** `https://developer.apple.com/ios/human-interface-guidelines/visual-design/adaptivity-and-layout/`
- **Google:** `https://material.io/guidelines/layout/metrics-keylines.html#metrics-keylines-touch-target-size`
- **Microsoft:** `https://docs.microsoft.com/en-us/windows/uwp/design/input/guidelines-for-targeting`

But, what do these numbers even mean in terms of design? How do you make sure your buttons are 9 mm x 9 mm or 44 points x 44 points? And why are they talking about these measurements in different units? It's almost like they are all competitors and don't want to work nicely together! To answer these questions, let's first look at what the various units of measurement represent:

- A **point** (**pt**) is used to measure what represents a physical measurement on a screen. 1 point is 1/72 of an international inch, or 0.3528 mm. It is primarily used in typography and print media. When working with a program such as Illustrator, creating an object in points and then exporting your image at 72 ppi makes pixels and points the same size. **Points and pixels are not the same, except when exporting at 72 ppi.**
- **Density-independent pixels** (**dp**) is a unit of measurement that is created to maintain consistently sized items on screens with different dpi (dots per inch). A density-independent pixel measures the size of 1 pixel on a 160 dpi screen. Using this conversion is like saying: it would appear at this size on a 160 dpi screen, it should appear the exact same physical size on any other screen. You can read more about density-independent pixels here: `https://developer.android.com/guide/practices/screens_support.html#range`.
- When **millimeters** (**mm**) are used to describe a button size, the size is a physical representation of the button on the screen. So, if you were to take a ruler and hold it up to the screen, it would be consistent with this unit of measurement.

OK, so they all represent some physical unit of measurement on the screen. That makes things a little easier. Let's convert all of these values to millimeters so we can compare them in a unit of measurement that is a bit easier to conceptualize. I'm also going to convert them to points, since you can use points in a program, such as Illustrator, to create your button art.

If you need to convert any of these units of measurement, and you're not too keen on the idea of doing math, googling *convert points to mm* will bring up a nice conversion calculator for you. You can also use the following converter tool. It is really handy to bounce between all of the different units of measurement: `http://angrytools.com/android/pixelcalc/`.

In the following chart, I rounded to the nearest integer the measurement for points, and to the nearest tenth for millimeters, to make things easier. We can use this image as a way to compare the different sizes (the image has been scaled and the sizes may not translate to their real-world measurements):

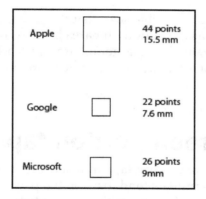

So, which size should you use? It's up to you. You don't have to use their recommendations, but I personally go with the Apple recommendation since it is the largest and therefore meets the recommendations of the other two.

Another consideration is whether your game will be played with thumbs or with fingers. If the game will be played with thumbs, you'll want bigger buttons, because thumbs are bigger! The numbers described previously are minimum recommendations so they would be used for a finger tap, not a thumb tab.

So, how do you ensure that your buttons are always the size you want in your game? The **Canvas Scaler** component! Remember from `Chapter 2`, *Canvases, Panels, and Basic Layouts*, we discussed ensuring a button of a specified size regardless of resolution, can be achieved by setting the **Canvas Scaler** component's **UI Scale Mode** to **Constant Physical Size**. You have the option to have your Canvas's measurement units be in millimeters or points (as well as a few other units).

My recommendation when designing for mobile devices is to have multiple devices on hand to test at various resolutions. Play the game and see how it feels to you. Ask people with smaller and larger hands than yours to play. Even after following the minimum guidelines specified by the various mobile platforms, you may still find your buttons are too small for what you need.

Google and Microsoft also specify visible sizes that they recommend, so you can have a smaller button image as long as the button's hit area is the recommended size. If you want a button that is smaller visually, but has a larger hit area, instead of attaching the button component to the tiny piece of art, attach it to a larger parent hit area and change the target image of the button to the tiny art.

Full screen/screen portion taps

Many have a single input where you can tap anywhere on the screen to make an action happen. For example, endless runners tend to allow the player to tap or press-and-hold anywhere on the screen to jump. To achieve this, you only have to add an invisible button that covers the whole screen and receives Events. If you have another UI that receives inputs, it needs to be in front of the fullscreen button so that the button does not block the inputs to the other UI items.

Some games require that you tap in specific regions of the screen to perform specific actions. For example, I created a game called Sequence Seekers for my doctoral dissertation. This game included a down-the-mountain mode in which the player had to tap the left-or right-hand side of the screen to move left or right in the game. I achieved this by adding invisible buttons that covered the two halves of the screen, as shown here:

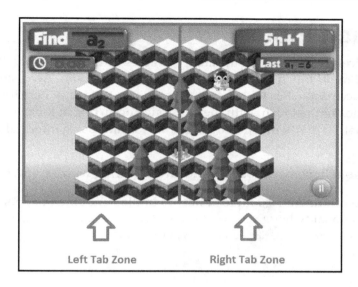

The thumb zone

When designing for a mobile game, it's important to consider how the player will hold the device. You don't want to put your UI in areas that will be difficult for the player to reach. Players tend to prefer to hold and play with one hand. Not all games allow for this, but if possible, you want to allow your players to do so. How do you know if your UI is in an area reachable by the thumb? Put the UI in the thumb zone! Essentially, the thumb zone is the area of the phone that is comfortable for the player to reach when holding with one hand. You can find the thumb zone on your particular phone by holding the phone and easily moving your thumb around without having to move your hand.

 The following blog post offers a really great explanation of the thumb zone, along with a handy (no pun intended) template for finding the thumb zone on various devices: `http://scotthurff.com/posts/how-to-design-for-thumbs-in-the-era-of-huge-screens`.

As a lefty, I implore you to consider making the game as easy to play with the left hand as it is for the right, when designing with the thumb zone in mind.

Multi-touch input

Touchscreen devices generally have the ability to access multiple touches. The most common usage of multi-touch allows the player to pinch to zoom. Accessing multi-touch is pretty easy. You access touches with `Input.GetTouch(index)`, where the `index` represents the index of the touch, with the first touch occurring at index 0. From there, you can access information pretty much in the same way as accessing information about a mouse.

You can also find out how many total touches are occurring with `Input.touchCount`.

 You can find an example of how to implement pinch-to-zoom functionality here: `https://unity3d.com/learn/tutorials/topics/mobile-touch/pinch-zoom?playlist=17138`.

Accelerometer and gyroscope

Most mobile devices have a built-in accelerometer, and many also have a gyroscope. Without getting too technical in describing how it actually works, the difference between the accelerometer and the gyroscope is what they measure. The accelerometer measures acceleration within the 3D coordinate system, and the gyroscope measures rotation.

You can access data from the device's accelerometer using the `Vector3` `Input.acceleration` property.

The coordinates of `Input.acceleration` line up with the scene based on the rotation of the device, as shown:

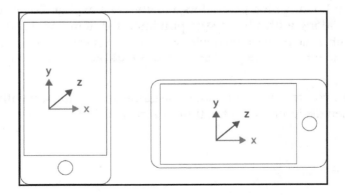

Simple examples of this involve moving an object around a scene when the device is moved, using something like the following within an `Update()` function on the object:

```
transform.Translate(Input.acceleration.x, 0, -Input.acceleration.y);
```

The gyroscope uses more complicated mathematics to get more precise movement of the screen using the `Gyroscope` class. Remember, the gyroscope is not supported on many devices, so it's best to use the accelerometer when possible.

 An example of how to use the gyroscope on an iOS device can be found here: `https://docs.unity3d.com/ScriptReference/Gyroscope.html`.

Device resources

If you are making a UI for a mobile device, you may want to use the device-specific UI elements to maintain a consistent style. You can find various art assets and templates for designing UI for each mobile platform at the following locations:

- **Apple:** `https://developer.apple.com/design/resources/`

- **Android:** `https://developer.android.com/design/index.html` (click **Downloads for Designers**)

- **Windows:** `https://developer.microsoft.com/en-us/windows/apps/design` (click **Design Toolkits and Samples**)

Examples

In this chapter, we are going to cover a few examples of frequently used mobile-specific UI interactions.

Adding press-and-hold/long-press functionality

Press-and-hold is utilized frequently in mobile games. Many games that use right-click on the PC or web use press-and-hold when they are converted to the mobile platform.

To demonstrate how to implement **Press and Hold** functionality, we will create a button that has a growing ring that represents hold time. Once a specified amount of time has passed, a function will fire:

When working this example, it is important to remember that even though the code is referencing a pointer, this functionality does not work exclusively with a mouse. Placing a finger on a touchscreen functions in the same way as a pointer down, and picking up the finger works the same as a pointer up.

To create a button with a growing ring that represents hold time, complete the following steps:

1. Create a new scene named `Chapter10Example1` in the `Assets/Scenes` folder and open the new scene.
2. Select **Create | UI | Button** to create a new button in the scene.
3. Set the button's **Transition** type on the button component to `None`.
4. Change the text on the button to say **Press and Hold**.
5. Right-click the button in the hierarchy and select **UI | Image** to add an image child to the `Button`.
6. Change the **Width** and **Height** on the image's **Rect Transform** to `50`.
7. Assign the `circular meter_1` image to the **Source Image** of the image component.
8. Change the **Image Type** to **Filled** and change the **Fill Amount** to `0`.
9. To create the press-and-hold functionality on the `Button`, we will utilize the **Pointer Down** and **Pointer Up** Events. Add the **Event Trigger** component to the `Button` object.
10. Select **Add New Event Type** and select **PointerDown**.
11. Select **Add New Event Type** and select **PointerUp**.
12. Now we need to actually write the functions that will be called by the Event Triggers we set up in the previous steps. Create a new script in the `Assets/Scripts` folder called `LongHoldButton`.
13. Before opening the script, go ahead and attach it as a component to `Button`.

14. Add the `UnityEngine.UI` namespace to the top of the script with the following:

```
using UnityEngine.UI;
```

15. To check how long the button is being pressed, we will use a Boolean variable that checks to see if the button is being held and a few different variables related to time. Add the following variable declaration to your script:

```
bool buttonPressed=false;
float startTime=0f;
float holdTime=0f;
public float longHoldTime=1f;
```

The `buttonPressed` variable will be set to `true` with the `PointerDown` Event and `false` with the `PointerUp` Event. The `startTime` variable will be set to the current time when the `PointerDown` Event is triggered. The `holdTime` variable will determine how much time has passed since `startTime`. The `longHoldTime` variable is the amount of time the `Button` must be held down before the long-press is complete. It is public so that it can be easily customized.

16. The last variable we need will represent the radial filling image. Add the following variable declaration to your code:

```
public Image radialFillImage;
```

17. Now we need to write a function that will be called by both the **Pointer Down** and **Pointer Up** Events:

```
public void PressAndRelease(bool pressStatus){
    buttonPressed=pressStatus;

    if(buttonPressed==false){
        holdTime=0;
        radialFillImage.fillAmount=0;
    }else{
        startTime=Time.time;
    }
}
```

This function accepts a Boolean variable from the Event Trigger. It then sets the value of `buttonPressed` to the passed value.

When the button is released, a value of `false` will be passed to the function. If the value passed is `false`, the amount of time that has passed, `holdTime`, is reset to 0 and the `radialFillImage` is reset to have a `fillAmount` of 0.

When the button is pressed, the `startTime` value will be set to the current time.

18. Create a function that will be called once the full amount of time needed for the long-press, specified by `longHoldTime`, has completed:

```
public void LongPressCompleted(){
    radialFillImage.fillAmount=0;
    Debug.Log(do something after long press);
}
```

This function doesn't really do anything but reset the filling image and print out a `Debug.Log`. However, you can later reuse this code and replace the `Debug.Log` line with more interesting and meaningful actions.

19. The `Update()` function can be used to make the timer count upward. Adjust the `Update()` function as follows:

```
void Update () {
    if(buttonPressed==true){
        holdTime=Time.time-startTime;
        if(holdTime>=longHoldTime){
            buttonPressed=false;
            LongPressCompleted();
        }else{
            radialFillImage.fillAmount=holdTime/longHoldTime;
        }
    }
}
```

This code makes the value of `holdTime` tick upward if the value `buttonPressed` is set to `true`. Remember, `buttonPressed` will be set to `true` by a `PointerDown` event and `false` with a `PointerUp` event. So, it will only be `true` if the player has pressed the button and not yet released it.

Once the `holdTime` value reaches the value specified by `longHoldTime`, the timer will stop ticking up, because `buttonPressed` will be reset to `false`. Additionally, the function `LongPressCompleted()` is called. If `longHoldTime` has not yet been reached, the image's radial fill will update to represent the percentage of total required time that has transpired.

20. Now that the script is completed, we can hook up the `PressAndRelease()` function with the Event Triggers on the button. Add the `PressAndRelease` function from the static list to both the **Pointer Down** and **Pointer Up** Event Triggers. Since the `PressAndRelease()` function accepts a Boolean variable, there is a checkbox representing the Boolean value that should be passed. Select the checkbox for the **Pointer Down** Event (sending `true`) but not for the **Pointer Up** Event (sending `false`).

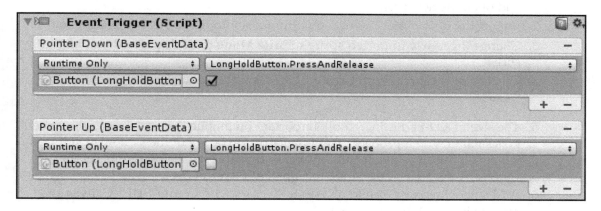

21. Now we need to assign the image to the **Radial Fill Image** slot on the `LongHoldButton` component.

Playing the game now will demonstrate the image radially filling when you hold the button and printing do something at long press in the console. If you release the button before the fill has completed, it will go away and reset for when you start clicking again.

Press-and-hold is a pretty common functionality, and while it isn't a pre-installed Event in the Unity Event library, luckily it isn't too difficult to hook up. I recommend holding on to that script so that you can reuse it for future use.

Creating a static four-directional virtual D-pad

A D-pad is simply four buttons on a directional pad. To create a D-pad for a mobile game, you just need to create a graphic that contains four buttons on the directions.

The art used in this example was obtained from `https://opengameart.org/content/onscreen-controls-8-styles`.

To create a virtual D-pad, complete the following steps:

1. Create a new scene named `Chapter10Example2` in the `Assets/Scenes` folder and open the new scene.
2. Import the `d-pad buttons.png` sprite sheet into the `Assets/Sprites` folder.
3. Change the newly imported sprite's **Sprite Mode** to **Multiple** and automatically slice it.
4. Create a new Canvas with **Create | UI | Canvas**. Name the new Canvas `D-Pad Canvas`.
5. The size of a D-pad is incredibly important on mobile devices. Even if the screen gets smaller, you'll probably want the D-pad to be about the same size. If it gets too small, the game can be unplayable or uncomfortable. Therefore, set the Canvas Scaler's **UI Scale Mode** to **Constant Physical Size**.
6. Add a new image as a child of `D-Pad Canvas` with **Create | UI | Canvas** and rename it `d-pad background`.
7. Set the **Source Image** to `d-pad buttons_4`.
8. Set its anchor and pivot to the lower-left corner of the screen and its **Pos X** and **Pos Y** to `30`.
9. Set its **Width** and **Height** to `200`:

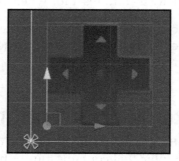

10. Right-click on `d-pad background` and add a new button as a child with **UI | Button**. Rename the new button `Up`.
11. Remove its child `Text` object.

12. Set the **Pos X, Pos Y, Width,** and **Height** of the Up Button to 0, 65, 60, and 60, respectively:

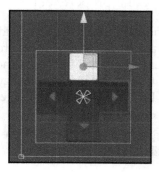

13. Duplicate the Up button three times and rename the duplicates Right, Left, and Down.
14. Set the Right button's **Pos X** and **Pos Y** to 65 and 0, respectively.
15. Set the Left button's **Pos X** and **Pos Y** to -65 and 0, respectively.
16. Set the Down button's **Pos X** and **Pos Y** to 0 and -65, respectively. You should now have four buttons positioned as follows:

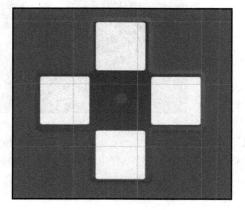

These four buttons cover the entire area of the arms of the directional pad. They will act as the hit area for the directions.

17. We only really want these four buttons for their hit area and don't want to actually have them visible in the UI. Select all four of the buttons and set the alpha value on the **Color** property of their image component to 0.

18. Since the directional pad image is static and not split into four separate buttons, any transitions applied to it would cover the whole image. However, we can make the individual directions look as if they are being pressed and have some sort of color transition by adding sub-images for the arrows on the directions. Right-click the Up button and add an image as a child with **UI | Image**. Rename the new image Arrow.

19. Assign the d-pad buttons_5 sprite to the **Source Image** on its image component and select **Preserve Aspect**.

20. Scale and move the image so that it is appropriately lined up with the arrow displayed on the d-pad background image:

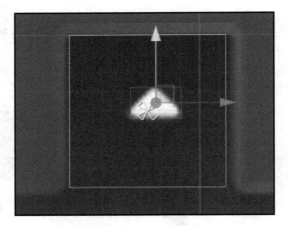

21. Select the **Color** slot on the Arrow image component and use the eye dropper tool to grab the color of the arrows from the d-pad background image.

22. Create `Arrow` children for each of the other three buttons, and size, position, and color them appropriately. Once completed, your D-pad and hierarchy should appear as follows:

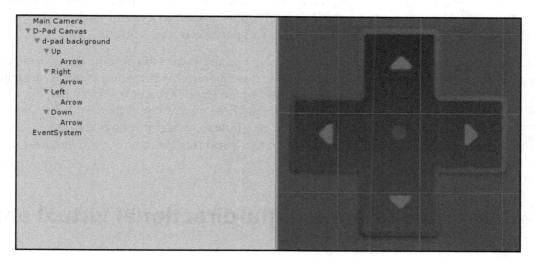

23. Now, so that the D-pad will react visually when the four directions are pressed, we will set the four Arrows to have a color tint button, **Transitions** when the four buttons are pressed. For each button, drag its child `Arrow` into the **Target Graphic** slot on its button component. Now, when you press the individual buttons, you will see a slight change in color of the arrows, indicating which direction is pressed. You may wish to change the pressed color to something a bit more drastic than the default gray, if you are having difficulty telling that a change is occurring.

24. Add the script named `DPad.cs` from the book's code bundle to the `Assets/Scripts` folder. This is an incredibly simple script that contains four functions that only write to the console. Hooking up these four functions to the individual directional buttons won't do anything fun, but it will allow us to see logs in the console that let us know the buttons are performing as they should.

25. Attach the script to the `d-pad background` object.

26. Select each of the four directional buttons and, with all of them selected, add an **On Click ()** Event to the button component.

27. Now, drag the `d-pad background` into the object slot of the **On Click ()** Event.

28. Select each button individually and assign the appropriate functions, `PressUp`, `PressDown`, `PressLeft`, and `PressRight`, to their **On Click ()** Events.

Playing the game and selecting the four directional buttons should result in the appropriate message being displayed on the console.

Many D-pads actually accept nine inputs: the four directs, the four diagonals (corners), and the center. If you want to accept diagonal inputs as well as a center-click for your D-pad, I'd suggest using a grid layout group to evenly space your nine buttons.

Since D-pads tend to allow press-and-hold, you may want to combine the process used in this example with actions similar to those described in the previous example. Instead of using the **On Click ()** Event, you could set up an Event Trigger for using the `OnPointerDown` and `OnPointerUp` Events. These events could then set a Boolean variable `true` and `false`. For example, on the `Right` button, you could have the `OnPointerDown` Event set a variable called `moveRight` to `true` and the `OnPointerUp` Event set `moveRight` to `false`.

Creating a floating eight-directional virtual analog stick

In this example, we will create a floating eight-directional virtual analog stick. First, we will create an eight-directional D-pad that simulates a control stick that moves in the direction the player drags:

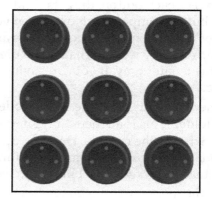

Then, we will expand the eight-directional D-pad so that it is floating, which means it will not be visible in the scene until the player presses somewhere in the screen. Then it will appear where the player's thumb is located and perform the eight-direction movement based on the player's thumb dragging.

Setting up the eight-directional virtual analog stick

To create an analog stick that moves in eight directions, as shown in the previous image, complete the following steps:

1. Create a new scene named `Chapter10Example3` in the `Assets/Scenes` folder and open the new scene.
2. Create a new image with **Create | UI | Image**. Name the new image `Stick Base`.
3. Add the `d-pad buttons_15` sprite to the **Source Image** slot of its image component.
4. Right-click `Stick Base` in the hierarchy and select **UI | Image** to add an image child to the `Stick Base`. Name the child `Stick`.
5. Resize the `Stick` image to match the `Stick Base` by setting its **Rect Transform** stretch and anchor to stretch fully across both directions.
6. Add the `d-pad buttons_0` sprite to the **Source Image** slot of the `Stick` image component.
7. Set the **Left**, **Top**, **Right**, and **Bottom** properties of the **Rect Transform** all to 20 to give some padding around the edges of the `Stick`.
8. Now, set the pivot and position to **middle center**. This is an important step! Without doing this, the `Stick` will not move around appropriately on the `Stick Base`:

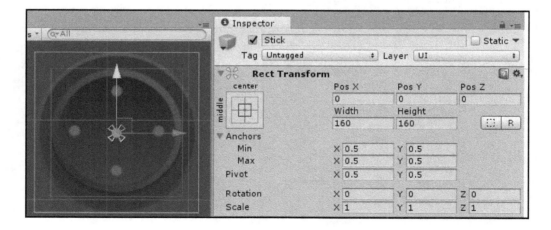

9. That's all there is for the setup to get our virtual analog stick working. We'll just leave it in the center of the screen for now. Now we need to write some code. Create a new script in the `Assets/Script` folder and name it `FloatingAnalogStick`.

10. Add the `UnityEngine.UI` namespace to the top of the script with the following:

```
using UnityEngine.UI;
```

11. To make the stick wiggle around on top of the base, we need the following variables:

```
public RectTransform theStick;
Vector2 mouseStartPosition;
Vector2 mouseCurrentPosition;
public int dragPadding=30;
public int stickMoveDistance=30;
```

The first three variables should be pretty self-explanatory. The `dragPadding` variable will be used to determine how far the player has to drag the stick before it actually registers as being moved. The `stickMoveDistance` variable specifies how far the stick will actually move outward in the *x* and *y* directions.

12. Before we write the code that checks how far the player has dragged their finger, let's add a few dummy functions that would allow this analog stick to actually control something in the future. Add the following functions to your script:

```
public void MovingLeft(){
    Debug.Log(move left);
}

public void MovingRight(){
    Debug.Log(move right);
}

public void MovingUp(){
    Debug.Log(move up);
}

public void MovingDown(){
    Debug.Log(move down);
}
```

13. The `Stick` will move outward when the player moves their finger from their starting finger-down position. So, let's create a function that will find the starting position when the player begins dragging their finger. Add the following function to your script:

```
public void StartingDrag(){
    mouseStartPosition=Input.mousePosition;
}
```

Remember, when working with a touchscreen, `Input.mousePostion` will give the value of the touch position.

14. Now let's create a function that checks how far the player has dragged their finger and moves the `Stick` based on that information. Add the following function to your script:

```
public void Dragging(){
    float xPos;
    float yPos;
    mouseCurrentPosition=Input.mousePosition;
    if(mouseCurrentPosition.x<mouseStartPosition.x-dragPadding){
        MovingLeft();
        xPos=-10;
    }else
    if(mouseCurrentPosition.x>mouseStartPosition.x+dragPadding){
        MovingRight();
        xPos=10;
    }else{
        xPos=0;
    }

    if(mouseCurrentPosition.y>mouseStartPosition.y+dragPadding){
        MovingUp();
        yPos=10;
    }else if(mouseCurrentPosition.y<mouseStartPosition.y-
dragPadding){
        MovingDown();
        yPos=-10;
    }else{
        yPos=0;
    }

    theStick.anchoredPosition=new Vector2(xPos,yPos);
}
```

15. The last piece we need to add is something that will reset the stick to its original position once the player stops dragging or lifts up their finger. Add the following function to your script:

```
public void StoppedDragging(){
    theStick.anchoredPosition=Vector2.zero;
}
```

16. Now we need to hook this script and these functions to the items within the scene. Add the `FloatingAnalogStick` script to the `Stick Base` image.

17. Add the `Stick` image to the **Stick** property in the `Floating Analog Stick` component.

18. Add an Event Trigger component to the `Stick Base` object with **Add Component | Events | Event Trigger**. This will allow the user to use Event Types other than **On Click()**.

19. Add the **Begin Drag, Drag,** and **End Drag** Event Types with the **Add New Event Type** button.

20. Add the appropriate functions on the `FloatingAnalogStick` script attached to the `Stick Base` to the Events:

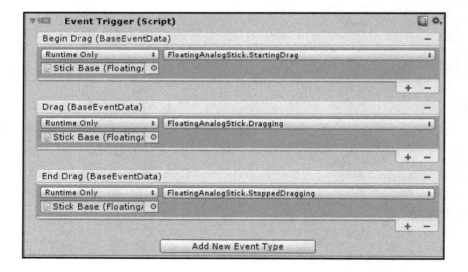

If you play the game now, you should see the eight-directional analog stick responding appropriately. Clicking on it and dragging in any direction will cause the stick to move in the direction of the drag.

Making the eight-directional virtual analog stick float

If all you want is an eight-directional analog stick, you're good to go! But, if you want the analog stick to float—appear where the players press and disappear when they lift their finger—you have to do a little bit more work.

To make the analog stick appear where the player clicks, complete the following steps:

1. First, we need to create an area where the player will click to bring up the analog stick. Right-click `Canvas` in the hierarchy and select **UI | Button** to add a `Button` child to the `Canvas`. Rename the `Button` to `Click Area`.

2. Remove the `Text` child object from the `Click Area`.

3. Stretch the `Click Area` to fill the whole `Canvas`.

4. Add some padding to the sides of `Click Area` by changing the **Left, Top, Right,** and **Bottom** properties on the **Rect Transform** to 50. I have added this padding so that the player cannot click on the very edge of the screen and have the analog stick appear mostly off screen.

5. In the hierarchy, move `Click Area` so that it is above `Stick Base`. Now the `Click Area` will render behind the analog stick:

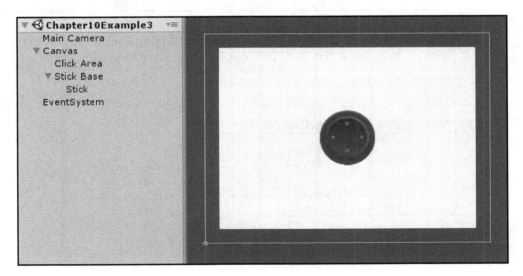

6. Open up your `FloatingAnalogStick` code so that we can add some functionality to it.

7. To make the position of our analog stick more easily hook to the position of the mouse on the screen, we should move our stick base so that it is centered at the lower-left corner of the `Canvas`. Set the anchor and position to the **bottom left** anchor preset.

8. Now, set the **X** and **Y Pivot** properties to 0.5.

9. Set the **Pos X** and **Pos Y** properties to -1. This should place the analog stick at the lower-left corner of the Canvas (or screen) with its pivot point set to its center:

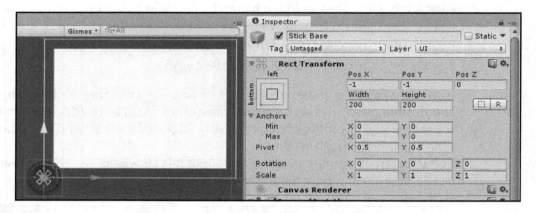

10. We need two more variables now to get the analog stick to appear where we want it to in the scene. Add the following variable to your script:

```
public RectTransform theBase;
public bool stickAdded=false;
```

11. Now, create the following function:

```
public void AddTheStick(){
    theBase.anchoredPosition=Input.mousePosition;
    theStick.anchoredPosition=Vector2.zero;
    mouseStartPosition=Input.mousePosition;
    stickAdded=true;
}
```

12. Add the following `Update()` function:

```
void Update(){
    if(stickAdded==true){
    Dragging();

        if(Input.GetMouseButtonUp(0)){
            stickAdded=false;
            StoppedDragging();
        }
    }
}
```

13. Add `Stick Base` to the `Base` slot:

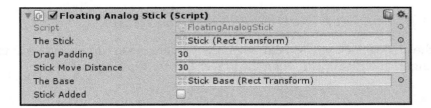

14. Add the **Event Trigger** component to the `Click Area`.
15. Add the following **Pointer Down** Event to the `Click Area`:

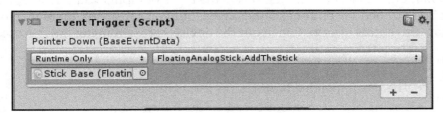

Playing the game now will have the analog stick appear where you click and move around with your dragging.

16. Add a **Canvas Group** component to the `Stick Base`.
17. Set **Alpha** to 0, **Interactable** to `false`, and **Blocks Raycast** to `false`.
18. Add the following variable:

```
CanvasGroup theBaseVisibility;
```

19. Add the following `Awake()` function:

```
void Awake(){
    theBaseVisibility=theBase.GetComponent<CanvasGroup>();
}
```

20. Add the following to the `AddTheStick()` function:

```
theBaseVisibility.alpha=1;
theBaseVisibility.interactable=true;
theBaseVisibility.blocksRaycasts=true;
```

21. Add the following to the innermost `if` statement within the `Update()` function:

```
theBaseVisibility.alpha=0;
theBaseVisibility.interactable=false;
theBaseVisibility.blocksRaycasts=false;
```

Now the analog stick will appear when the player presses down, move in the direction of their finger, and disappear when the player lifts up the finger.

Summary

Creating a UI for mobile devices isn't too different from creating a UI for a console or computer, but it does have limitations in the types of inputs you can accept. Most of the input is controlled via buttons on the screen, but you can accept more than one screen input and can also access information about the device's accelerometer and gyroscope.

In this chapter, we discussed the following topics:

- The recommended button sizes for mobile games
- Laying out interactions based on the thumb zone
- How to access multi-touch buttons
- When to use the accelerometer and gyroscope
- How to add long-press or press-and-hold functionality
- How to add a four-directional virtual D-pad and a floating eight-directional analog stick

Other Books You May Enjoy

If you enjoyed this book, you may be interested in these other books by Packt:

Getting Started with Unity 2018 - Third Edition
Dr. Edward Lavieri

ISBN: 978-1-78883-010-2

- Set up your Unity development environment and navigate its tools
- Import and use custom assets and asset packages to add characters to your game
- Build a 3D game world with a custom terrain, water, sky, mountains, and trees
- Animate game characters, using animation controllers, and scripting
- Apply audio and particle effects to the game
- Create intuitive game menus and interface elements
- Customize your game with sound effects, shadows, lighting effects, and rendering options
- Debug code and provide smooth error handling

Mastering Unity 2017 Game Development with C# - Second Edition
Alan Thorn

ISBN: 978-1-78847-983-7

- Explore hands-on tasks and real-world scenarios to make a Unity horror adventure game
- Create enemy characters that act intelligently and make reasoned decisions
- Use data files to save and restore game data in a way that is platform-agnostic
- Get started with VR development
- Use navigation meshes, occlusion culling, and Profiler tools
- Work confidently with GameObjects, rotations, and transformations
- Understand specific gameplay features such as AI enemies, inventory systems, and level design

Leave a review - let other readers know what you think

Please share your thoughts on this book with others by leaving a review on the site that you bought it from. If you purchased the book from Amazon, please leave us an honest review on this book's Amazon page. This is vital so that other potential readers can see and use your unbiased opinion to make purchasing decisions, we can understand what our customers think about our products, and our authors can see your feedback on the title that they have worked with Packt to create. It will only take a few minutes of your time, but is valuable to other potential customers, our authors, and Packt. Thank you!

Index